University of York Studies in Economics

4

EXPORT PERFORMANCE AND THE PRESSURE OF DEMAND

A STUDY OF FIRMS

University of York Studies in Economics

1. THE GROWTH OF PUBLIC EXPENDITURE IN THE UNITED KINGDOM
Alan T. Peacock and Jack Wiseman, assisted by Jindrich Veverka

2. THEORIES OF THE BARGAINING PROCESS
Alan Coddington

3. THE ECONOMICS OF UNEMPLOYMENT INSURANCE
Mark M. Hauser and Paul Burrows

5. THE ECONOMIC THEORY OF FISCAL POLICY
Alan T. Peacock and G. K. Shaw

In Preparation

PROBLEMS IN FEDERAL AND REGIONAL FINANCE
ed. Jack Wiseman

THE BRITISH TAX SYSTEM AND THE COMMON MARKET
ed. Douglas Dosser

A THEORY OF ECONOMIC INTEGRATION FOR DEVELOPING COUNTRIES
Douglas Dosser and S. S. Han

EXPORT PERFORMANCE AND THE PRESSURE OF DEMAND

A STUDY OF FIRMS

---

by

R. A. Cooper

Reader in Economic and Social Statistics, University of York

and

K. Hartley

Lecturer in Economics, University of York

assisted by

C. R. M. Harvey

Lecturer in Economics, University of Zambia

London

GEORGE ALLEN AND UNWIN LTD

FIRST PUBLISHED IN 1970

ISBN 0 04 382010 7

PRINTED IN GREAT BRITAIN
in 10 on 12 pt. Times type
BY T. AND A. CONSTABLE LTD
HOPETOUN STREET, EDINBURGH

PREFACE

In recent years, considerable attention has been given to the export performance of the U.K. economy. Numerous explanations of both a short- and long-run kind have been proposed to account for this export performance and it is the purpose of this book to present a detailed study of one of the former kinds of explanation, namely the short-run relationship between the pressure of domestic demand in the U.K. and variations in exports. At its simplest, the pressure hypothesis predicts that in the short run, a relatively high pressure of internal demand will adversely affect U.K. exports and relatively low pressure will assist them.[1] In the study, this hypothesis has been tested for a limited number of industries and firms. Although the pressure hypothesis formed the central part of the study, we also obtained evidence on a variety of other aspects of the export behaviour of firms, such as the determinants of a firm's export performance in the long run, its pricing and queuing policies. These aspects of firm behaviour could, in themselves, form the basis for a separate research project. In this respect, it has been stated that, '. . . too little is known of the actual administrative processes of exporting in different industries; and it is very likely that measures which might stimulate one industry to export will deter another'.[2] In a limited way, this study attempts to provide information on such issues and on the export mechanics and motivations of a number of firms in different industries. In other words, the study contains two strands: first, a detailed assessment of the pressure hypothesis and its operation in the short run; and second, evidence on various aspects of the export performance of firms and industries. Since the study was concerned with the period 1958-66, the field work was completed before the devaluation of 1967.

[1] In the text, this relationship is frequently referred to as the pressure hypothesis.

[2] F. T. Blackaby, *Britain's Share in World Trade in Manufactures*, Woolwich Economic Papers, London, 1965 (p. 14).

The contents can be divided into two parts. In the first, consisting of Chapters 1-5, there is a general methodological analysis of the pressure hypothesis. A simple statement of the pressure hypothesis is presented (Chapter 1) together with the results of previous empirical work in the field (Chapter 2). The methodology of the survey, with its emphasis on both questionnaire and econometric evidence is described (Chapter 3) and this is followed by a theoretical analysis of the predicted relationship between domestic demand and exports at the firm level and the associated implications for such variables as pricing, profitability and queuing (Chapter 4). The problems of constructing satisfactory econometric tests of the pressure hypothesis at the firm and industry level are also discussed (Chapter 5). The second part of the study, comprising Chapters 6-10, presents the results of our industry- and firm-level studies of the pressure hypothesis and the related export behaviour of these units. These chapters generally include an outline of each industry's export performance and of any factors which might be relevant for the pressure hypothesis, together with sections presenting the questionnaire and econometric results. Each interview and questionnaire section provides qualitative evidence not only on the pressure hypothesis but also on a variety of related aspects of the export behaviour of firms: a copy of the questionnaire which formed the basis for this section is contained in Appendix A. The econometric sections are solely concerned with presenting quantitative evidence on the pressure hypothesis for industries and, where possible, firms. The industry chapters are of varying length and detail, a feature which reflects our individual interests, the availability of data and the lack of funds! Finally, a concluding chapter summarizes some of the major points from the study and suggests possibilities both for future research and for public policy.

Throughout the study, which began in mid-1965, we have been fortunate in the advice and assistance we received from sources too numerous to identify. We are especially grateful to the Houblon-Norman Fund, Bank of England, for a research grant for the period 1965-6 which supported one full-time research assistant and other expenses. Continuing support was received from both Professors Jack Wiseman and Alan Peacock who kindly provided research facilities at the Institute of Social and Economic Research and within the Economics Department. Charles Harvey's major contribution, not only during his one-year, full-time appointment as research assistant on the project (1965-6) but also on a voluntary part-time basis in the subsequent year, merits his inclusion as a co-author. Computational advice and assistance were provided by Miss J. M. Crush, Mrs E. M. Sutcliffe and Mr C. Cross. We also greatly benefited from the Institute Workshop, the Departmental Seminar and from the comments of many of our colleagues.

We owe a special debt of gratitude to those businessmen who freely gave of their time and enthusiasm and who, but for our promise of confidentiality, we should be delighted to thank publicly. We must also express our appreciation to each of the industry trade associations for their kindness, tolerance and substantial resource commitments, without which our project would have been much more limited. Here, we wish to thank particularly Messrs S. H. Jerrett, British Pottery Manufacturers' Federation; H. M. Palin and P. R. T. Sheen of the British Cycle and Motor Cycle Industries Association; J. G. Orr of the Business Equipment Trade Association; C. G. E. Parrott, British Electrical and Allied Manufacturers' Association. We alone remain responsible for all errors.

R. A. C.
K. H.

September 1969

CONTENTS

Chapter 1

INTRODUCTION

This study is concerned with some of the factors affecting the export performance of firms in a limited number of industries during the period 1958-66. In its original form, the study was designed to test at the level of the firm and industry the hypothesis that, in the short run, variations in exports are a function of the pressure of domestic demand. Although the testing of the pressure hypothesis remains the central part, the project was subsequently enlarged in order to obtain additional and related information on the factors affecting the export performance and behaviour of firms. The restricted industry coverage inevitably limits the general macroeconomic implications and applicability of the results. However, it is felt that even a limited project can be justified by the emphasis of public policy on the balance of payments and by the general lack of detailed investigations into the export performance of firms and industries.[1] In this general introductory chapter, we place our work in its macroeconomic context by presenting a brief review of the U.K. balance of payments position and some of the hypotheses which have been suggested as explanations of the economy's export performance.

In the post-war period, the U.K. has experienced a series of balance of payments crises, with their consequent implications for the foreign exchange price of sterling, the gold and dollar reserves and the pressure of domestic demand. These crises generally emerge when government decision-makers simultaneously attempt to pursue a variety of conflicting policy objectives concerned with the level of

[1] See, e.g. J. M. McGeehan, 'Competitiveness: A Survey of Recent Literature' (including bibliography), *Economic Journal*, June 1968; also, S. J. Wells, *British Export Performance*, Cambridge: Cambridge University Press, 1964.

employment, internal price stability, economic growth and the balance of payments. Ideally, any assessment of public policy requires a specific statement of policy objectives and the valuation which policy-makers place on particular objectives so as to provide evidence of their preference function or 'trade-off' pattern in situations where there are conflicting objectives. A classic example of a conflict in policy objectives arises when a government attempts to expand aggregate demand in order to reduce unemployment. Eventually, such a policy conflicts with price stability and balance of payments objectives. Given the marginal propensity to import, the expansion of aggregate demand will increase imports. In addition, if, as internal prices begin to rise more rapidly, they rise at a faster rate than the rate of increase of prices for the U.K.'s foreign competitors, then with a given exchange rate, exports will tend to become less competitive and imports more competitive, so that a balance of payments deficit on current account will eventually result. In order to eliminate such a deficit, a government has usually two basic policy alternatives: first, it can vary the external price level, namely the exchange rate, with the aim of reducing the size and/or duration of any domestic deflation required to obtain a given improvement in the balance of payments position. However, if, as seems to have been the case in the U.K. during the post-war period, the maintenance of the prevailing exchange rate is sometimes regarded as a prior objective of policy,[1] then a constraint is imposed on the choice of policy solutions to eliminate the deficit. With such a constraint, it becomes necessary to resort to the alternative possibility of changing the internal price level by reducing its rate of increase in an attempt to bring the U.K.'s domestic costs and prices into line with those of its major foreign competitors. Traditionally, and in the short run, such a result has been achieved by reducing or deflating the pressure of domestic demand in the economy. Deflation is not, of course, a costless process: it tends to achieve external balance at the expense of the domestic economy and the associated internal policy objectives. For example, unemployment is increased and there is also a belief

[1] See, e.g. *The Committee on the Working of the Monetary System*, Cmnd. 827, 1959, p. 19. The exchange rate was, of course, changed in November 1967: this devaluation, however, occurred outside the period covered by our study, 1958-66.

that deflation adversely affects growth in the economy. Although the economists' models of growth are far from satisfactory, one hypothesis which has been formulated suggests that the incentive to invest and innovate and hence the growth of capacity is a function of the pressure of demand and entrepreneurs' expectations about future demand.[1] Whilst it is difficult to formulate a satisfactory test of such a hypothesis, it has been used to provide a plausible series of relationships between the balance of payments, domestic demand and growth. From the international comparisons of these relationships, it seems that for advanced industrial countries involved in foreign trade 'there appears to be no substitute for rapidly rising exports as a means of ensuring confidence in longer-run demand prospects'.[2] In the U.K., it is frequently suggested that one of the basic problems has been that government-induced expansions in demand have tended to stimulate any increases in aggregate demand: this contrasts with some of the rapid growth economies in which export demand, especially for manufactures, appears to have stimulated expansions in aggregate demand.

The fact that deflation is not a costless process has resulted in the formulation of long-run public policy measures designed to achieve a relative improvement in the international competitiveness of the U.K. economy. In recent years, examples of such domestic policy measures have included the work of the Prices and Incomes Board, the Industrial Reorganization Corporation and the National Economic Development Council, together with such fiscal measures as the Selective Employment Tax and the associated Regional Employment Premium. In the case of both regional and prices and incomes policies, the measures were aimed at changing the traditional relationship between unemployment in the economy and the annual rate of change of domestic costs and prices.[3]

In the context of the objectives of policy, the relationship between the pressure of domestic demand and growth partially explains the

1 See W. Beckerman, *The British Economy in 1975*, Cambridge: Cambridge University Press, 1965 (p. 45).

2 Ibid., p. 56.

3 These are policies which have been presented as means of achieving a leftward shift in the Phillips' Curve. This curve shows that the lower the rate of unemployment in the economy, the greater the annual rate of increase in money wage rates.

emphasis of public policy on the balance of payments and especially the export performance of the economy. In the export sphere, which is the concern of this study, one of the most significant facts has been the long-run decline in the U.K.'s share in the world exports of manufactures. The U.K.'s share figure has declined from 20 per cent in 1954 to 13·1 per cent in 1966.[1] Whilst there is nothing sacrosanct about a particular share figure, the relevant point is that, given the importance of exports in the balance of payments, the decline in the U.K.'s share has occurred during a period when world trade has been expanding rapidly. This situation in the period up to 1966 has been appropriately described: 'The opportunities to sell more on the world market have been there, but British manufacturers have not taken them up'.[2]

A variety of reasons have been suggested to explain the decline in the U.K.'s share in world trade and many of these can be included under the general heading of 'competitiveness'.[3] Unfortunately, 'competitiveness' is rarely defined but is generally presented as an all-embracing term incorporating price and non-price factors: for example, the term appears to include managerial attitudes, innovation, marketing, product quality and style, advertising, delivery dates, service, credit facilities and public relations. Probably because of misunderstanding and the lack of precise definitions, some of the reasons suggested for the U.K.'s relative 'lack of competitiveness' are rather vague, descriptive statements which have not been formulated into hypotheses capable of being subjected to a satisfactory test. For the purposes of this study, it is sufficient to outline briefly some of the more convincing and plausible explanations of the U.K.'s declining share of world trade.

The movement of relative costs and prices provides one obvious explanation. Here, evidence from international comparisons suggests that there is a negative correlation between the rate of increase of relative export prices and the rate of increase of a country's exports. One study has indicated that for a sample of industrial countries during the period 1956-63, 43 per cent of the variation in export

1 Annual statistics of share figures are given in Table 1.1.

2 F. Hirsch, *The Pound Sterling: A Polemic*, London: Gollancz, 1965.

3 See, e.g. G. F. Ray, *The Competitiveness of British Industrial Products: A Round-Up*, Woolwich Economic Papers, London, 1966.

performance was attributable to relative export prices and that, other things being equal, a reduction of 1 per cent in price competitiveness will be associated with a decline in exports of about 3 per cent.[1] In fact, a further study has attempted to quantify the contribution of various factors in explaining the decline in the U.K.'s share of world trade in manufactures between the late 1950s and the mid-1960s: it was suggested that a decline in the price competitiveness of U.K. exports might explain over half of the reduction in the U.K. share with the relatively low growth rate accounting for a substantial proportion of the remainder.[2] In this same study, it was found that, for the period 1958-66, U.K. export prices appeared to have risen more rapidly than the export prices of her major competitors in world markets. Further evidence from an N.E.D.C. study[3] showed that for the period 1953-61, the U.K.'s wage costs per unit of manufacturing output rose by about 3 per cent per annum faster than other countries taken together. Even before the sterling devaluation of 1967, such evidence was being used to support the view that, at the prevailing exchange rate, the U.K.'s relative costs and prices were out of line with those of her foreign competitors. In addition, the N.E.D.C. study showed that between 1954 and 1962, the wholesale prices of non-food manufactures sold in the domestic market rose faster than U.K. export prices. Evidence such as this suggested that, for U.K. firms, home market sales might be relatively more profitable than exports with the result that, at the margin, firms might tend to allocate their output to the home market. This, then, was the sort of evidence on relative costs, prices and profitability which, prior to 1967, provided the basis for such suggested policy solutions as devaluation and a prices and incomes policy together with long-run structural adjustments in the economy, namely, increased investment and a greater emphasis on technical progress in order to raise the economy's growth rate, a reduction of restrictive practices, an increase in mergers and more product

1 H. Junz and R. Rhomberg, *Prices and Export Performance*, American Statistical Association, 1964.

2 L. B. Krause, 'British Trade Performance' in *Britain's Economic Prospects*, ed. R. E. Caves, London: Allen & Unwin, 1968, p. 222. See also, H. S. Houthakker and S. P. Magee, 'Income and Price Elasticities in World Trade', *Review of Economics and Statistics*, May 1969.

3 N.E.D.C., *Export Trends*, H.M.S.O., London, 1963, pp. 16-22.

standardization.[1] Whilst our study does not include a detailed analysis of prices, costs and profitability, we shall provide some limited evidence on such relevant variables as the objectives of a firm's export policy, the pricing and allocative policies of exporters and their views on the profitability of exports in relation to home sales.

The commodity and geographical composition of the U.K.'s exports provides another possible explanation of its declining share in world trade. However, the available evidence suggests that 'our commodity pattern has not, on balance, been a significantly adverse factor, but our regional pattern has been to a moderate extent. However, when both factors are taken together, their total effect seems to have been small.'[2] It is possible that the data used to test this hypothesis have been inadequate and that a more satisfactory test needs to be undertaken at a greater degree of disaggregation: we shall present the results of a limited test which was undertaken for one of the industries in our study.[3]

The pressure of domestic demand has been proposed as a further possible explanation of the U.K.'s declining share.[4] In this form, as an explanation of falling export share over time, it is a long-run explanation and one which is frequently concerned with the relationship between relatively high demand pressure and the relatively rapid rate of increase of domestic costs and prices, with consequent adverse effects on the U.K.'s share in world trade. The present study differs, in that the pressure of domestic demand is considered in relation to short-run variations around the long-run declining trend value of the U.K.'s share in world trade. Similarly, where the level of exports

1 For an excellent discussion on the relationship between policy objectives and policy measures, see R. N. Cooper, 'The Balance of Payments', in *Britain's Economic Prospects*, ed. R. Caves, London, 1968. Cooper states, '. . . that there is no logical connection between the causes of a country's balance of payments deficit and the appropriate solution. Rather, if a country must correct an imbalance in its international payments, it should seek the least-cost method for doing so in terms of its own national objectives.' (p. 155).

2 N.E.D.C., *Export Trends*, H.M.S.O., London 1963, p. 6. Also, 'Fast and Slow Growing Products in World Trade', *National Institute Economic Review*, August 1963.

3 See Chapter 7.

4 See, e.g. F. T. Blackaby, *Britain's Share in World Trade in Manufactures*, Woolwich Economic Papers, London, 1965.

rather than share is the dependent variable, the project is concerned with the relationship between the internal pressure of demand and short-run variations in exports: in these forms, the pressure explanation provided the basis for the present study.

As a short-run explanation of the U.K.'s export performance, the pressure of domestic demand can be analysed in terms of price, income and export allocative effects. In order to understand the relationships involved in the pressure hypothesis, including its effect on imports, it is useful to consider a situation in which the economy experiences a deficit on the current account of the balance of payments.[1] In the short run, with a given exchange rate, such a deficit can generally be reduced by a deflation of domestic demand. On the basis of public policy statements, it is generally assumed that, in the short run, a domestic deflation will improve the U.K.'s external trading account through three general effects:

1. A deflation will be expected to reduce the relative rate of increase of costs and prices for U.K. goods and services and there is, in fact, a substantial amount of evidence supporting this relationship.[2] In this context, the duration of a domestic deflation will depend upon its magnitude and the time required for the relative costs and prices of foreign goods to rise and so reduce the U.K.'s competitive disadvantage in world markets. In addition, since the relationship between domestic demand and the rates of change of internal costs and prices will affect exports through the effect on the international price competitiveness of British goods, it seems more logical to classify this effect of the pressure hypothesis under the general competitiveness explanation of the economy's trade performance.

2. Through its effects on the level of domestic income, a deflation will be expected to reduce the volume of imports.[3] Although the import effect of a deflation was outside the scope of the present

[1] Annual statistics of exports, imports, market share and unemployment rates, 1958-66 are given in Table 1.1.

[2] A deflation can be represented by a movement along a given Phillips' Curve. For evidence, see D. Smith, 'Incomes Policy', in *Britain's Economic Prospects*, ed. R. Caves, London, 1968.

[3] See, e.g. R. Caves, *Britain's Economic Prospects*, pp. 160f. Evidence has suggested that for every £2 10s 0d to £5 reduction in domestic income, imports have declined by £1; see, M. FG. Scott, *A Study of U.K. Imports*, Cambridge: Cambridge University Press, 1963, p. 70.

study, we have mentioned it because of its substantial contribution to reducing a trade deficit.

3. It seems that a domestic deflation is further expected to increase exports in the short run by releasing goods and resources from supplying the domestic market. It was this part of the pressure of demand explanation of variations in the U.K.'s export performance which stimulated our interest in the present study, and we shall devote the remainder of this section to a brief preliminary description of the hypothesis.

The above explanation of the pressure hypothesis was concerned with its operation at the economy level, whereas our study was largely undertaken at the level of the firm and the industry. At the microeconomic or product market level, if the quantity supplied by a domestic industry exceeds the quantity demanded domestically, then the difference will represent the output available for export. If, in the market, domestic demand for the product changes but other things remain given and constant, there will result variations in the volume of output available for export and these variations will be inversely related to the pressure of domestic demand. In other words, the pressure of demand explanation of the U.K.'s export performance maintains that, in periods of increasing and peak domestic demand, goods and resources which would otherwise be used to supply export markets will be diverted to domestic sales: such allocative effects might be induced by the greater profitability of domestic sales relative to exports. In these circumstances, it is argued that government domestic deflationary measures, such as reductions in private and public expenditure and/or tax increases will release goods and resources from supplying the home market, so allowing firms to increase their exports. At the same time, it is maintained that a domestic deflation will encourage firms to seek overseas outlets for the products which can no longer be sold at home. In this study, we shall test the pressure hypothesis which predicts that there is a negative relationship between the pressure of domestic demand on the one hand and short-run variations in exports and market share on the other, and our tests will be undertaken for a number of firms and industries.

Finally, it may be useful to describe the general economic position against which the study was undertaken. For the period under review, 1958-66, the key statistics relating to exports, imports, share and a measure of the pressure of internal demand, namely the unemployment rate, are shown in Table 1.1.

TABLE 1.1. *The U.K. Balance of Trade and the Unemployment Rate, 1958-66*

Item	*1958*	*1959*	*1960*	*1961*	*1962*	*1963*	*1964*	*1965*	*1966*
£ million									
Imports (f.o.b.)	3,378	3,640	4,141	4,045	4,098	4,370	5,016	5,065	5,262
Exports (f.o.b.)	3,407	3,522	3,733	3,892	3,994	4,287	4,471	4,784	5,110
Visible balance	29	−118	−408	−153	−104	−83	−545	−281	−152
U.K. share of world trade in manufacture (%)	17·8	17·3	15·9	15·7	15·1	14·9	13·7	13·3	13·1
Unemployment rate (%)	2·0	1·9	1·4	1·2	1·8	2·1	1·4	1·2	1·1

Sources: Central Statistical Office, *United Kingdom Balance of Payments*, 1967. *Board of Trade Journal.*
Ministry of Labour Gazette: the unemployment percentages are based on the June figures for Great Britain.

Table 1.1 shows that fluctuations in the balance of payments on visible trade are related to the proxy variable used in the table for the pressure of demand: the unemployment rate. In 1958, visible trade showed a small surplus and the pressure of demand, with an unemployment rate of 2 per cent, was relatively low. The economy entered an expansionary phase during 1959, partly as a result of Government reflationary measures, and by 1960, unemployment had dropped to a rate of 1·4 per cent, the balance of visible trade showing a deficit of some £400 million. Following the balance of payments crisis in the spring of 1961, and attendant deflationary measures in the April and July budgets, the visible trade deficit fell to less than £100 million by 1963 and, with the lower pressure of demand, the unemployment rate rose to a little over 2 per cent. Thus, the period 1958-63 exhibited a typical cycle of go-stop. Developments in 1963-6 were less clear-cut. The economy expanded at a rapid pace during 1963 and in 1964, and this was accompanied by a quick and substantial deterioration in the balance of visible trade and a fall in unemployment During 1965 and 1966, Government policy was directed to restoring the balance of payments to equilibrium. At the time of the 1965 budget, the Chancellor's assessment of the economic outlook was 'that, to free resources for the intensive export effort needed to meet his objective, home demand would have to be reduced'.[1] The policy was only partly successful. The balance of payments improved, though not sufficiently so. The pressure of demand remained high and another balance of payments crisis developed in the summer of 1966. The Government brought in a package of monetary constraints in July 1966, which led to sharply falling demand by the autumn. Between July and December, the unemployment rate rose from 1·2 to nearly 2 per cent. Subsequently, outside the period of the study, devaluation was forced upon the authorities in November, 1967.

This briefly was the economic background of the period covered by this study. Our field work, the interviews with firms, started in the latter part of 1965, and most were concluded before the impact of the July 1966 measures were felt. In assessing the results of these interviews set out in later chapters, it should be borne in mind therefore that at the time businessmen were likely to be conscious of the effect of a high pressure of demand situation; their most recent experience of the stop part of the stop-go cycle had been in 1961-2.

1 H.M. Treasury, *Economic Report*, 1965.

Chapter 2

A REVIEW OF EMPIRICAL MACROECONOMIC STUDIES OF THE PRESSURE HYPOTHESIS

Serious empirical study of the connection, if any, between the pressure of home demand and export performance is relatively recent. One of the first journal articles on the subject, by Ball, Eaton and Steuer, appeared in 1966.[1] Long-run studies of United Kingdom export performance, of the kind referred to in the last chapter, have sometimes touched upon the pressure effect. Thus Wells (op. cit.) writes in a chapter on economic conditions and export performance: 'While restrictions upon domestic demand, whether general or discriminatory, might have had a dampening effect on imports, the experience of 1955 to 1959 suggests that it is extremely doubtful whether they had a correspondingly favourable effect on exports'. And he goes on to suggest that restrictive policies in the second half of the 1950s might well have harmed the balance of payments by slowing down the rate of growth and keeping down the level of investment with unfavourable reactions upon productivity, costs and the will to export. This is of course no more than a plausible hypothesis and Wells does not attempt, nor is it his intention, to establish empirically the nature of the relation between home demand and export performance.

Studies of the long-term trend of British exports in world trade have not, then, thrown much light upon short-run influence of home demand upon export performance. And in principle there is no reason why they should. For it is quite possible for exports to be influenced by home demand regardless of the nature of the long-run performance of exports. In the case of the United Kingdom, it

1 'The relationship between United Kingdom export performance in manufactures and the internal pressure of demand,' *Economic Journal*, September 1966.

appears from the econometric studies reviewed below, that a long-run decline in the share of exports in world trade has been coupled with a pressure of home demand effect upon export performance. But equally it is quite possible for a country with a long-run rising trend in export share to exhibit a cyclical pattern of export fluctuation related to variations in home demand. At times of abnormally high demand pressure, exports might well rise less quickly if they were affected by, say, lengthening delivery dates or adverse fluctuations in relative prices. The O.E.C.D. study, to which reference is made below, suggests that this has been the situation for a number of continental European countries. If the 1967 British devaluation has the hoped-for effect, it could be the case in this country also.

We now turn to consider the problem of testing at the national level the hypothesis that the internal pressure of demand adversely affects United Kingdom export performance and we briefly review the results of studies which have been published in this field.

MODELS OF EXPORT DETERMINATION

The simplest approach might appear to be to test empirically the statistical relation between the fluctuations of United Kingdom exports on the one hand and some measure of pressure of demand on the other. This could be by a normal regression analysis of U.K. exports (perhaps detrended) on some variable reflecting pressure of demand, such as the unemployment rate or rate of change of gross national product. This approach is typified in the following extract from *The Economist* (November 30, 1963):

'The bottom chart shows the effect on Britain's industrial output of variations in total demand since 1961. Under Mr Lloyd's theory – which is still held by some people in the Treasury – this chart line should have moved in the opposite direction to the chart line of exports. . . . But it did not; surely anybody looking at these chart lines can see that since mid-1961 they have moved, with remarkable consistency, in the same directions instead.'

The snag with this kind of analysis is that it is impossible to be sure that a bivariate empirical statistical relationship between exports and a pressure of demand variable proves anything at all about the effect of pressure of demand upon exports. For even a simplistic view of the situation suggests that there is not one, but two different causal chains connecting exports and home demand. The first, and the one of primary concern in the present context, suggests that exports might be in part dependent upon the pressure of home demand, or mathematically:

$$X(t) = f(C(t), \ldots) \qquad (1)$$

where $X(t)$ is the level of exports, varying over time
and $C(t)$ is the level of capacity utilization, a proxy variable for pressure of home demand.

There is however a second causal chain acting within the home economy which also links exports and the pressure of home demand. Exports are a part of national output. Directly, and indirectly through the multiplier process, the level of exports affects the level of home demand. In other words, the pressure of home demand can be expected, in part, to be dependent on exports and we have the relation

$$C(t) = F(X(t), \ldots) \qquad (2)$$

Given both these relations, it is impossible to say whether an observed statistical correlation between $X(t)$ and $C(t)$ reflects the export determination Equation 1 or the internal economy Equation 2. In the language of econometrics, there is a problem of identification, that is to say, a problem of identifying empirically the nature of the relation between exports and the pressure of home demand in the context of Equation 1, separately from the other relation of Equation 2.

One way to overcome this difficulty is to make use of more information, specific to each of the two relations which will make them different to each other. Thus, in the export determination Equation 1, it would seem reasonable to introduce the level of overseas demand (however this is defined and measured) as an explanatory variable additional to the pressure of home demand. Indeed, overseas demand might be expected to be the principal factor determining United Kingdom exports. And in the home economy Equation 2, as well as exports, the level of output for the home market would be an explanatory variable for the pressure of home demand. This leads to a model of the following nature

$$X(t) = \alpha+\beta M(t)+\gamma C(t) \qquad (1.1)$$
$$C(t) = f(X(t), H(t)) \qquad (2.1)$$

where $M(t)$ is a measure of overseas demand and $H(t)$ a measure of output for the home market. For the purpose of exposition, Equation 1.1 is in linear form but this is not essential for the discussion following, and a number of empirical studies have used logarithmic transformations of the variable.

The first equation and in particular an estimate of the parameter γ is of primary interest in the present context. A zero value for γ would support the hypothesis that the pressure of home demand has no influence on exports, while a negative value would suggest an adverse influence. Some empirical studies have estimated equations of the type of 1.1 by a multiple regression analysis of exports on explanatory variables including measures of world trade and pressure of demand. This however is not wholly satisfactory for the procedure leads to an upwardly biased estimate of the value of γ, i.e. too great a positive value or too small a negative value.[1] In fact, this may not matter much. It means that if γ is estimated at a certain negative value, the true value is likely to be more negative. On the other hand, if γ is estimated to be positive, this could be consistent with an underlying value of this coefficient equal to zero or even negative.

A related approach to the problem of assessing the effect of pressure of demand on exports is to look at the performance of the share of U.K. exports in world trade and examine whether there is any evidence that the share is adversely affected at times of high pressure of home demand. The U.K. share of world trade has been declining in the long run and the decline might be the faster at times of high pressure of demand. This suggests seeking a multi-regression analysis of the U.K. share upon home pressure of demand and a time variable (in order to remove the trend effect). Ball *et al.* (op. cit.) discuss a two-equation model set up in constant elasticity terms

[1] Due to the second relation (2.1) between $X(t)$ and $C(t)$, the error term in 1.1 will be positively correlated with $C(t)$. This has the consequence that the estimate of γ will not be unbiased and the bias under normal conditions would be upwards.

from which can be derived a relation involving the U.K. share of world trade. The first equation of their model, relating to export determination, is

$$X(t) = k_1 M(t)^\alpha U(t)^\beta e^{-rt} \tag{1.2}$$

$X(t)$ is an index of U.K. exports. As before, $M(t)$ is an index of world imports which stands proxy for 'overseas demand'. $U(t)$ is an index of unutilized resources, inversely related to the level of capacity utilization and the final term is an exponential trend. Their second equation, expressing the determination of unutilized resources in terms of export demand and output for the home market, $H(t)$, is

$$U(t) = k_2 X(t)^{-\lambda} H(t)^{-\pi} e^{st} \tag{2.2}$$

In this two-equation model, the parameter of central interest is β in Equation 1.2. A zero value for β would indicate no effect on exports by the level of capacity utilization, whereas a positive value would indicate that an increase in the level of unutilized resources would, other things being equal, lead to an increase in exports. Taking an assumed (and unrealistic) value of $\pi = 0$, Ball *et al.* show that it is a consequence of this model that the share of U.K. exports in world trade, $\frac{X(t)}{M(t)}$, can be expressed as a function of $U(t)$ and t itself and that the share will be dependent upon $U(t)$ even if $\beta = 0$. For it can be shown that Equations 1.2 and 2.2 can then be rearranged to give the relation

$$\log\left(\frac{X(t)}{M(t)}\right) = \frac{\beta}{\alpha} + \frac{(1-\alpha)s}{\alpha\lambda} \log U(t) + \text{other terms.}$$

The coefficient of $\log U(t)$ would be positive if $\alpha < 1$ and $s \neq 0$ even if $\beta = 0$. A positive correlation between the share of U.K. exports and unutilized capacity could therefore be exhibited even where there is no real marginal effect on exports due to the pressure of home demand.

In the Ball study, the assumption is made that the parameter α in Equation 1.2 is unity in which case the source of bias discussed in the last paragraph does not arise. This is equivalent to the assumption that the demand elasticity of U.K. exports with respect to world trade is unity. On the basis of this assumption they set up a model in which the share is a dependent variable:

$$\frac{X(t)}{M(t)} = \alpha+\beta t+\gamma C(t) \tag{1.3}$$

$$C(t) = F(X(t), H(t)) \tag{2.3}$$

where $C(t)$, the pressure of demand variable, is defined as the ratio of industrial production to trend.

In fact only the first equation is estimated by carrying out the ordinary single equation least squares regression of U.K. share of trade on the level of capacity utilization and on time which has the effect of removing a linear trend from each series. A value of γ significantly different from zero and negative, would support the hypothesis that the pressure of home demand adversely affects export performance. But Ball *et al.* point out that two qualifications need to be borne in mind in assessing any experimental results. The first is that, as we have remarked above, if in fact the demand elasticity of U.K. exports with respect to world trade is less than unity, then the effect of the pressure of demand would be overestimated by this method. The second qualification is that the separate estimation of Equation 1.3 by ordinary least squares is liable to produce a biased estimate of γ given the causal dependence of $C(t)$ on $X(t)$ expressed by the second equation (2.3) of the model. Ball *et al.* argue that it is doubtful whether the bias in the least squares estimate is very serious, since the feedback from exports to capacity utilization is likely to have been small compared to the influence of $H(t)$. But it is interesting to note that if there is any bias it is likely to have the result that the pressure of demand effect on exports is *underestimated* for the reason discussed earlier. In other words it would work the opposite way to the first.

To sum up, two classes of model have been studied, one class consisting of export determination equations based on the level of exports and the other based on equations explaining the behaviour of the U.K. export share. And in so far as the export determination equation is estimated by ordinary least squares technique, due to bias, any adverse effect of the pressure of demand may be underestimated. On the other hand, a model based on the U.K. share of world trade may overestimate the effect of pressure of demand if the elasticity of U.K. exports in relation to overseas demand is less than one. To put it simply, an estimation based upon a level of exports model which suggests a beneficial effect upon exports due to pressure of demand cannot be trusted, while a share model which suggests an adverse effect might be overstating its magnitude.

MEASURES OF THE VARIABLES

Our discussion so far has ignored the problem of deciding upon the most appropriate statistical measures of concepts such as 'overseas demand' and 'pressure of home demand'. At various points, it has been tacitly assumed that overseas demand can be equated to the level of world trade or that pressure of home demand is synonymous with capacity utilization.

The first aim of an equation of export determination is to set up one which will best estimate the relation between exports and 'overseas demand', other things, i.e. the internal economy, being equal. That is, we are seeking an overseas variable which would be in functional relation with U.K. exports if there were no supply restrictions from the effect of pressure of demand. Complete success cannot be achieved. United Kingdom exports are a unique collection of particular goods in particular quantities exported to particular markets. The U.K. export figures themselves measure overseas demand *ex post*; there can be no completely satisfactory measure of intended demand for U.K. exports. All that can be done is to use a proxy variable which minimizes inadequacies and then try to evaluate their consequences on the estimation process.

A normal proxy variable for overseas demand is the level of world trade – normally world trade in manufactures if the study relates, as is usual, to British exports of manufactures. The argument runs that total imports of manufactures of any country or group of countries will equal demand for imports of manufactures in general, and in particular reflect demand for imports of British manufactures. There is of course a problem of aggregation here. The market pattern of world trade in manufactures is not the same as that of British exports. So an index number of world imports weighted according to the country pattern of trade of U.K. exports would be more appropriate than an overseas demand variable directly based on total world trade, or some other aggregative variable such as exports of manufactures by industrial countries. In principle, a similar argument applies to the fact that there is a difference in commodity composition between U.K. exports and world trade in manufactures. It may not however be worth while producing an index of world trade reflecting the structure of U.K. exports. The statistical work, particularly in the case of commodity composition, would be considerable. And although the estimating process would to some extent be more efficient, there is no reason to think that any bias is introduced by using a simple aggregate not reweighted.

There remains a more fundamental difficulty with the use of country import figures as measures of demand for U.K. exports. It is this. If country imports from the U.K. (i.e. U.K. exports) do not measure 'demand' for U.K. exports, in what sense do total imports into a country measure total import demand? In the extreme case where there is perfect substitution between overseas countries' imports from the U.K. and from elsewhere, and there are no supply limitations on imports from third countries, then actual total imports will be a satisfactory proxy variable for total demand. In this situation, demand for imports will be satisfied and total imports will equal total demand for imports. Also, even where there is no substitution as between U.K. imports and imports from other countries, total imports would remain an appropriate measure of demand for U.K. exports so long as (*a*) there are no supply limitations on exports from other countries and (*b*) the import demand for U.K. goods can be assumed to vary in the same way as the demand for goods imported from elsewhere. If, however, there are supply limitations on imports from other countries taken as a whole, the position is more complicated. In this situation, U.K. exports will be dependent upon the demand for U.K. exports which itself will be a function of imports from all sources and of the pressure of demand in competing countries. In terms of a simple linear model explaining the level of U.K. exports we have:

$$X(t) = \alpha + \beta M(t) + \gamma C(t) + \delta C'(t)$$

where $C'(t)$ is an aggregative indicator of the pressure of demand effect on exports from competing countries. We may ask what will be the effect of setting up an export-determination equation which omits the final term, when in fact pressure of demand effects in other countries work their way through to affect U.K. exports performance in the way which has just been described. The answer will depend upon the behaviour of $C'(t)$ in relation to the variables $M(t)$ and $C(t)$. If $C'(t)$ is independent of $M(t)$ and $C(t)$, then the estimates of β and γ in the complete equation will be unbiased, though some precision will be lost. $C'(t)$ may however be correlated with $M(t)$ or $C(t)$ or both. In a model concerned with explaining U.K. exports to industrial countries, $M(t)$ and $C'(t)$ are more likely to be positively correlated since they will both be directly related to the broad, overall level of activity in industrial countries. The effect on the estimation procedure of omitting a $C'(t)$ term, if it is positively correlated with $M(t)$, will be to overestimate β, not a serious deficiency if we are primarily interested in the coefficient γ of $C(t)$.

A more important question is what would be the consequences of a relation between $C(t)$ and $C'(t)$. Again, if one exists, it is more likely to be positive and the effect will be that the parameter γ will be *numerically* underestimated. This is a fortunate direction for the bias for it means that, if a significant pressure of demand effect is established wrongly in a model which omits the $C'(t)$ variable, the true pressure of demand effect would, if anything, be greater than that estimated.

To sum up this discussion of the measurement of overseas demand in the export determination model, it can be said that there are dangers in ignoring the possible effect of changes in the pressure of demand in competing countries. But it is unlikely that an omission of this kind would have an effect on the quality of any conclusion which might be drawn. For the probable effect will be that the role of U.K. pressure of demand in the performance of U.K. exports will be underplayed if anything. It is of course a corollary that an analysis which suggests no influence or a positive influence of the pressure of home demand must be looked on with suspicion.

MEASUREMENT AND MEANING OF PRESSURE OF DEMAND

At the outset let it be said that there is no theory about the possible effect of supply limitations on exports which suggest that one particular method of measuring pressure of demand is better than any other. There are two issues: the practical one of the most appropriate statistical measure, and the more interesting question of principle of whether it is the *level* of pressure of demand or its *rate of change* which is the relevant factor.

There are many variables which might stand proxy for the pressure of demand, but two in particular have been used: the deviations of G.D.P. or industrial production from trend value (or what is much the same thing, the ratio of G.D.P. to its trend value) and the unemployment rate. In the present context, the main difference between these two variables is in their timing but in a model using appropriate lagged values of variables there is no *a priori* reason why one variable suitably lagged should perform better than the other. The timing relation at the national level between pressure on capacity and export performance is bound to be tenuous because it will vary much between industries. Whether in the event an output variable, such as deviations from trend of G.D.P., performs better than a labour supply variable, such as unemployment, is bound to be somewhat fortuitous.

The choice between level of pressure of demand and rate of change of pressure is more arguable. To crystallize the discussion, let us compare the two hypotheses and their implications at two particular points of the cycle: the peak and the trough when the rate of change of pressure of demand is the same. The level of demand hypothesis affirms that exports performance would be adversely affected by the peak as compared with the trough; the rate of change hypothesis does not distinguish between these two situations. At first sight, it seems implausible that export performance should depend upon the rate of change of pressure regardless of its level. Comparing a peak situation with a trough, in general prices will be rising faster, delivery dates will be further ahead, and firms might have less reason to push out export sales. In qualitative terms, the level of pressure of demand seems to promise better explanatory power of any supply limitations upon exports than the rate of change of pressure.

The comparison however is no longer so clear-cut if we consider intermediate stages of the business cycle, for example the upturn phase between trough and peak. Over this phase, the level hypothesis suggests a progressive worsening of export performance as the pressure of demand rises from below to above 'average' value. On the other hand, the rate of change hypothesis suggests little change in effect once the upturn has got under way. This is clear from an idealized sinusoidal model of the cycle shown in the diagram (Figure 2.1). Over the time-period *AB*, the pressure of demand increases substantially whereas the rate of change varies only slightly from its maximum value.

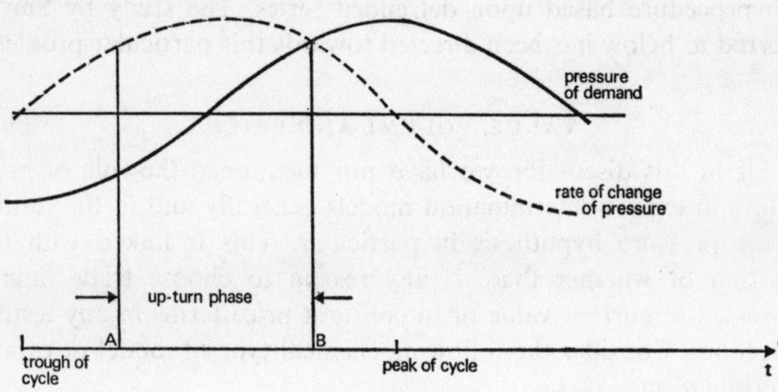

Fig. 2.1

Perhaps now the rate of change model is more convincing. Over most of the upturn phase, prices will be rising faster, firms will be finding difficulty in matching production to continually rising demand and, again over the upturn phase as a whole, export performance might be continually and fairly constantly affected.

It seems therefore that there is something to be said for both the level and the rate of change of pressure of demand hypotheses. Perhaps their relative relevance varies at the various points of the cycle, sometimes one being more appropriate, sometimes the other. There is however an important qualification to be made. We have so far ignored the undoubted existence of time-lags in the process. Whether the level or the rate of pressure of demand is used, it will be a matter for empirical investigation, and little more, to establish what the timings are. But once lags are introduced into the model, the distinction between level and rate of change inevitably becomes rather blurred. For example, in an idealized model where the pressure of demand fluctuates sinusoidally with a period of say four years, the rate of change variable lagged one year would perform in exactly the same way as the level of demand variable unlagged.

In our discussion, it has been implicitly assumed that the pressure of demand would affect export performance over its whole range of variation. But it is possible that the relation is asymmetric in the sense that only when the pressure is greater than a particular critical value is export performance affected. However, as Ball *et al.* point out (op. cit.) it is difficult to test this effect empirically by an estimation procedure based upon detrended series. The study by Smyth referred to below has been directed towards this particular problem.

VALUE, VOLUME AND PRICE

So far in this discussion we have not mentioned the role of price factors in export-determination models generally and in the testing of the pressure hypothesis in particular. This is linked with the question of whether there is any reason to choose trade figures expressed in current value or in constant price terms in any testing procedure. Consider the following classical type of model of export determination:

$$X = kM^{\alpha}\left(\frac{P_x}{P_m}\right)^{-\gamma} C^{-\beta} \tag{3}$$

where X is the volume of U.K. exports, M the volume of total overseas countries' imports, P_x and P_m the respective prices, and C a measure of U.K. pressure of demand. This is a constant elasticity model in which α is the volume elasticity of demand for exports and γ the price elasticity. The logarithmic form of this relation is

$$\log X = \log k + \alpha \log M - \gamma \log\left(\frac{P_x}{P_m}\right) - \beta \log C \tag{4}$$

and a regression analysis of the logarithms of the variables would yield, *inter alia*, an estimate of α, the volume elasticity of demand for U.K. exports.

On the basis of this model, it is possible to derive the consequential relation between X_v, the value of U.K. exports, and M_v, the value of overseas imports and the price and pressure variables. For $X_v = P_x X$ and $M_v = P_m M$, and substitution in the logarithmic relation above yields after rearrangement:

$$\log X_v = \log k + \alpha \log M_v + \log\left(\frac{P_x}{P_m^\alpha}\right) - \gamma \log\left(\frac{P_x}{P_m}\right) - \beta \log C \quad (5)$$

or, since α can be expected to be near to 1, $\log\left(\frac{P_x}{P_m^\alpha}\right)$ will be very near to $\log\left(\frac{P_x}{P_m}\right)$ and so Equation 3 becomes

$$\log X_v = \log k + \alpha \log M_v + (1-\gamma) \log\left(\frac{P_x}{P_m}\right) - \beta \log C. \quad (6)$$

Comparing Equations 4 and 6, it can be seen that the alternative approaches of using in the regression analysis, volume figures (Equation 4) or value figures (Equation 6) will each lead to estimates of the basic elasticities α, β, and γ. The difference will be that the coefficient of $\log\left(\frac{P_x}{P_m}\right)$ in the value equation will give an estimate of the price elasticity less than unity.

RECENT STUDIES

In this section we describe and compare the main results of four studies which directly or indirectly bear upon the relationship of pressure of demand to United Kingdom export performance. These are Ball, Eaton and Steuer, 'The relationship between United Kingdom export performance in manufactures and the internal pressure of demand'; the O.E.C.D. study by Adams, Eguchi and Meyer-zu-Schlochtern, *An Econometric Analysis of International Trade*; Renton, 'Forecasting British exports of manufactures to industrial countries'; and Smyth, 'Stop-go and United Kingdom exports of manufactures'.[1] Each study involved the estimation of

[1] Ball, Eaton and Steuer: 'The relationship between United Kingdom export performance in manufactures and the internal pressure of demand', *Economic Journal*, September 1966 (op. cit.);

Adams, Eguchi and Meyer-zu-Schlochtern: *An Econometric Analysis of International Trade—an interrelated explanation of imports and exports of O.E.C.D. countries*, O.E.C.D., 1969;

G. A. Renton: 'Forecasting British exports of manufactures to industrial countries', *National Institute Economic Review*, November 1967;

D. J. Smyth: 'Stop-go and United Kingdom exports of manufactures'. *Bulletin of the Oxford University Institute of Economics and Statistics*, No. 1, February 1968.

multiple regression equations in which the dependent variable was based upon the level of United Kingdom exports of manufactures; the main independent variables were a world trade variable and a pressure of demand variable. In addition, the Ball study examined the share of U.K. exports in world trade in relation to a pressure of demand variable. Table 2.1 summarizes the main models which were estimated.

Three of the studies, Ball, O.E.C.D. and Renton, estimated a model which explained the level of exports in terms of overseas demand and a pressure of demand variable. The Ball and Renton equations were very similar but whereas the second study revealed a significant pressure of demand effect, the former did not. Thus a typical equation in the Ball study was

$$X(t) = 1{,}461 + \underset{(0{\cdot}003)}{0{\cdot}064}\, M(t) - \underset{(254{\cdot}8)}{266{\cdot}4}\, C(t)$$

where $X(t)$ and $M(t)$ were respectively U.K. exports and world exports both at constant 1958 prices and $C(t)$ a measure of capacity utilization based upon the ratio of industrial output to trend. Renton estimated the following equation (using his notation):

$$X = -0{\cdot}9579 + \underset{(0{\cdot}0937)}{1{\cdot}0213}Z - \underset{(0{\cdot}1626)}{0{\cdot}7734}Q_{-1} - 0{\cdot}0034t$$

where variables are expressed as their logarithms and X was the value of U.K. exports *to industrial countries*, Z the value of industrial countries' total imports, and Q_{-1} an index of pressure of demand (lagged one-quarter) based upon deviations from trend of manufacturing production. In the Ball model, the coefficient of the pressure of demand term is not significant, in the Renton model it is. The bases of the two equations are not identical; the Renton equation, though not the Ball equation, has a time-trend term and the presence or absence of this can affect other coefficients. The Renton analysis covers exports to industrial countries only and possibly these are more sensitive to pressure of demand effects. The periods covered are also slightly different: 1954-64 for the Ball analysis and 1956-66 (third quarter) in the Renton study.

The O.E.C.D. study also estimates an export determination equation for the level of U.K. exports. It differs from the two referred to

TABLE 2.1

Study coverage	*Period covered*	*Export variable*	*Overseas demand variable*	*Pressure of demand variable*	*Remarks*
***Ball* et al.:** Exports of manufactures	1954–64 quarterly	(i) Exports (*Q*) (ii) Share in world trade (*Q*)	World exports (*Q*) ...	Deviations from trend of industrial production	
O.E.C.D. Exports to O.E.C.D. countries	1955–65 quarterly	Exports (*Q*)	Index of imports (*Q*) weighted according to constant U.K. share	Deviations from trend of industrial production	Pressure of demand variable a measure of U.K. relative to other O.E.C.D. countries
Renton Exports of manufactures to industrial countries	1956–66 quarterly	Log exports (*V*)	Log imports (*V*) of industrial countries	Log deviations from trend of manufacturing production	U.K. pressure of demand relative to that of other industrial countries also tested
Smyth Exports of manufactures	1955–65 annually	Annual percentage change in exports (*V* & *Q*)	Annual percentage change in exports of main exporting countries (*V* & *Q*)	(i) Unemployment in manufacturing industries (weighted according to export performance) (ii) Change in unemployment on previous year	Asymmetric effects of pressure of demand also tested

Note: (*V*) indicates variable in form of value figures or index.
(*Q*) indicates variable in form of quantity index.

above in three main respects: it relates to U.K. trade with other O.E.C.D. countries only, it pre-specifies a unit elasticity of demand for exports with respect to overseas imports, and it employs a pressure of demand variable which is a measure of the pressure of demand in the U.K. relative to other competing countries. The estimated equation is:

$$X = 87{\cdot}31 + \underset{\text{(determined)}}{1{\cdot}00S} - \underset{(1{\cdot}4)}{0{\cdot}48PX} - \underset{(1{\cdot}5)}{0{\cdot}33PDX} + \text{dummy variables},$$

where X is a volume index of U.K. exports, S is a weighted aggregate of import indexes of overseas markets based on constant market shares, PX is a measure (lagged one-quarter) of relative export prices (i.e. U.K. export prices relative to those of competing countries) and PDX is a relative pressure of demand index (lagged one-quarter) based upon deviations of industrial production from a semi-log trend. The figures in brackets are not standard errors but t-values. The coefficients of the prices and pressure of demand terms are therefore not significant at around the 5 per cent level. In the O.E.C.D. study, it is stated that the overseas demand coefficient was predetermined at unity 'in view of the lack of a structural explanation for the long-term developments of the U.K. share of export markets'. The restriction imposed is very similar to estimating a share model with an assumption of unit elasticity of overseas demand for U.K. exports. And, as was pointed out above, this estimation procedure might well overestimate any pressure of demand effect.

Returning to the study by Ball, Eaton and Steuer, it was their estimation of a share model which showed a significant pressure of demand effect. In fact, they estimated a number of alternative share model equations: on linear or logarithmic bases, current value or constant price terms and with prior or dummy variable methods of seasonal adjustment. In essence, all approaches gave similar results and one typical one was:

$$\log S = \text{constant} - \underset{(0{\cdot}115)}{0{\cdot}439 \log C} - \underset{(0{\cdot}0003)}{0{\cdot}01t}$$

where S is the share of U.K. exports of manufactures in world trade at constant prices, and C, as in the level of exports equation referred to above, is based upon the deviations of industrial output from trend. The pressure of demand effect is clearly significant.

Finally in this summary of macro studies of the pressure of demand effect upon exports there is the study by Smyth. This differed from the others in three main respects. First, it was based solely upon annual data. Second, the figures of exports and overseas demand used in the analysis were in the form of percentage changes on the previous year. And third, it compared the effect of level of pressure of demand with rate of change of pressure of demand, and it explored the possibility of a non-continuous effect. The pressure of demand was measured by unemployment, unlike other studies which have employed measures based upon fluctuations in output. In the terms of his approach, Smyth found no significant relation between the level of pressure of demand and export performance. Thus, a typical result was

$$Y = 3.34 - 0{\cdot}465X - 1{\cdot}627U$$
$$(0{\cdot}206) \quad (2{\cdot}579)$$

where Y is the percentage change in value of exports, X the percentage change in exports of main exporting countries, and U the unemployment in manufacturing industries with individual industries weighted according to their level of exports. The coefficient of U is not significant but an estimation replacing U by W, the absolute change in U on the previous year gave the following:

$$Y = -3{\cdot}28 + 0{\cdot}909X + 4{\cdot}687W.$$
$$(0{\cdot}176) \quad (1{\cdot}970)$$

It is not at all clear that these two results taken together support a hypothesis that the rate of increase of demand pressure, rather than its level, is the important supply factor in export performance, as was suggested by Brechling and Wolfe.[1] For if we postulate a model in which the level of U.K. exports are in linear relation with the level of world trade and the level of unemployment, then, as a consequence, a linear relation will also connect the year-to-year changes in the variables. But percentage year-to-year changes in a variable will in general be closely correlated with year-to-year

[1] F. P. Brechling and J. N. Wolfe, 'The End of Stop-Go', *Lloyds Bank Review*, January 1965.

changes. Hence an empirically established relation which establishes a partial correlation between the rate of change of pressure of demand and the rate of change of exports could be taken as supporting the hypothesis that it is the level of pressure of demand which affects the level of exports.

THE QUANTITATIVE EFFECTS ON EXPORTS OF VARIATIONS IN DEMAND PRESSURE

The establishing of a statistically significant marginal relationship between two variables does not in itself imply that actual variations in one variable have an economically significant effect on the other. The studies reviewed above, with the exception of that by O.E.C.D., lead to the conclusion, in terms of the various models, data and time-periods studied, that pressure of home demand is significantly related to export performance. But, given the relationships which have been estimated, what numerical effect upon export level do they predict for the kind of variation in pressure of demand which is actually experienced?

Two of the studies present numerical estimates of this nature. Thus, Ball *et al.* calculate central estimates of the implied 'loss' in exports in the boom years of 1955, 1960 and 1964 as a consequence of the pressure of demand being greater than that in 1958. 1958 was a year of relative recession with a level of capacity utilization roughly corresponding to 2½ per cent unemployment. These calculated 'losses' were about £86 million for 1955, £122 million for 1960 and £179 million for 1964. Renton made a similar calculation, though it should be remembered that his study related to manufacturing exports to industrial countries and not, as in the Ball *et al.* analysis, to the world. He estimated that, as compared with a 'normal' year, the export 'loss' in 1965 was about £44 million and the export 'gain' in 1958 was about £32 million, i.e. a differential between 1958 and 1965 of some £76 million.

It is of course extremely difficult and perhaps not particularly useful to compare the effects of pressure of demand variation by various estimated models. A certain consistency is almost inevitable since they are based on common or closely related data over much the same period of time. On the other hand, there are bound to be differences if only because none of the models have identical structures. However, it is interesting to ask what percentage effect on exports is predicted by each model comparing a high pressure of demand year with a low pressure of demand year. So far as can be estimated from the data presented in the articles, the answers all appear to lie in the range 2½ to 5 per cent. But any figure of this kind, as Ball *et al.* point out, can only be suggestive, for many important qualifications need to be borne in mind. First, there is the usual statistical range of error in any estimation of a regression coefficient, and hence in the estimated marginal influence of pressure of demand upon exports. The precision of the estimated regression coefficients varies from one estimated equation to another, but very roughly the data are consistent with regression coefficients at least 30 per cent less than the central estimate (at the 20 per cent level of significance with a one-tailed test).

Second, there is the problem of bias in the estimation procedure. This has been discussed above and from that discussion it emerged that it was possible, though not certain, that a share model would, if anything, overestimate the pressure effect, whereas a level of exports model might underestimate it.

Third, and perhaps more important, any econometric analysis at the most describes what has happened. Relationships deduced between variables are conditional upon the whole system analysed. In so far as it is plausible to assume the system continues into the future, it might be reasonable to assume that the economy will continue to display much the same marginal relations: that, for example, years with a high pressure of demand will, other things being equal, exhibit an export performance predicted by the estimated relation. But it could be quite implausible to assume that the estimated relations will hold in other circumstances. If, for example, the economy were to be run at a significantly lower pressure of demand in the future long term than in the past, there is no reason to expect that the consequential gain to exports could be predicted by the regression coefficients estimated on the basis of past performance.

Chapter 3

SURVEY AIMS AND METHOD

The article by Ball, Eaton and Steuer (op. cit.) concludes: 'The analysis of this paper is based on aggregate data. This entails not only aggregation over products but also over markets. In so far as this is the case, the results conceal variation between products and between markets. At the aggregate level we mix up the adjusting patterns of different industries. It is important to emphasize, therefore, that research at the industry level is an essential adjunct to the work. Such research provides a firmer base from which to better interpret the results of this study.' There is, however, a prima facie case for suggesting that an attempt should be made to take disaggregation further to the level of the firm. Differences in technology and market structure between industries will affect the manner in which they react to pressure of demand, and the problem of aggregation of industries will be all the more severe if, as seems plausible, any reaction to pressure of demand is non-linear. But similarly, there can be expected to exist substantial variations in the reactions of individual firms within a particular industry. At any point in time the exports of individual firms may exhibit varying reactions to the current pressure of demand, if only for reasons of a structural nature, such as varying proportions of output exported and how far important customers are in the home or the export markets. Hence the performance of an industry as a whole may well in part depend upon the distribution of properties specific to firms in the industry.

There is another aggregation problem which merits more attention than it has received. Studies of export performance at industry level (including long-run studies) normally rely upon the use of international trade statistics according to commodity groupings.

But the available international trade statistics make it extremely difficult to carry out any analysis more detailed than a three-figure heading of the Standard International Trade Classification (S.I.T.C.). Within such headings, however, there are far from homogeneous collections of goods. Thus, headings in the machinery and equipment sectors such as 'metal working machinery' and 'electrical equipment' clearly cover an extremely wide range of greatly differing products. Even apparently homogeneous groups may, in the present context, comprise products of a very differing nature. Pottery (S.I.T.C. heading 666), an industry included in this study, is a good example. At one end it includes cheap earthenware, a low-quality product in which the British industry is finding it extremely difficult to compete in overseas markets, and, at the other end, high-quality china where, for a number of firms, the major limitation on exports has been one of productive capacity. In such a case, any study of the export performance of an industry as a whole, either as regards long-run or short-run performance, would throw little light on the factors at work. Thus, if the decline in the British share of world markets were the consequence in part of a comparative inflexibility in the development of new products within industries, it would be difficult to discern evidence for this from aggregative data based upon commodity groups.

In general, studies at the firm level may be desirable where there is significant lack of homogeneity between firms in an industry as regards relevant factors. Another major justification for a firm study arises from the need to study a whole class of factors affecting export performance which are not measured by statistical data available at industry level, or, indeed, not statistically measurable at all. Apart from the influence of factors specific to the individual firm, such as size of firm and proportion of output exported, there is the question of the relation between export performance and the relevant aspects of attitudes. What is the role of exports generally in the firm's long-run aims? To what extent do firms give priority to exports at periods of high pressure of demand? What degree of choice in the short and long run do managements have as regards the allocation of production between export and home sales? What is the role of pricing policy?

Our first objective then was to examine the relationship between home demand and exports and our second was to try to discover what other variables influenced U.K. exports.

It seemed to us that if we were to learn anything about the problems outlined above, and in particular about the amount of management discretion in choosing between home and export sales and the factors affecting management decisions, then it would be necessary to go to the decision-units, the firms, and ask a lot of questions. It was recognized that there are certain disadvantages of an investigation at the individual firm level. So much detail peculiar to individual firms may be uncovered that it might be difficult to discern any important common factors. In addition, asking firms about their policy and actions (not the same thing) in this field is not a simple matter, and is not a method that is likely to reveal the whole truth. What senior executives think are the factors which influence their own decisions and their firm's performance are not necessarily those which are actually relevant. Nor do causal influences necessarily work in the way management thinks they do. Moreover, the lack of previous work of a similar kind meant that ours was to some extent a pilot study. We did not know how much about their affairs firms would be willing to tell us, or indeed if they would agree to help at all, so to begin with we were working very much in the dark, and always ran the risk of failing to ask the right questions or of failing in some way to obtain crucial pieces of information.

We tried to overcome some of these disadvantages in a number of ways. In the first place, we chose interviews rather than a postal enquiry by questionnaire. The complexity of the problem meant that a straight question-and-answer technique was not likely to be very useful nor indeed could a satisfactory response be expected from a mail enquiry. The intention was to try to get businessmen talking, and let them throw light on the questions we were interested in without too much direct questioning on our part. This was vindicated in practice in that, with our more tricky questions, we seldom reached an answer which both we and our subject could agree was fair and not misleading without a considerable amount of discussion. Firms were also asked for statistical data bearing upon their export performance and the pressure of demand and other related variables. It was hoped to be able to compare the results of statistical and econometric analysis of the relevant variables with the qualitative data which would come out of the interviews. In short, neither a qualitative nor quantitative enquiry would on its own be satisfactory, but there was a chance that the two combined would lead us nearer the truth. A final reason for pursuing interviews was that we did not know before we started how much statistical information firms would be willing or able to give us, or indeed, if they would give us any. In the event, we got some very interesting qualitative data from firms who could not or would not give us any figures.

The project was restricted to firms in a small number of industries rather than a random selection of firms over a wide field. This clearly reduced the possibility of generalizing from the results at a national level but gave some other advantages. It would, however, give an indication of the kind of variability in performance and experience which there might be from one industry to another and would suggest which factors bearing upon export performance were common – and which were not – to firms in the same industry. In addition, tackling a few industries yielded considerable economies in research time and money. Only a few trade associations had to be approached, relatively few published statistics needed to be extracted, the number of particular conditions of manufacture and other special factors surrounding different products was much reduced. An unusual bonus was that in the case of pottery, the geographical concentration of the industry meant we were often able to see several firms on a single trip.

PROCEDURE

The first step was to select some industries to be studied, their number consistent with the limited research resources at our disposal. The ideal industry for our purposes has a very low 'spread', by which we mean that it makes no products of other industries, and firms classified to other industries do not make its products; it does a significant export business; it is geographically concentrated; and has a fair number of firms, not because we were anxious to investigate one type of market structure only, but because a number of firms makes the statistical results of more interest. In addition we wanted the final selection to include a fair range of types, industries with relatively high and low exports as a proportion of turnover, with increasing, decreasing and constant exports, and industries covering consumer, consumer durable and capital goods. More industries were initially selected than we could eventually study, in case of failure to establish contact or refusal to help, but we eventually tackled the following: pottery, motor cycles and cycles, office machinery, and domestic electrical appliances. This list shows one major gap, with no representation from the machine tool and motor vehicles industries. At the time of our survey, both these industries were the objects of a number of official and semi-official enquiries and in these circumstances it was felt that a small private project would not meet with a satisfactory response. In addition, a study of any sector of the machine tools industry would have raised considerable difficulties in statistical analysis due to the problem of 'spread' referred to above.

All the industries included in our enquiry, except possibly pottery, had a number of drawbacks; but the only serious one was that motor cycle and cycle production – which are really two separate industries which happen to be classified together in the Standard Industrial Classification – is dominated by two firms, so that our results in this case were heavily dependent on what these two could and would tell us.[1] At first sight, covering an industry fairly effectively by seeing two firms (in fact we saw a number of others too) seems to represent a bonus in time and money saved, but as it happened neither gave us figures, so statistical analysis had to be confined to published figures. In the domestic electrical appliance industry, we decided to concentrate the enquiry upon three products (refrigerators, vacuum cleaners and washing machines) because of the complicated 'spread' in the industry.[2]

The next step in each case was to contact the relevant trade association and have a general discussion about the industry, the project and its chances of success in the industry, and about firms we might see. In the case of the first firm or two, the trade association contacted the firm first and prepared them for our visit. Later on, when we had established our bona fides so to speak and nobody

1 This degree of concentration was not apparent from the most recent census of production for 1958 available at that time, partly because it was by then very out of date, but also because it classified firms in the same financial groups, but with separate company structure, as being independent.

2 See introduction to Chapter 10.

had complained about us to the trade association, we obtained names of firms and of someone to write to in the firm, and wrote mentioning the association. In this letter we explained the general purposes of the project and asked for an interview. Only at the end of an interview, after, we hoped, some rapport and understanding of our objectives (and our academic independence) had been established, did we ask for statistical data. We felt, and still do, that businessmen were entirely entitled to refuse us either interview or figures or both, but especially figures, involving as they do the firm's private affairs and usually some work in preparation as well. We also felt though that we had more chance of success in obtaining figures after we had had an opportunity to explain ourselves at some length.

At an earlier stage we had drafted a questionnaire (reproduced in Appendix A), but the interviews were deliberately not conducted on the basis of a series of questions and answers. At the interview itself we tried to initiate a general discussion, and guide it as gently as possible along the general lines of the questionnaire, filling in answers as and when they appeared to have been supplied by the discussion, rather than asking direct questions. Although of course this ideal procedure was rarely followed completely, we felt that, the nearer we approached it, the nearer would we get to a true picture of the businessman's policies, objectives, attitudes and so forth, all of which were most relevant for answering the most important questions we were trying to ask. In this context we found it was better to have two people interviewing, so that one could keep the conversation going while the other took notes. This was not always possible, and, while it became less important as we acquired more practice in interviewing, having a single interviewer probably reduced the effectiveness of some of the interviews. At the end of each interview we asked for the statistical data described below. We also asked if we could send a 'cleaned-up' version of the answers we had entered in the questionnaire for checking. Usually we specified the exact figures we wanted in a letter accompanying the questionnaire and received them with the corrected questionnaire. With only one or two exceptions the questionnaire was not shown to the businessmen during the interview.

The final version of the questionnaire itself was not prepared until we had seen two trade associations (motor cycles and cycles, and pottery) and a leading firm in each industry. As it happened, one firm would not give us figures, and the other could not for purely technical reasons. This made us realize how much we might have to rely on qualitative data; we also confirmed from these meetings that it would be useful to have a questionnaire to guide the discussion, so that our qualitative results would be of a similar nature for every firm, and so to some extent classifiable. It will be seen from Appendix A that the questionnaire had entered on it alternative answers to many of the questions and as a consequence note-taking during interviews was greatly helped. Inevitably the printed answers did not cover every sort of answer given – this was expected. But they did succeed in the objectives mentioned above and also allowed our summary of each interview to be checked by the businessman. In the event, one or two questions were superfluous, and one or two, intended as cross-checks, were unnecessarily repetitive.

Contrary to the fears recorded above that firms would be unhelpful, everywhere we went we were met with great kindness and sympathy. We had nothing to offer except the possibility of a contribution to knowledge, and the amount of influence that an academic paper might be expected to have on policy. And there was a fair chance that such influence might even be against the interests of the firms. Yet businessmen gave up quite large amounts of their time to see us, frequently at short notice, and many of them went to considerable trouble to provide us with the statistics we wanted. This was true regardless of the size of the firm; one felt very bad about bothering some of the smaller firms whose resources were less able to cope with our demands. Indeed the smallest firm of all, whose total work force consisted of the directors and one other employee, must have lost quite a lot of production time during our visit.

STATISTICAL DATA FROM FIRMS

We started the project with the aim of gathering data on enough relevant variables from each firm on a time-series basis to set up and test an econometric model of the determination of firms' exports with particular reference to the pressure of demand effect. Any initial shopping list of 'required relevant data' can be little more than an expression of hope as we could not know at the start what figures firms would be able or would be ready to divulge to private investigators such as ourselves. The broad aim was to obtain data which would allow, at firm level, a study of the effect on firms' export performance of plausible explanatory variables: overseas demand and variables reflecting the various aspects of competitivity, particularly in relation to capacity utilization and prices. At the start of the survey the following specification was drawn up:

1. *Time-series 1958-65, quarterly.* Quarterly time-series data would yield enough observations to allow the possibility of analyses of the separate performances of individual firms and allow greater precision of estimation generally. If only annual figures proved to be obtainable, any analysis would almost certainly need to be based upon a model making simultaneous use of cross-section combined with time-series data and the estimation procedure would lack precision.

2. *Value of exports by main destinations.* It would be an important part of the analysis to link variations in overseas demand to variations in exports. And in a short-run study such as this, the relevant measure of overseas demand would be demand in each firm's overseas markets. Destination of exports data would therefore play an important role.

3. *Value of home sales.* Together with the export figures, this would measure total output (with a bearing upon measures of capacity utilization).

4. *Product prices.* The obtaining of comprehensive figures of price movements of many individual products was in general clearly out of the question. But if a firm had the practice of periodical changing all or most prices by the same overall percentage, then one series of price figures would serve; if not, it was planned to ask for the price series for a few important or representative products.

5. *Level of capacity utilization.* There are considerable conceptual problems in the way of arriving at a suitable definition of, let alone a proper way of measuring, capacity utilization of a single firm. Apart from difficulties of principle, it seemed likely that there would

be no readily available statistics from firms which would give an acceptable measure of this variable, and this was confirmed in our early interviews.

6. *Order books and delivery dates.* At the planning stage we simply noted this as a head to explore quantitatively if possible; the statistics which might be obtained would be dependent upon the nature of the firms' book-keeping and would need to be discussed with individual firms.

In the event, it was found that what the outsider might term irrational suspicion of disclosure of information did not play an important part in limiting the data we were able to gather. In the main the directors and senior executives of the firms contacted very readily passed on data which came naturally out of their accounting records and very often went to some trouble to do so. The statistical data and the scope of the analysis turned out to be considerably restricted, however, by the nature of the figures which were readily obtainable from most firms' records. Very few firms had quarterly accounting figures. Value figures of exports and home sales were readily obtainable, as were certain statistics of price changes. But in general, firms could not give detailed breakdowns of exports by countries of destination though they were of course able to indicate the relative importance of different markets. Nor was it possible to obtain any comprehensive data relating to the order book position over time. Furthermore, most firms were unable to provide any precise measures for the past of changes in plant utilization, although, in many cases, they could tell us in general terms at what times over the period under review they had been operating at or below 'normal capacity'. The statistical data at firm level which were obtained is described in the individual industry chapters below: only in the pottery industry was there sufficient to proceed to a comprehensive econometric test of export performance.

Chapter 4

DOMESTIC DEMAND, EXPORTS AND FIRM BEHAVIOUR: THE PREDICTIONS OF ECONOMIC ANALYSIS

INTRODUCTION

In studying the relationship between domestic demand and exports at the firm level, we might proceed in one of two directions. We could simply state our hypothesis and subject it to a variety of tests, using both multiple regression and questionnaire methods; or we could use the theory of the firm to predict the relationship between the domestic demand for a firm's product and its export performance and then proceed to test the predictions against the facts. This study has adopted the latter approach, and the current chapter will be concerned with deriving testable predictions of the short-run relationship between domestic demand and exports at the firm level.[1] It will, in fact, be shown that different predictions can be obtained according to the assumptions made about the objectives of the firm and its market and cost conditions. We found this analytical exercise invaluable, since it provided a logical framework for the project and it improved our understanding of the hypothesis. In addition, the analysis suggested a number of variables which might explain the relationship between a firm's exports and the domestic demand for its products, as well as indicating various aspects of a firm's export behaviour: these provided a basis for our subsequent empirical work. In this chapter, we shall present our theoretical treatment, beginning with a general outline and then proceeding to comment on specific issues and problems.

[1] For a similar treatment, see, R. J. Ball, 'Credit Restrictions and the Supply of Exports', *Manchester School of Economic and Social Studies*, May 1961.

MODELS OF FIRM BEHAVIOUR

At the outset, any explanation of firm behaviour requires a specific statement of objectives. Orthodox theory regards the firm as a price-output, decision-making unit shown by a set of cost and revenue schedules and concerned with profit-maximization. Given this objective function, the firm can be analysed in a variety of market situations. Such an analysis suggests that in pursuing its objectives, a firm might be regarded as a price-taker or price-maker concerned with price and/or non-price competition and its behaviour will be dependent upon certain strategic variables, namely the number and size distribution of buyers and sellers and entry conditions into the market. For the profit-maximizing firm, domestic and export markets simply represent opportunities for obtaining revenue, and decisions to allocate resources and products between such markets will be based upon expectations about cost and revenue conditions in alternative markets. We were especially interested in using the analysis to predict the direction of change in exports following any variations in domestic demand. In order to derive predictions, we shall initially analyse the short-run behaviour of a profit-maximizing firm in different world-market situations, and, in a later section, we shall relax the assumption of profit-maximizing behaviour.

For the sake of simplicity, let us assume that a profit-maximizing firm produces a single product, and is a monopolist in the domestic market but subject to competitive conditions in the world market. The short-run, price-output decisions of such a firm can be analysed in the same way as a discriminating monopoly. In more general terms, the analysis will cover all those situations in which the firm is a price-maker in the home market but a price-taker in the export market. The allocation of the firm's output between the two markets and the resulting prices in the short run are shown in Figure 4.1:[1]

In Figure 4.1, AR_d and AR_w show the firm's demand curves in the domestic and world markets, respectively. The diagram shows that a

[1] A firm's profits will be maximized when it produces at the point where its marginal cost curve (*MC*) intersects its marginal revenue curve (*MR*). In a two-market situation, the combined *MR* curve is the relevant one for the equilibrium of the firm; see, e.g. W. J. L. Ryan, *Price Theory*, London: Macmillan, 1962. In Figure 4.1, *SAC* and *SMC* refer to the firm's short-run average and marginal cost curves, respectively.

profit-maximizing firm will produce an output oq_t of which oq_d will be allocated to the domestic market. The domestic price of the product will exceed its export price. Given these relative prices and the short-run average cost curve of Figure 4.1 it is also possible to show that profits per unit of domestic output will exceed the unit profitability of exports.[1] In addition, this model of the firm predicts

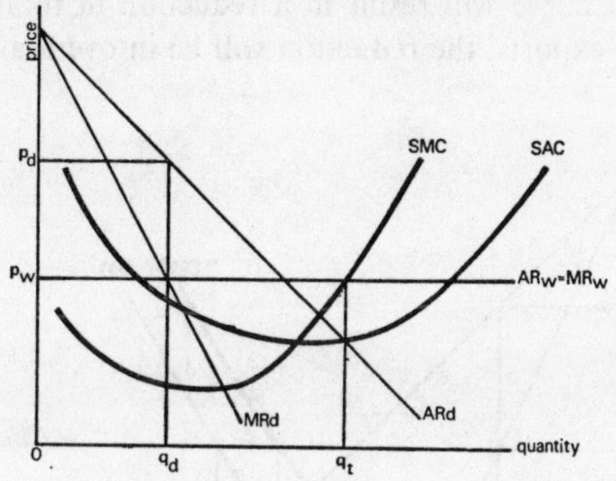

Fig. 4.1

that, given the marginal cost curve and the competitive world demand curve, fluctuations in domestic demand resulting in shifts in the firm's home-market average revenue curve will be associated with variations in the volume of output exported. More particularly, for a range of output, the model predicts an inverse relationship between changes in domestic demand and export sales. In Figure 4.1, the limiting cases will occur when a firm has no domestic market and consequently exports the whole of its output oq_t or, when domestic demand results in the home market marginal revenue curve intersecting the producer's marginal cost curve at, or to the right of, oq_t, in which case the firm will allocate the whole of its output to the domestic market. It is also worth noting that shifts in the firm's domestic demand curve will be associated with variations in the domestic price of its product: export prices will remain unchanged.

So far, attention has been given to the effect on exports of changes in the domestic demand for a firm's products. The causation operates

[1] For the U.K., this analysis is in sterling prices, given the exchange rate. Given the foreign currency price of U.K. goods, the devaluation of 1967 increased the relative profitability of British exports compared with home market sales.

from changes in the domestic product market through to exports. If, however, the pressure of domestic demand, together with trade-union bargaining power and the expectations of unions about the future level of demand, *initially* results in a rise in wage rates, the immediate effect at the firm level will be a rise in its marginal costs. For the firm shown in Figure 4.2 below, an upward shift in its short-run marginal cost curve will result in a reduction in total output and, since the firm exports, the reduction will be in overseas sales.

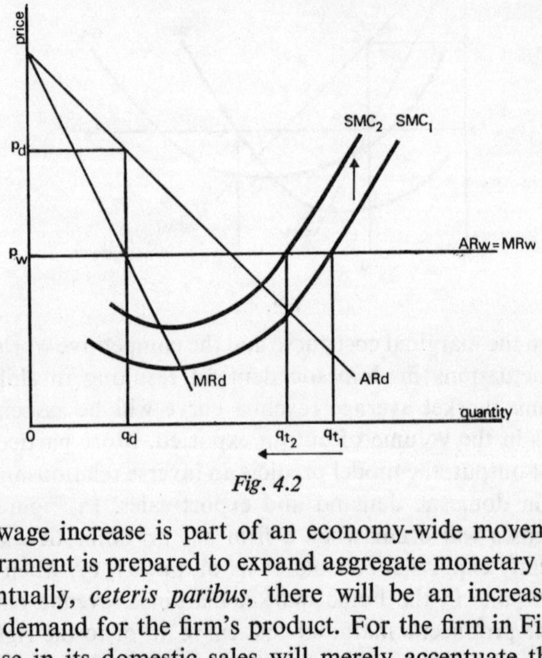

Fig. 4.2

If the wage increase is part of an economy-wide movement and the Government is prepared to expand aggregate monetary demand, then eventually, *ceteris paribus*, there will be an increase in the domestic demand for the firm's product. For the firm in Figure 4.2, an increase in its domestic sales will merely accentuate the initial reduction in exports which followed the rise in its marginal costs. Clearly, at the firm level, an increase in marginal costs and an expansion of domestic demand will adversely affect exports, but the critical question is whether the process is reversible and whether a domestic deflation will favourably affect export performance? We have already shown that there is an inverse relationship between domestic demand and a firm's exports. If, in addition, it can be shown that trade-union wage claims are related to expectations about the future level of domestic demand in the economy, then a deflation will reduce or postpone the *rate* of increase in wage rates and so prevent a further rise in marginal costs at the firm level.[1] In an imperfect labour market, with downward rigidities in wage rates, a domestic deflation will not result in a reduction in wage *levels*, and to this extent an increase in marginal costs is irreversible in the short run. Other things being equal, an increase in marginal costs will adversely affect a firm's exports.

The above model of decision-making for a profit-maximizing firm provides us with a number of predictions which form a basis for analysing the allocation of a firm's output between domestic and export markets and various other aspects of behaviour. In addition to suggesting an inverse relationship between changes in domestic demand and exports – a central part of the project – the analysis predicted that for a given product, the domestic price will exceed its export price, that the domestic price will vary with shifts in demand and that a unit of home sales will be more profitable than a unit of exports: these predictions provided the basis for our questionnaire. We do, of course, recognize the above model is not the 'definitive work' on this subject: it does, however, provide a starting-point for analysing the export behaviour of firms. It is now necessary to relax our assumption of perfectly competitive world-market conditions.

Consider now a profit-maximizing firm producing a given product for two markets, namely home and overseas, with given and downward-sloping demand curves in each market. For such a firm, the predicted effect on exports of a change in domestic demand will depend upon its cost conditions. Figure 4.3 (*a*) and (*b*) show the short-run effects on a firm's export sales following a decrease in domestic demand under the contrasting conditions of increasing and declining marginal costs respectively.[2]

1 For a survey of relevant literature see M. Bronfenbrenner and F. D. Holzman, 'A Survey of Inflation Theory', in *Surveys of Economic Theory*, Volume I, London: Macmillan. 1965. Also, A. G. Hines, 'Wage Inflation in the United Kingdom, 1948-62: A Disaggregated Study', *Economic Journal*, March 1969.

2 Equilibrium will be determined by the intersection of the firm's *MC* curve with its combined marginal revenue curve (MR_t) from the domestic and overseas markets: this will determine the equilibrium output, *oqt*, which will be allocated between the two markets so that the *MR* in each market is the same. See, e.g. W. L. J. Ryan, *Price Theory*, London, 1962.

From Figure 4.3, it can be seen that a given reduction in the domestic demand for the firm's product will be associated with a rise in its export sales under increasing short-run marginal cost conditions but a decrease in exports with declining marginal costs.

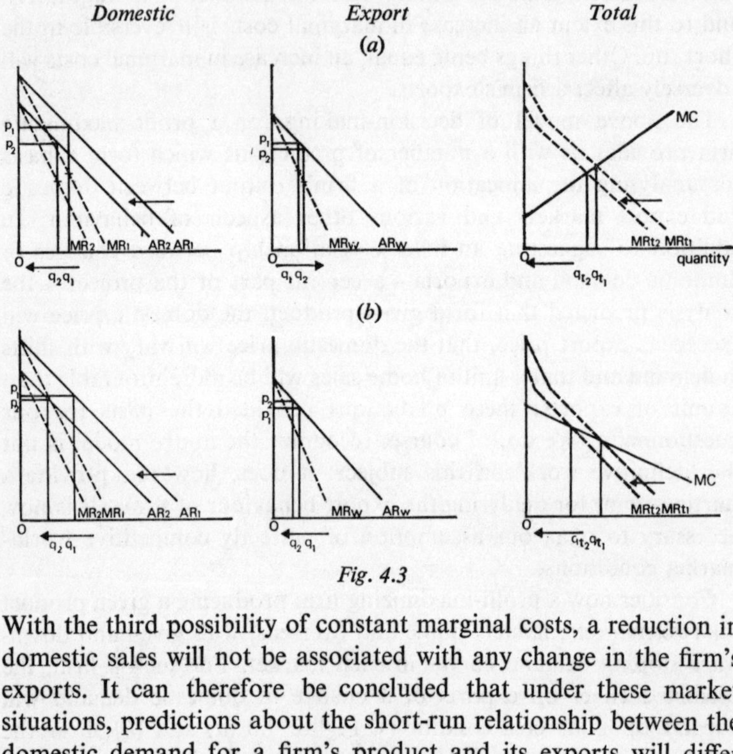

Fig. 4.3

With the third possibility of constant marginal costs, a reduction in domestic sales will not be associated with any change in the firm's exports. It can therefore be concluded that under these market situations, predictions about the short-run relationship between the domestic demand for a firm's product and its exports will differ according to the cost conditions under which the firm is operating. For an inverse relationship between exports and domestic demand, the profit-maximizing firm needs to be subject to conditions of increasing marginal costs.

Our analysis has so far been based on the assumption that short-run profit-maximization is the basic objective of the firm. The model has, in fact, predicted all the possible short-run relationships between exports and domestic demand and this might be regarded as sufficient for analytical purposes. However, the profit-maximizing objective and more particularly the resulting price-output decisions of the firm, have been subject to much criticism.[1] Some of the criticism of the traditional objective function has been unsatisfactory, especially where there has been a failure to test the predictions of the model against the facts. In addition, where the predictions resulting from profit-maximizing behaviour have apparently been refuted by the facts and alternative motives governing business behaviour have been suggested, these have frequently failed to specify their predictions unambiguously and in a manner capable of being tested. Having mentioned these problems, we must now examine some of the alternative explanations of business behaviour and their associated predictions of the relationship between domestic demand and exports.

Some authorities have suggested the full-cost principle as an alternative explanation of business behaviour.[2] As such, the principle is really an explanation of pricing which, if consistent with the facts, suggests that firms *might* be pursuing objectives other than maximum profits but it completely fails to specify these objectives. Expressed in a form which yields different predictions from those of profit-maximization, the principle states that product prices are a function of average variable costs plus a costing margin which includes an allowance for overheads and a profit mark-up.[3] Essentially this is a supply hypothesis of pricing and, despite a failure to specify the firm's objective function, it can be shown that for given demand and cost conditions, a firm's price will tend to be lower and output greater than under profit-maximization. Also, in contrast to profit-maximization, the principle predicts that in response to an increase in demand for the firm's product, price will tend to remain unchanged.

[1] For a review article and bibliography, see F. Machlup, 'Theories of the Firm: Marginalist, Behavioural, Managerial', *American Economic Review*, March 1967. Also, H. I. Ansoff (ed.), *Business Strategy*, Penguin Modern Management Readings, Harmondsworth: Penguin, 1969, Part IV.

[2] R. L. Hall and C. G. Hitch, 'Price Theory and Business Behaviour', *Oxford Economic Papers*, May 1939. For further analysis, see, e.g. W. T. Baxter and A. R. Oxenfeldt, 'Approaches to Pricing: Economist versus Accountant, *Business Horizons*, vol. 4, 1961.

[3] Strictly, a rigorous version of the full-cost principle requires an explanation of the determinants of both the profit mark-up and the degree of capacity-working within the firm. We mention some of our reservations about the principle at a later stage.

Certainly, there is evidence that the prices of manufacturers in the U.K. are not sensitive to short-run variations in demand conditions.[1] Such evidence can, however, be interpreted in a number of different ways. First, it might be a basis for refuting the predictions of the profit-maximization hypothesis. Second, it might not be accepted as a satisfactory test of the traditional objective function since such evidence is *ex post* and neglects the basis on which the businessman's *ex ante* decisions were made. Third, some evidence on price changes suggests that a firm's prices and especially the profit mark-up vary over time in which case it might be plausible to regard the full-cost principle as a 'rule of thumb' attempt at profit-maximization under conditions of uncertainty. Whatever interpretation is given to the evidence, the full-cost principle provides us with a further insight into a firm's export behaviour.

A single-product firm supplying both home and export markets and with price determined on a full-cost basis is shown in Figure 4.4.[2]

In Figure 4.4 it is assumed that price p_f is estimated on the basis of short-run average costs at some standard output oq_t plus a profit 'mark-up'. Initially, we shall assume that oq_t is also capacity output and that the total demand for the product results in the firm being able to sell the whole of its output at the price p_f. Since price is based on some standard output, it will be the same in both home and overseas markets. The total demand for the firm's product will consist of domestic plus overseas demand, and it is assumed that in both markets the firm faces a downward-sloping average revenue curve. In Figure 4.4, the firm will allocate oq_d to the domestic market and q_dq_t for export. Assuming that export demand remains given and unchanged, consider the effect on exports of an increase in home demand.

The immediate effect of a rightward shift in the firm's total

1 See, e.g. R. Neild, *Pricing and Employment in the Trade Cycle*, N.I.E.S.R., Occasional Papers XXI, Cambridge: Cambridge University Press, 1963. Also, P. J. Hovell, 'Export Pricing Policies', *District Bank Review*, September 1968. For further analysis of evidence see, I. F. Pearce, 'A Study of Price Policy', *Economica*, vol. 23, 1956.

2 In Figure 4.4, *AC* and *AVC* are short-run average and average variable costs, respectively. P_f is the full-cost price. D_d and D_t are the firm's domestic and total demand curves, respectively.

demand curve will be excess demand at the ruling price. In such a situation, prices and/or queues can be used as an allocative mechanism. The full-cost principle, where prices are a function of costs, predicts that prices will remain unchanged and queues will form. In other words, an increase in domestic demand will result in order

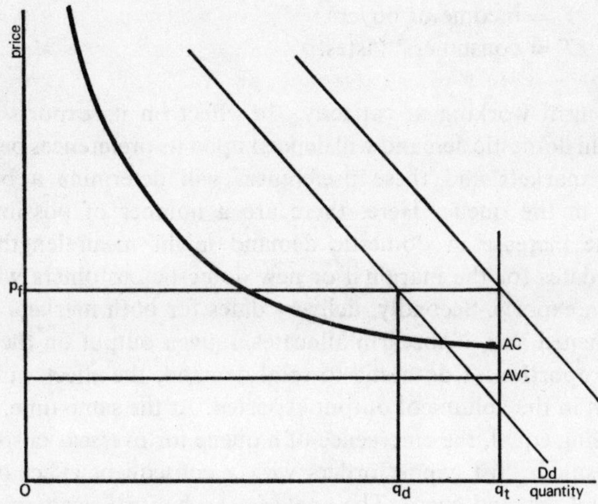

Fig. 4.4

books, lengthening delivery dates and waiting times.[1] It seems plausible to suggest that at the economy level, such behaviour will adversely affect Britain's balance of payments position (exports and imports) if, given the relative cost-price position, firms in the U.K. lengthen the delivery dates for their products (both home and export sales) at a faster rate than their competitors. We shall undertake a further analysis of delivery dates below, when we analyse a number of specific problems. At this stage though, the analysis suggests an export demand function for the firm's product of the following form:

[1] See e.g., M. D. Steuer, R. J. Ball and J. R. Eaton, 'The Effect of Waiting Times on Foreign Orders for Machine Tools', *Economica*, November 1966. We present evidence on pricing and queuing policies in the questionnaire sections of each industry chapter.

$$D_x = f(p_x, p_1, \ldots, p_{n-1}, d_x, d_1, \ldots, d_{n-1}, Y, T)$$

where D_x = export demand for the firm's product,

p_x = export price of product,

$p_1, \ldots, p_{n-1}$ = prices of all other commodities,

d_x = delivery date for exports,

$d_1, \ldots, d_{n-1}$ = delivery dates for all other commodities,

Y = income of buyers,

T = consumers' tastes.

For a firm working at capacity, the effect on its exports of an increase in domestic demand will depend upon its preferences between the two markets and these preferences will determine a buyer's position in the queue. Here, there are a number of possibilities. First, the increase in domestic demand might mean lengthening delivery dates for the marginal or new domestic customers with no change in exports. Secondly, delivery dates for both markets might be lengthened and, if the firm allocates a given output on the basis of the proportion of domestic to total demand, the effect will be a reduction in the volume of output exported. At the same time, other things being equal, the emergence of a queue for overseas customers might result in lost export orders with a consequent effect on the firm's total demand curve. The analysis can be further complicated if the firm allocates its available capacity output on the basis of a queuing preference for 'the first come, first served' or for the largest firms: we explored these possibilities in our questionnaire. Further problems arise if domestic and export demands are *both* increasing. In these circumstances, without a specific statement of a firm's objectives and an adequate theory of queuing, we can only suggest possibilities. At the most, we can suggest that the market period or 'first round effect' on exports of an increase in domestic demand for a firm already producing at capacity output will depend upon its system of priorities in a queuing situation. Moreover, this is only the 'first round effect': in the second round or short run with capacity an 'elastic' concept, the firm might demand additional variable factors of production. Within the labour market, the elasticity of a firm's labour supply curve will determine the effect of an increase in demand on wage rates and consequently on its average variable costs and hence product prices. If a large number of firms in the labour market are increasing their demand for a given supply, the result will be a rise in wages and, with the full-cost principle, a corresponding effect on product prices. At this stage, without a general equilibrium model in which prices and queues are the adjustment mechanisms, the implications of a firm's decisions become difficult to handle.

Consider now the immediate effects on a firm's exports of a decrease in domestic demand with the firm initially at capacity output with no excess demand for its products (see Figure 4.4). At a given price, a leftward shift in the firm's total demand curve will result in a reduction in total output, a rise in average costs and a consequent reduction in unit profitability.[1] At the same time, with a given price and overseas demand, exports will initially remain unchanged so that the decrease in domestic demand will immediately result in spare capacity or production for stocks: we used our questionnaire to obtain some evidence on the reactions of firms to a deflation of home demand.

To summarize, our analysis of the full-cost principle has suggested different predictions from those derived from the profit-maximizing model. With the full-cost principle, it is possible to show that with given cost conditions, domestic and export prices and hence unit profitability in both markets, will be identical. Of course, this analysis has been concerned with production costs. Once selling costs are introduced, then a strict application of the full-cost model would indicate that differences in unit selling costs between home and export markets might be reflected in different prices for the product: a point which we examined in our questionnaire. Our analysis of the full-cost principle also indicated that with capacity working, the

[1] Figure 4.4 assumed that short-run average costs decline with increasing output. In these circumstances, the strict application of the full-cost principle suggests that in the next 'season', an attempt to retain a *constant* profit mark-up per unit of output will result in a rise in price: for a given demand curve, such a price increase will lead to a further reduction in output and so on until equilibrium is restored. The general result is increasing excess capacity: a result which needs to be related to the full-cost principle's original assumptions about the degree of capacity working within the firm. Alternatively, if the firm reduces prices in an attempt to increase capacity utilization, questions immediately arise about the determinants of the profit mark-up. Certainly in these circumstances doubts are raised about the internal consistency of the 'model': hence our frequent reference to the full-cost *principle*.

effect on exports of an increase in domestic demand will depend upon the firm's queuing policy. In a deflation, exports will initially remain unchanged.

It remains for us to examine the export implications of the sales-maximization hypothesis and satisficing behaviour. Since we have already raised a sufficiently large number of problems for this rather limited study, we propose to deal briefly with these remaining hypotheses.[1] With sales-maximization, it can be shown that with given cost and revenue conditions, a firm will receive a larger total revenue than under profit-maximization: if such a result arises in the export market, then it will have obvious public policy implications for countries attempting to maximize their foreign exchange earnings. At the same time, in contrast with the profit-maximizing hypothesis and the full-cost principle, sales-maximizing behaviour can be used to show that if total revenue and total costs are independent, an increase in a firm's costs will not result in any change in a firm's price or output so long as it continues to earn the minimum profit constraint. In this situation, for a limited increase in costs, a sales-maximizing firm will not change the allocation of its output between home and export markets.

Finally, mention must be made of the alternative assumption that firms act as 'satisficers', attempting to achieve 'satisfactory' performance expressed in the form of minimum 'target' levels in several spheres such as profits, security, growth, sales, control and employee relations.[2] The specification of a number of 'targets' suggests that a firm might have a variety of objectives[3] but the multiplicity as well as the vagueness of aims increases the difficulty of deriving testable predictions from the assumption of satisficing behaviour. Nevertheless, it is possible to suggest some plausible export implications of

1 Since it can be shown that the price-output implications of the growth-maximizing hypothesis are similar to those of profit-maximization, we shall not be concerned with this hypothesis. See, J. H. Williamson, 'Profits, Growth and Sales Maximisation', *Economica*, February 1966.

2 See, e.g. H. A. Simon, 'Theories of Decision-Making in Economics and Behavioural Science', in *Surveys of Economic Theory*, volume III, London: Macmillan, 1966. Also, G. Katona, *Psychological Analysis of Economic Behaviour*, New York: McGraw-Hill, 1951.

3 The profit-maximization hypothesis can be interpreted to suggest that a firm has a variety of objectives but that its behaviour will be dominated by the pursuit of profits.

such behaviour. At the outset, it must be recognized that a 'satisficing' firm is concerned with achieving a 'satisfactory' rather than an optimum position. Indeed, since decision making is not a costless process, such behaviour might reflect the desire for a quiet life. Here, one possible result of this behaviour might be the existence of 'organizational slack' which in periods of domestic deflation might be subjected to a 'shock effect', so stimulating the firm to enter export markets: such organizational 'slack' would not be present for a profit-maximizing firm. As a further possibility, a firm's concern with a quiet life might reveal itself in a desire for security: such a desire might result in a preference for a substantial home market base for its output. At the same time, the desire for security and additional sales might be achieved through market diversification with exports providing a basis for such diversification.[1] This is not to suggest that a satisficing firm will neglect profits: after all, if security is desired for survival, then some minimum level of profit is an essential element in the process! Moreover, we do not wish to suggest that a profit-maximizing firm will not diversify its markets: for such a firm, diversification could be explained in terms of its expectations about alternative market conditions. At the most, an assessment of satisficing behaviour introduces further descriptive considerations into the analysis of the export behaviour of firms.

The various hypotheses about a firm's objective function have provided us with an insight and understanding of its allocative decisions and associated export behaviour. Our analysis has shown that predictions about the short-run relationship between exports and domestic demand depend upon the firm's objective function together with its market and cost conditions: in fact, it has been shown that a decrease in the domestic demand for a firm's products can be associated with either an increase or a reduction in its exports or with no immediate change in overseas sales but the creation of excess capacity! The actual response at the firm level and the distribution of firms with similar responses will determine the relationship between domestic demand and exports at both the industry and the economy level. Our attention has also been focused upon domestic and export prices, queuing and the relative profitability of home and

[1] For a summary of various theories on diversification see, L. Amey, 'Diversified Manufacturing Business', *Journal of the Royal Statistical Society*, June 1964.

export sales: these were some of the aspects of behaviour on which we tried to obtain information from our questionnaire.

This completes our more formal survey of the theory of the firm and the export implications of alternative hypotheses about firm behaviour. Our short-run analysis has been based on a single-product firm in a two-market situation. With the aid of this analysis, we now wish to develop further our survey of some of the variables and underlying relationships which seem relevant to the pressure of demand hypothesis. These further developments will be concerned with suggesting possible exceptions, qualifications and problems which arise when the pressure hypothesis is assessed in terms of individual firm behaviour. It must, of course, be stressed that any qualifications which subsequently arise are only informative: in the last resort, the relationship between exports and domestic demand at the firm and industry level can only be confirmed or refuted by testing the hypothesis against the facts. Moreover, it must also be remembered that the pressure hypothesis is not attempting to explain the behaviour of every individual firm: for it to result in an inverse relationship between domestic demand and exports at the industry or economy level, it merely requires a sufficiently large number of firms to react in the way suggested by the hypothesis.

SOME PROBLEMS FOR THE PRESSURE HYPOTHESIS

The pressure hypothesis predicts that government domestic deflationary measures will release resources from supplying the home market, so providing factors of production to enable firms to increase their exports. At the same time, it seems to be implicitly assumed that by reducing home demand, firms will be induced to seek overseas outlets for their products which can no longer be sold at home. If this inverse relationship between exports and domestic demand is to be valid, a number of considerations seem relevant: for our purposes, we wish to consider the relevance to the pressure hypothesis of overseas demand, the factor market and the supply side. Throughout, we shall be concerned with identifying the sets of relationships which are required for a domestic deflation to actually result in an increase in a firm's exports.

First, consideration must be given to the state of demand in the export market. The pressure hypothesis only operates on a firm's domestic sales and so tends to be a supply hypothesis whilst exports are a function of both demand and supply (costs). Of course, in the absence of a statement of the objectives of the majority of firms in the economy, analysis becomes rather difficult and we shall confine ourselves to suggesting a number of possibilities. From the comments of previous sections, it seems plausible to suggest that if a firm possesses both domestic and export markets, a reduction in sales in the former will be associated with an increase in exports where there is a given and perfectly elastic export demand curve for the firm's products. Similar results will follow if the firm is experiencing excess demand (queues) for its exports. However, problems arise if a firm does not export any of its output. For such a firm, a decline in domestic sales might result in one or a combination of three possible responses, two of which will assist exports. As one possibility, the firm might react by continuing to concentrate its resources on the domestic market:[1] the response might consist of stock-building and/or an increased sales effort in the domestic market.[2] Alternatively, the firm might release resources for other exporting firms; we return to this possibility below. As a third possibility, the firm might consider entry into the export market. Where such entry is possible, it seems reasonable to suggest that a firm might commence exporting if the export market is treated as a sort of 'sink' or residual in the sense that overseas sales can be obtained with little, if any, extra sales effort.[3] Here, much depends on overseas demand conditions. For an established firm, attempting to maximize short-run profits, entry into the export market might be a rational response to a decline in domestic sales in a situation where the firm is faced with a perfectly

[1] Especially if domestic sales are more profitable than exports.

[2] Much will also depend upon the relationship between selling costs and the domestic demand for the firm's product. For a rational firm, the allocation of sales resources between alternative home and export markets will depend upon the expected marginal returns from additional selling expenditure in each market.

[3] For the mechanical engineering industry it has been argued that '... export success depends mainly on world demand and sustained marketing effort: exports cannot be easily turned on and off according to the vagaries of the home market. Successful marketing overseas depends upon a long-term strategy of market exploitation and the backing of a solid sales and service organization which cannot be created overnight in response to a domestic "squeeze".' Mechanical Engineering E.D.C., *Market – The World*, H.M.S.O., 1968, pp. 5 and 37.

elastic demand curve for its overseas sales and where the export price is at least equal to average variable costs. In this situation there are no market limitations to the firm's output. Such a firm is shown in Figure 4.5:[1]

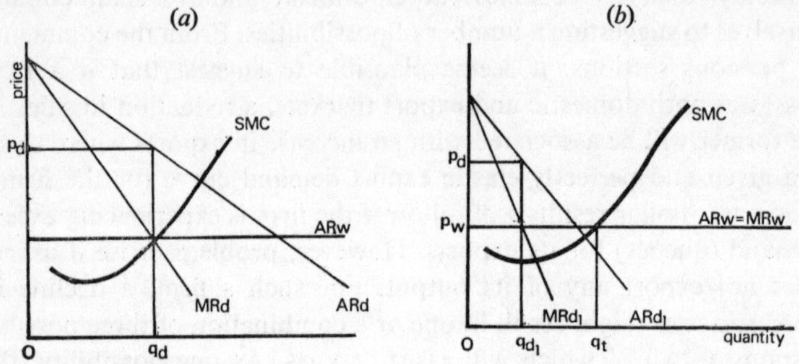

Fig. 4.5

Figure 4.5 (*a*) shows a profit-maximizing firm in equilibrium, allocating the whole of its output to the domestic market. Figure 4.5 (*b*) shows that with the decline in domestic sales, the firm will enter the export market. Alternatively, in the absence of a perfectly elastic demand curve, a firm might use sales expenditure to attract foreign customers to its products. If, however, the export market requires a considerable investment, especially in sales effort – investment of a long-run nature even for an established firm – it is most unlikely that a *short-run* domestic deflation will result in a short-run increase in the firm's exports. In other words, entry into the export market might only be possible in the long run. In such circumstances, a firm's decision to enter the export sphere will be a function of such variables as its objectives, expectations about the length of a domestic recession and the future position of overseas markets and presumably the relative profitability of home and export sales. Moreover, to establish a causal relationship between domestic demand and exports,

1 In Figure 4.5, subscripts *d* and *w* refer to the domestic and world markets, respectively. The firm is faced with a given and perfectly elastic overseas demand curve. Between (*a*) and (*b*), only the domestic demand curve for the firm's product shifts. In (*b*), the firm's output will be oq_t, of which oq_{d_1}' will be allocated to the domestic market.

it seems necessary to postulate that a deflation results in firms considering export possibilities which they would not otherwise have considered. Such a causal relationship might arise if a decline in domestic sales 'shocks' a firm into considering export markets or if the decline induces an adverse change in the firm's expectations about its future home sales.

Whilst discussing demand, consideration must be given to the problems which arise with the emergence of excess demand for a firm's product. For the individual firm, the responsiveness of buyers to the length of waiting time or the 'delay elasticity of demand', will determine the extent to which any change in delivery dates will affect orders. In the short run, the firms might maximize the number of orders by differentiating between buyers according to their responsiveness to waiting time. In the long run, the length of the order book might induce the firm to increase its capacity. However, to some extent, order books can be a misleading indicator of unsatisfied demand. Some orders or options might be duplicated, the buyer placing orders with a number of firms[1] whilst, in other instances, buyers might order ahead so transferring orders between time-periods; the expansion plans of rival firms further complicate the issue. In the last resort, though, these qualifications are simply a way of describing the risk and uncertainty of business activity. For the research worker, there arises the problem of measuring demand for a firm's product. To some extent, current sales might reflect past orders rather than the inflow of new orders and comparisons of order books in different time-periods are not very meaningful in the absence of data on capacity changes.

A brief assessment of the effects of a decline in domestic sales on the excess demand for a firm's product is illuminating. Consider a firm which is operating at capacity,[2] with excess demand for its products. Given the level of export demand, the first effect of a decline in home sales will be a reduction in the size of excess demand. The effect on exports will depend upon the firm's policy concerning the relative treatment of home and export orders: we shall distinguish three cases. First, the neutral case, where the firm maintains an equal queue or waiting time for home and export orders. In this case,

1 E.g. orders for new civil aircraft.

2 See Figure 4.4.

the decrease in the firm's excess demand will mean a reduction in the average waiting time for each market: if exports are delay-elastic, the firm will attract additional overseas orders, so benefiting exports. Second, the export-biased case, where the firm favours export orders, supplying them in the minimum possible time. In this situation, the decline in domestic demand will simply reduce the waiting time for home market orders, with no immediate effect on exports. Third, there is the case where the firm favours home market orders. As in the neutral case, the decline in home demand will tend to favourably affect exports through a reduction in export waiting time. Thus, in each of these cases, a decline in domestic demand, through its effect on waiting times, will be associated with either no initial change or with an increase in exports.

The factor market is a second consideration which is relevant to the working of the pressure hypothesis. As a result of a domestic deflation, the hypothesis predicts that resources, especially labour, will be released from domestic production so enabling an increase in exports. Two points seem relevant to this aspect of the hypothesis. First, where a firm is not an exporter, the initial release of resources following a decline in domestic sales will depend upon its contractual obligations, especially in the labour market, its expectations about the period of deflation and its consequent response.[1] Second, even where resources are released from domestic production, their subsequent employment in exporting sectors will depend upon the geographical and occupational mobility of factors, both within and between firms and regions. For example, in the absence of a perfect market, if a domestic deflation releases unskilled labour from construction work in North East England and if there is excess demand for skilled labour for export production in the Midlands, the adjustment process operating through the various labour markets will be far from instantaneous!

Finally, certain supply-side considerations are relevant to the pressure hypothesis. These include the distinction between capacity and scale effects, the nature of the production process, the proportion of output exported and the 'flexibility' of production. The distinction between the short- and long-run effects of the pressure hypothesis

1 See previous paragraphs – e.g. depending on expectations, its response might be to produce for stock.

has probably been most frequently argued by the motor car industry.[1] In both time-periods, the motor car manufacturers have appeared to suggest that a decline in domestic sales *adversely* affects vehicle exports. In the short run, it has been argued that by decreasing home sales, firms are unable to achieve capacity working with the result that unit costs rise and, at a given product price, there is a corresponding decline in the profitability of both home and export sales.[2] Such results appear to be similar to the predictions derived by using the full-cost principle with a firm initially working at capacity and no excess demand. The long-run effects on exports of a decline in domestic sales will presumably arise from the relationship between the utilization of existing capacity and future expansion, with its associated opportunities for obtaining further economies of scale. Once again, short-run reductions in domestic demand will prevent further future reductions in the unit costs of exports if, as a result, the firm finds itself with less incentive to move towards its optimum size. Here, the important point is that there are possible long-run implications of the pressure hypothesis. In fact, for the motor car industry it has been argued that in the long run, '. . . any decline in the profitability of the motor industry will tend to undermine its ability to compete in export markets because it will discourage risk-taking, because it will weaken the ability to sustain temporary losses in a market in the expectation of future profits and because it will jeopardize the future investment on which continuing international competitiveness will depend'.[3]

If we return to the short-run analysis, there are a number of interesting observations which can be derived from the view that

[1] See, e.g. Motor Manufacturing E.D.C., *The Effect of Government Economic Policy on the Motor Industry*, H.M.S.O., 1968. A contrasting view has been expressed in Mechanical Engineering E.D.C., *Market – The World*, H.M.S.O., 1968 (p. 38), where the relationship between exports and a large and stable home market was examined; it was found that '. . . very few of the companies in our sample independently mentioned the value of a thriving home market as an important support for exports . . .'. The report explained that the favourable effects of high volume on unit costs '. . . can equally well result from a preponderance of sales overseas'. However, it was stated that the bulk of mechanical engineering takes the form of batch, not mass, production.

[2] This argument assumes given input prices whilst, of course, one of the aims of a deflationary policy is the reduction in the rate of increase of factor prices.

[3] Motor Manufacturing E.D.C., *The Effect of Government Economic Policy on the Motor Industry*, H.M.S.O., 1968, p. 30.

a domestic deflation *adversely* affects exports. The result sometimes appears to depend upon a firm initially pricing its products on the basis of average costs and these costs declining up to capacity with the spreading of fixed outlays over a larger output.[1] Of course, in this situation, with a given price determined for 'a season', any reduction in domestic sales will have less of an adverse effect on unit costs and unit profitability the more the short-run average cost curve tends to be horizontal as output approaches capacity. In this context, it seems plausible to suggest that the size and nature of fixed outlays (contractual commitments) might differ between firms of differing sizes and production processes. For example, *ceteris paribus*, the shape of a firm's short-run average cost curve might differ between mass production activities and batch production with the latter tending to result in unit costs decreasing less rapidly as output tends towards capacity.

Even if a decline in domestic sales results in a significant increase in unit costs, for a firm's short-run exports to be *adversely* affected it is necessary to show that the reduction in unit profitability results in a decrease in, say, overseas sales and marketing expenditure or a rise in export prices. Otherwise, for a firm working at full capacity with no excess demand and a limited overseas market, the 'first-round effect' of a decrease in domestic sales will tend to result in spare capacity or stock-building with no change in exports. Once spare capacity arises at the firm level, it is possible to show that there are a number of ways in which this might favourably affect exports in the short run. First, if excess capacity is arising in a large number of firms, then, other things being equal, at the economy level there will be a reduction in the rate of increase of costs and prices[2] with favourable effects on the U.K.'s international 'competitiveness'. Second, as suggested above, the creation of excess capacity might release resources for exporting. Finally, with spare capacity, the firm might be stimulated to enter the export market in an attempt to achieve capacity output: we have already commented on this response.[3]

[1] See Figure 4.4. Similar *output* effects result for a profit-maximizing firm under conditions of declining marginal costs, see Figure 4.3.

[2] The Phillips' Curve.

[3] Our analysis has been concerned with the short-run relationship between exports and domestic demand. This is not to deny that there are possible long-run effects, especially the possibility that successive domestic deflations will adversely

Further insight into the complexity of the relationships involved in the pressure hypothesis can be obtained by considering the proportion of output which a firm exports. Where a firm exports a relatively large proportion of its output, it is to some extent 'insulated' from the effects of changes in domestic demand: the home market is the 'residual'. The limiting case will be a firm which exports the whole of its output with no excess demand for its product. This is not to say that an export-orientated firm will not be affected by a reduction in its domestic sales but it does indicate that the direction and magnitude of the adjustment effect might vary between firms according to the proportion of output exported. For example, evidence from our field work showed that some firms which exported a relatively large proportion of their output included a preference for the home market as part of their objective function: such firms might respond to a decline in their domestic sales by attempting to maintain a minimum level of home market sales. In addition, the magnitude of any change in the firm's exports will depend upon the proportion of output exported. A few examples should illustrate the point.

Consider a firm which is exporting 50 per cent of its capacity output. If such a firm experiences a 10 per cent fall in its domestic sales, it will require only an equivalent rise in its export demand to use the production capacity released. By comparison, where a firm exports only 20 per cent of its capacity output, a decline in home sales of 10 per cent would release sufficient productive capacity for a 40 per cent rise in export sales. In the absence of excess demand or a perfectly elastic export demand in the short run, such a percentage increase for a domestic-market orientated company is substantial to say the least.[1] In the limiting case, with no change in exports, such

affect the rate of growth of the economy: here a growth model is required which incorporates the pressure of domestic demand.

1 In the engineering industry, it appears that '. . . only the exports of those companies for whom exporting is marginal (with less than 25 per cent exports) are likely to be sensitive to changes in the level of home demand. In particular, domestic deflation has a negligible effect on the export sales of major exporters. This does not mean that the manipulation of the level of home demand has no influence on exports, but simply that since its influence mainly affects modest exporters, the total effects are likely to be small.' Mechanical Engineering E.D.C., *Market – The World*, H.M.S.O., 1968, p. 37. It must, of course, be recognized that in terms of the U.K.'s balance of payments position, variations in exports

a firm would simply find itself with excess capacity equivalent to about 8 per cent of capacity output. On the other hand, if exports are 80 per cent of capacity output, a 10 per cent decrease in home sales would only release capacity for a 2·5 per cent rise in production for export. Similar arguments apply to an increase in domestic demand. In the example of the export-orientated firm, exporting 80 per cent of its capacity production, a 10 per cent rise in domestic demand could only result in a 2·5 per cent decline in export volume. Whether, in such a situation, a firm's export sales will actually decline is a possibility on which we have already commented. In the absence of a statement of the firm's objectives, it can be suggested that the larger are a firm's exports both absolutely and as a proportion of capacity output, the larger will be its investment in overseas selling subsidiaries, market information, and managerial experience, some or all of which might be highly specific to the export market. We can propose the hypothesis that such an export-orientated firm is less likely to allow short-run increases in domestic demand to affect its exports, provided that it is achieving some minimum level of home sales. We shall provide some evidence on this hypothesis in a subsequent section.

So far, our assessment of the pressure hypothesis has been based upon the assumption of a single, identical product sold in both home and export markets. If this is not the case, and a firm's domestic and export sales are not perfect substitutes, then for the pressure hypothesis to affect a firm's exports there needs to be a relatively high degree of flexibility in the production and marketing processes so that firms can vary their product 'mix' in the short run. The emphasis upon short-run production and marketing flexibility or substitutability is necessary since the pressure hypothesis has generally been applied in a short-term policy context.

Further factors might affect the relationship between exports and domestic demand in the economy. For example, in the office machinery industry, a growing capital goods sector, it was suggested by some firms that a domestic deflation in the economy might actually result in an *increase* in the domestic sales of their products: it was

will affect foreign exchange earnings and, in this respect, marginal changes can be significant: much will depend upon whether a particular policy measure is regarded as the least-cost solution.

argued that in a buyers' market, firms tend to become more conscious of the need for increasing efficiency and economizing on costs.[1] If this argument is valid, it implies that a firm's 'cost-conciousness' is a function of the pressure of domestic demand: such a view could not be incorporated into any model of short-run profit-maximizing behaviour but it might be compatible with satisficing behaviour. The office machinery industry is also interesting in that it includes a number of foreign-owned companies. However, the fact that some U.K. firms are foreign-owned subsidiaries does not, in itself, seem likely to affect the relationship between domestic demand and exports. The crucial point is not the nationality of ownership but the objective function, and whilst foreign-owned companies might be subject to a number of additional or different constraints, there seems no reason for not incorporating them into one of our basic models of firm behaviour.

CONCLUSIONS

This completes our survey of theory and our outline of some of the considerations which seem relevant to the pressure hypothesis. We appreciate that some of the outline has been inconclusive. Throughout, we have accepted the basic pressure hypothesis as a statement of relationships at the economy level and we have tried to show some of its microeconomic foundations.

The orthodox model of the firm as a profit-maximizer predicted that the short-run relationship between exports and domestic demand might be negative, positive or even zero – the actual prediction depending upon the firm's market and cost conditions. We then explored the pressure hypothesis in greater detail by trying to identify the various conditions under which a decline in a firm's domestic sales would actually be associated with a favourable effect on exports. For this exercise, we avoided any specification of the objective function of firms: instead, we approached the task more intuitively by specifying some of the conditions which seem to be required if a decline in domestic demand is to result in a rise in the firms' exports. Our analysis suggested that individual firms might be in different

[1] For further evidence, see, D. I. Mackay, 'Exporters and Export Markets' *Scottish Journal of Political Economy*, November 1964.

situations, with capacity utilization, export demand, the proportion of output exported, queuing policies and different production processes as some of the variables which differ between firms. At the industry level there will be a collection of firms, each in different situations, and in these circumstances the short-run relationship between exports and domestic demand is a matter for empirical testing. In addition to providing testable predictions on the relationship between exports and domestic demand, this chapter also formed the theoretical basis for our questionnaire and the associated field work, the results of which can be found in the industry studies. As will be apparent, the questionnaire was concerned not only with the pressure hypothesis but also with a variety of aspects of firm export behaviour and, in general, the more significant interviewing and questionnaire results from the sample of firms are presented under a number of major headings:

1. Evidence on the basic allocative decisions of firms. Under this heading, which is not independent of subsequent sections, evidence is presented on the proportion of output exported by firms and their opinions on this proportion, the constraints on exports, the attitude of firms towards exporting and their choice of selling methods.
2. The profitability of exports. The central questions for this section were: Have exports been less profitable than home sales? If so, why? And why, in fact, do firms export?
3. Pricing and excess demand. For similar products, evidence was obtained on the relationship between home and export prices and, in addition, we obtained some evidence on how firms allocate their available output in situations of excess demand.
4. The pressure hypothesis. This was the central part of the questionnaire and we present qualitative evidence on the export effects of various levels of domestic demand and the response of firms to a deflation.

Finally, mention must be made of the fact that the questionnaire results are concerned with the behaviour of individual firms whilst our econometric analysis of the pressure hypothesis was a mixture of firm and industry level tests, the latter being required in the absence of data from companies.

Chapter 5

TESTING THE PRESSURE HYPOTHESIS AT THE FIRM AND INDUSTRY LEVEL

In this chapter we consider the econometric testing of the relation between exports and the pressure of demand at the firm and industry level. As stated at the end of Chapter 3, only for the pottery industry was sufficient statistical data obtained to attempt a detailed study based upon the performance of individual firms; the results are in Chapter 6 below. Later chapters also include studies at industry level of the pressure hypothesis for the pottery, motor cycles and cycles and office machinery industries.

MODELS OF EXPORT DETERMINATION AT THE FIRM LEVEL

We shall be concerned with developing a model which simultaneously incorporates time-series data across firms in an industry, and one basic problem is to set up a model which will explain the time evolution of exports of individual firms and the effects of capacity utilization and yet allow for the heterogeneity of firms particularly as regards their size and their degree of involvement in the export field.

A model directed to an explanation of level of firms' exports presents formidable problems. For an individual firm, equations could be set up similar to the corresponding relations for a macro study, subject to data considerations and the special problems of a micro study to which we refer below. But the parameters of such a system would vary from one firm to another. Thus, for the simple model

$$X(t) = \alpha M(t) - \beta C(t)$$

(where, for a given time-period t, $X(t)$ is firm's exports, $M(t)$ is an appropriate indicator of overseas demand for its exports, and $C(t)$

is a measure of the firm's capacity utilization), both α and β would vary as between one firm and another if only because both parameters would be dependent upon the scale of individual firms' exports. Nor is this overcome in the case of a share model, for the ratio $X(t)/M(t)$ is also related to the scale of exports if $M(t)$ is any proxy variable for overseas demand unscaled as regards the individual firm.

There are, broadly, three possible ways of tackling this kind of difficulty. The first would be to incorporate into the model other variables which would explain the cross-sectional variability. In the present study, this would imply bringing in to the model other variables specific to the firm which would explain differences between firms in, for example, the general level of exports. We did not pursue this approach if only because it would have involved an unnecessarily wide study of firms' export performance in relation to long-term as well as cyclical factors.

A second possible approach would be to use appropriate deflators of the firm variables. In other contexts, such deflators are not too difficult to find. Thus, for cross-sectional studies concerned with geographical areas, population size is often an appropriate and easy to use deflator. But in the present study there is no such simple variable, since there are two sources of difference of scale between firms: the size of firm associated with its level of production and the share of exports within total production. Moreover, if the use of a deflator is not to give rise to estimation problems, it should be a variable external to the model. In the present context, this rules out any deflator based upon level of output.

A third approach, and one we have used, is to set up a model of export determination in the short term from which can be derived a testable relation which does not depend upon the level of individual firms' exports. A constant elasticity model is particularly suitable for this purpose so let us first consider a simple model in which overseas demand is the only explanatory variable:

$$X(t) = A(M(t))^{\alpha_0}.$$

Here, $X(t)$ is the level of a firm's exports, in value terms,

A is a constant which takes on a different value for each firm,

$M(t)$ is an overseas demand variable such as imports of relevant goods by relevant markets. By 'relevant' we mean that this variable is specific to the firm and in general takes on a different set of values for each firm,

α_0 is an elasticity parameter which is assumed to be constant over time and between firms.

By taking logarithms and differentiating, we obtain the usual relation expressing the proportionate change in $X(t)$ as a constant multiple of the independent proportionate change in $M(t)$:

$$\frac{dX(t)}{X(t)} = \alpha_0 \frac{dM(t)}{M(t)}$$

and the constant A specific to the firm no longer appears. However, the use of variables expressed in the form of proportionate changes is in one way unsatisfactory as it tends to give rise to serial correlation in the residuals. An alternative method is to express the variables in terms of proportionate deviations from trend (denoted here by $X\%(t)$ and $M\%(t)$). Thus

$$X\%(t) = \frac{X(t)-X_0(t)}{X_0(t)}$$

where $X_0(t)$ is the trend value of $X(t)$; and similarly for $M\%(t)$. The basic model $X\%(t) = \alpha M\%(t)$ is not identical to the model described above, relating proportionate changes in exports and overseas demand. In effect, it postulates a constant elasticity at the margin in exports in relation to overseas demand. It may be thought that this is more plausible than the first model.

We can now build up a model of export determination in which the variables are expressed in terms of proportionate deviations from trend, but at the start it can be seen that there are going to be important differences between a macro model based upon national data and a firm model. In the discussion of the macro models in Chapter 2, it was seen how a two-equation model might be set up. The first equation related the level of exports to overseas demand and capacity utilization and the second related capacity utilization to exports and output for the home market. The argument was noted that although the two-way relation between exports and capacity utilization could in principle lead to bias in the estimation, this was unlikely to be serious since the major influence in the second equation on the variation in capacity utilization was likely to have been output for the home market rather than exports.

The same argument, however, cannot be maintained in the case of a firm model. The second equation in the firm model will have the same form as in the macro model and express the level of capacity utilization as a function of exports and home sales. But at the firm level it would be quite implausible to assume a weak link between capacity utilization and exports, particularly for those firms with a large proportion of output exported. There is a further complication in the firm model in that there is the possibility of a reversed causal chain between home sales and capacity utilization. For not only will capacity utilization be partly dependent upon home sales but also home sales will be a function of home demand for the firm's output and capacity utilization.

This discussion suggests the following three-equation model: an export determination equation, a capacity utilization equation and a home sales equation. We consider first linear relations and ignore for the sake of exposition the constant terms. The variables are:

$X\%(t)$	Proportionate deviation from trend of exports in value terms,
$M\%(t)$	Proportionate deviation from trend of relevant overseas imports,
$P\%(t)$	Proportionate deviation from trend of total production, a proxy variable for level of capacity utilization,
$HS\%(t)$	Proportionate deviation from trend of home sales in value terms,
$HD\%(t)$	A variable reflecting the fluctuation in home demand.

The measures of the overseas and home demand variables will be discussed below.

With this notation, the export equation can be written

$$X\%(t) = \alpha M\%(t) - \beta P\%(t). \quad (1)$$

Similarly, home sales will be dependent upon demand and also possibly upon the level of capacity utilization and we have:

$$HS\%(t) = \gamma HD\%(t) - \delta P\%(t). \quad (2)$$

(So far as β or δ are not zero, they might be expected to be positive.) Thirdly, we can relate production to home sales and export sales. The accounting identity $P = HS + X$ is clear enough but for the present purpose we need a relation between $P\%$ and $HS\%$ and $X\%$. If k is the proportion of output exported at a particular time then

$$P\%(t) = kX\%(t) + (1-k)HS\%(t). \qquad (3)$$

If there is no substantial shift between exports and home sales over the period studied, it is reasonable to treat this equation as the third of our set, k being the average proportion of output exported.

In this system there are three endogenous variables $P\%(t)$, $X\%(t)$ and $HS\%(t)$. $M\%(t)$ is certainly exogenous, except in the unusually extreme case where an individual firm is dominant in world markets. It will be assumed that home demand for the firm's products is also exogenous. In other words, the analysis will deal only with firms in a competitive home market. The reduced form equations for $X\%(t)$ and $HS\%(t)$ in terms of the exogenous variables $M\%(t)$ and $HD\%(t)$ can be obtained by eliminating $P\%(t)$ from the first two equations and solving for $X\%(t)$ and $HS\%(t)$. This leads to the following results:

$$X\%(t) = \lambda . \alpha(1+\delta(1-k))M\%(t) - \lambda . \gamma\beta(1-k)HD\%(t) \qquad (4)$$

and

$$HS\%(t) = \lambda . \gamma(1+\beta k)HD\%(t) - \lambda . \alpha\delta k M\%(t) \qquad (5)$$

where

$$\lambda = \frac{1}{1+\beta k+\delta(1-k)}$$

also

$$P\%(t) = \lambda[\alpha k M\%(t) + \gamma(1-k)HD\%(t)]. \qquad (6)$$

For the individual firm, this model explains export and home sales fluctuations in terms of (*a*) two exogenous variables related to overseas and home demand, (*b*) a parameter specific to the firm, k, the proportion of output exported and (*c*) parameters α, β, γ and δ which are assumed invariant between firms in the same industry.

Before turning to the problem of estimating the parameters of this model, it is interesting to see what the model predicts in some particular circumstances. Consider for example the case where firms 'favour' home sales at the expense of export sales when there are capacity limitations, that is, the case where $\delta = 0$. In this extreme case, the export Equation 4 of the reduced form becomes:

$$X\%(t) = \frac{\alpha}{(1+\beta k)} M\%(t) - \frac{\gamma\beta(1-k)}{(1+\beta k)} HD\%(t).$$

This shows that a regression of export fluctuations upon fluctuations in overseas demand and home demand has a regression coefficient of overseas demand which is not only dependent upon the elasticity of exports with respect to overseas demand (α) but also upon the pressure of demand parameter β and the coefficient k which measures the importance of exports in the firm's output. To put it another way, a regression analysis of $X\%(t)$ upon $M\%(t)$ and $HD\%(t)$ could yield non-significant coefficients of $M\%(t)$ and $HD\%(t)$ as a result of ignoring the effect of varying values of k for different firms. A firm exporting a large proportion of its output would appear to show a very different marginal relation between overseas demand and exports as compared with a firm exporting a small proportion.

This model and its reduced form present estimation problems because the parameters of the reduced form are functions of k which varies from one firm to another. But since β and δ, and therefore βk and $\delta(1-k)$ can be expected to be considerably less than unity,

$$\lambda = \frac{1}{1+\beta k+\delta(1-k)}$$

can be approximately written as

$$\lambda = 1-\beta k-\delta(1-k).$$

Hence

$$X\%(t) = (1-\beta k-\delta(1-k)\alpha(1+\delta(1-k))M\%(t)$$
$$-(1-\beta k-\delta(1-k))\gamma\beta(1-k)HD\%(t).$$

Expanding, and ignoring second-order terms such as $\beta\delta$ and β^2:

$$X\%(t) = \alpha(1-\beta k)M\%(t)-\gamma\beta(1-k)HD\%(t).$$

Similarly

$$HS\%(t) = -\alpha\delta kM\%(t)+\gamma(1-\delta(1-k))HD\%(t).$$

These two reduced form equations can now be formulated in a way susceptible to ordinary least squares estimation for:

$$X\%(t) = \alpha M\%(t)-\alpha\beta.kM\%(t)-\gamma\beta.(1-k)HD\%(t) \quad (1.1)$$

and a regression of $X\%(t)$ on $M\%(t)$, $kM\%(t)$ and $(1-k)HD\%(t)$ will estimate the coefficients α, $(\alpha\beta)$ and $(\gamma\beta)$ and hence β and γ separately. A similar conclusion applies to the reduced form equation for

$$HS\%(t) = -\alpha\delta . kM\%(t) + \gamma . HD(t) - \gamma\delta . (1-k)HD(t). \quad (1.2)$$

A three-equation model in multiplicative form can also be set out on similar lines to the above linear additive model. The export determination equation is

$$X(t) = [M(t)]^{a} . [P(t)]^{-b}$$

where, contrary to the notation used at the beginning of this chapter, the variables $X(t)$, $M(t)$ and $P(t)$ are to be taken as expressed in the form of ratio to trend values, that is, $X(t) = 1 + X\%(t)$ etc. (It will be recalled that in the additive model, the corresponding equation was $X\%(t) = \alpha M\%(t) - \beta P\%(t)$ where the variables $X\%(t)$ etc. were proportionate deviations from trend.) The multiplicative form might be thought more convincing than the additive one; in the latter the effect on exports of the pressure of demand would be independent of the underlying value of exports resulting from the given state of overseas demand; the multiplicative form on the other hand provides, at a given level of pressure of demand, for an effect upon exports which is dependent upon the level of overseas demand. The other two equations of the multiplicative model are:

$$HS(t) = [HD(t)]^{c} . [P(t)]^{-d}$$
$$P(t) = [X(t)]^{k} . [HS(t)]^{1-k}.$$

In the last equation, k as previously is the proportion of output exported; on taking logarithms and differentiating, it leads to the necessary relation between a proportionate change in exports, a proportionate change in home sales and the associated proportionate change in total output. Taking logarithms of each equation in turn leads to a set of equations exactly similar in form to the linear additive equations above with $\log X(t)$, etc. in place of $X\%(t)$ etc., and the parameters, a, b, c and d in place of α, β, γ and δ. The reduced form of this multiplicative model will also be similar. The equation for exports is:

$$\log X(t) = a \log M(t) - ab . k \log M(t) - bc(1-k) \log HD(t) \quad (2.1)$$

and, as in Equation 1.1 above, a regression of log $X(t)$ on log $M(t)$, k.log $M(t)$ and $(1-k)$ log $HD(t)$ will estimate the coefficients a, b and c.

SHARE MODEL

We have described above, in the chapter on macro studies of the pressure hypothesis, the construction and estimation of models explaining the performance of the share of U.K. exports in world trade. Thus the basic model evaluated by Ball *et al.* expressed the U.K. share as dependent upon the level of capacity utilization. This model, of course, assumes unit elasticity of demand for exports which may or may not be valid. And a least squares estimation of this single relation ignores the reverse dependence of capacity utilization upon exports themselves. However, it is argued that this second dependence can reasonably be ignored since it is likely to be relatively weak.

The setting up of a share model at firm level presents if anything more problems. The first difficulty relates to the calculation of a measure of share. Earlier in this chapter we have considered models based upon $X\%(t)$ and $M\%(t)$, respectively the proportionate deviations from trend of exports and overseas imports. But a ratio of these two variables, being a ratio of small or possibly zero values, is not operational. An alternative procedure would be to take as the basic export and overseas demand variables, $X(t)$ and $M(t)$, the ratio to trend values, where, as before, $X(t) = 1+X\%(t)$ and $M(t) = 1+M\%(t)$. A test of the existence of any pressure of demand effect upon exports would be provided by an estimation of the model

$$\frac{X(t)}{M(t)} = \alpha+\beta P\%(t) \tag{3.1}$$

where, as before, $P\%(t)$ is the proportionate deviation from trend of total production and stands proxy for the degree of capacity utilization. This is plausible because, with no capacity effect and a short-run unit elasticity of demand for exports, the share as measured by $X(t)/M(t)$ would have a constant value (of unity). In so far as the pressure of demand affects export performance, the share measure would be less than unity at times of high pressure and greater than unity at low pressure. Unfortunately, a least squares estimation of Equation 3.1 would not correctly estimate the parameter β as $P\%(t)$ itself is a function of exports. Indeed, in the absence of any real pressure of demand effect, the least squares estimate of β in Equation 3.1 could be expected to be positive. The problem cannot be resolved by a simultaneous equation approach such as we developed for the level of exports since the system cannot be solved for the share except in terms of a functional dependence upon $M(t)$ as well as the other exogenous variable in the system: $HD(t)$.

A second-best alternative is to test for a relationship between the share variable and some variable which measures the pressure of home demand position for the industry generally. This has the advantage that, for the individual firm, the causal link is more nearly one way and ordinary least squares regression estimates should have the usual desirable properties.

It remains to consider the appropriate statistical measures of the two central variables not so far specifically defined: $M\%(t)$, the overseas demand variable specific to each firm and $HD\%(t)$, the home demand variable. $M\%(t)$ can be constructed in two stages. First, for each overseas market separately, the percentage deviations from trend of their total imports of the relevant products are computed and second, a weighted average of their overseas market series is calculated for each firm, the weights being related to their relative importance in the firm's exports.

A measure of the home demand facing the firm is much more difficult. A firm's home sales are not necessarily equal to home demand, and indeed Equation 2 of the model allows the possibilities of capacity limitations leading to inequalities between the two. In the analysis of pottery firms in Chapter 6, we have used as the main proxy variable for the pressure of home demand, the percentage deviations about trend of industry sales to the home market. It must be confessed that movements in industry sales as a whole – or indeed any other demand variable external to the firm – may imperfectly measure fluctuations in demand on the individual firm. However, at the expense of some loss of precision, this proxy variable will avoid to a considerable extent the bias which would be inherent in any model which equates home demand on the firm to home sales by the firm.

TESTS OF THE PRESSURE HYPOTHESIS AT THE INDUSTRY LEVEL

In later chapters, ordinary least squares estimation has been used to test the pressure hypothesis at the industry level of disaggregation in single individual overseas markets. We describe here the nature of these tests and the problems concerned with the interpretation of the results. Two sets of models have been used: one based on explaining the level of U.K. exports and the other on the share of U.K. exports in the overseas market. In some cases, both linear and multiplicative equations have been fitted.

The explanatory variables for the level of exports equation are: overseas demand measured by total imports from all countries into the overseas market (M), pressure of demand measured by two alternative proxy variables – either (i) by sales to the home market (HS), or (ii) by national or regional unemployment rate (U),[1] a time trend-removal term and quarterly dummy variables. In some ways, single-equation analysis at industry level gives rise to less serious estimation problems than at national or firm level. Consider the two-equation level of exports model analogous to the model at national level of Equations 1.1 and 2.1 of Chapter 2:

$$X = \alpha + \beta M + \gamma C + \lambda t$$
$$C = F(X, HS)$$

where M and HS are treated as exogenous variables. At industry level, the feedback from fluctuations in exports to the level of capacity utilization over the short term might reasonably be discounted, particularly if the industry's exports go to a wide range of markets. Hence, if national unemployment, U, is used as a proxy variable for C in the first equation and exports regressed on overseas demand and unemployment, the regression coefficient will be unbiased. If, on the other hand, home sales (HS) are used in place of a proxy variable for capacity utilization in a single-equation estimation, this is equivalent to estimating the export equation of the reduced form of the model; that is, a regression of exports on overseas demand, home sales and time. However, the model coefficients of overseas demand

[1] In the industry regression analyses, these variables are referred to as the pressure of demand variables.

and home sales in the reduced form equation will not be the same as the coefficients respectively of overseas demand and capacity utilization in the export determination equation. It can be shown that the reduced form coefficients will be *numerically* less than the corresponding coefficients of the export determination equation if there is an adverse pressure effect (i.e. γ negative), they will be the same if there is no pressure effect, and they will be numerically greater if the pressure effect is (unexpectedly) favourable to exports (i.e. γ positive). In other words, in the presence of a pressure of demand effect upon exports, the coefficient of home sales in the regression equation will have the correct sign though not the correct magnitude. It is also important to note that, when there is an adverse pressure effect, it is a consequence that the demand elasticity of U.K. exports will be underestimated, in an equation with home sales replacing capacity utilization as the pressure variable.

There is little to be said about the estimation problems relating to a shares model at industry level. As in the case of the shares model at national level, the estimation procedures can be expected to overestimate the pressure effect if the true demand elasticity for U.K. exports is less than unity.

Finally, it should be noted that there is a gap in the empirical estimations below, in that the variables are based upon value rather than volume data and prices do not enter explicitly into the analyses. This deficiency is the consequence of the absence of suitable constant price data. However, as the Brookings Report points out,[1] 'much econometric research on British exports has failed to support prices as a significant explanatory variable' and so far as this is the case, the omission of price variables will not matter.

1 *Britain's Economic Prospects*, Richard Caves and associates, Allen & Unwin, 1968, p. 212.

Chapter 6

THE U.K. POTTERY INDUSTRY

INTRODUCTION

The pottery industry consists of four quite different parts which overlap hardly at all. They are: domestic pottery, tiles, sanitary ware and electrical porcelain. Firms manufacturing electrical porcelain were not included in the survey. In general, firms do not make more than one of these products and if they do, in separate establishments. The common factor linking the whole industry is the process of firing, glazing and decorating clay. Otherwise, domestic pottery is a consumer good, whereas tiles and sanitary ware depend to a great extent upon the building industry. Domestic pottery is much the most important sector of the industry. It accounts for about 55 per cent of the value of total production, compared to less than 20 per cent for tiles, and about 12 per cent each for sanitary ware and electrical porcelain. Two-thirds of the industry's exports are domestic pottery. Production and export figures for 1958, 1962 and 1966 are set out in Table 6.1.[1]

The main emphasis of our survey investigation and analysis has been on the domestic pottery side, although firms making tiles and sanitary ware were also interviewed. Apart from its relative importance, the published statistics for domestic pottery are more comprehensive than those for tiles and sanitary ware and, for foreign trade analysis, the Standard International Trade Classification heading number 666 conveniently consists entirely of domestic pottery so making it possible to relate fairly readily home and overseas developments.

[1] For detailed statistics relating to pottery exports, see H. Macdiarmid and R. L. Smyth, *Exports of Pottery from the United Kingdom 1948-68*, Keele University Library, 1969.

TABLE 6.1 *Production and Exports of the Pottery Industry*

	£ million					
	1958		*1962*		*1966*	
	P	*E*	*P*	*E*	*P*	*E*
Domestic pottery	32·5	14·1	35·6	14·5	42·9	18·8
Tiles	11·7	2·3	...	3·6	...	4·3
Sanitary earthenware	8·5	2·9	...	2·4	...	2·8
Electrical porcelain	7·9	1·3	...	1·4	...	1·5
Total	60·6	20·7	...	21·9	...	27·4

Note: P = Production for home and export.
E = Exports.

In the sections below, after some introductory remarks on the constitution of the sample for the industry as a whole, there follow four sections relating to domestic pottery. The first sets out the main statistical features of the domestic pottery industry's performance in the home and export markets over the period covered by our survey. The second analyses the results of the interviews with firms. The third comprises a statistical and econometric study of the home and export sales which were obtained from most of the firms which were interviewed; in this section we examine the evidence at firm level for the pressure of demand hypothesis. The fourth describes the results of an econometric analysis of the pressure of demand effect on the industry's exports. The chapter concludes with a brief discussion of the results of the interviews with firms in the tiles and sanitary ware sectors of the pottery industry.

Survey Procedure and Sample Characteristics

The sample of firms to approach for interview was chosen in consultation with the British Pottery Manufacturers' Federation. It comprised firms thought to be representative of the industry. By its nature the sample was not a random one, and as a consequence the results of the survey cannot be grossed up to give estimated values for the whole industry with appropriately calculated sampling errors. A random-sampling approach was deliberately not attempted for we were going to ask firms to divulge confidential information and there was a strong likelihood that a random approach would in any case prove abortive due to non-response. The firms included were of course those who, it was hoped, would be ready to help, and in the event almost all did. But this selection criterion has its own kind of bias which needs to be borne in mind in interpreting the data. The outside investigator likes to think that co-operative managements are 'progressive' managements, though the authors know of no firm evidence for this view.

TABLE 6.2 *Sample Constitution*

	Firms interviewed	*Firms in B.P.M.F.*	*Larger firms in 1963 Census*
Domestic pottery			
Fine china	3	5	
China	4	20	94
Earthenware and other	14	68	
	21	93	
Tiles	3	17	18
Sanitary earthenware	4	11	14
	28	121	126

Note: The few domestic pottery firms which produced under more than one heading have, arbitrarily, been allocated to the first relevant heading in our table. Mergers not fully implemented at the time have not been taken into account.

Our choice of firms roughly reflected the numbers in the various sectors of the industry though it was deliberately unrepresentative of the smaller firms. We did not have access to data on the sizes of individual firms in the industry and so it was not possible to build up a sample with predetermined sampling fractions according to size groups. Table 6.2 shows the number of firms interviewed compared with the number of member firms of the British Pottery Manufacturers' Federation (B.P.M.F.) at the time of the survey, and with the number of larger firms employing more than twenty-five persons recorded in the 1963 Census of Production.[1] The

[1] It is understood that the Federation members account for nearly all the total production of the industry. It is not possible to compare the Federation numbers with those of the Census of Production; the Federation numbers include larger and smaller firms in the census sense while the census breakdown in part relates to establishments rather than to firms.

interviews started towards the end of 1965 and were completed in mid-1966. The survey covered between one-fifth and one-quarter of the firms in the Federation (as will be seen below, the coverage was rather greater in terms of production and employment of the industry). The preponderance of domestic pottery manufacturers in the sample reflects the numbers in the whole industry, and the greater variety of types of product in this section. These vary from the cheapest white earthenware cup and saucer, through 'fancies' such as pottery animals and ashtrays, to the very finest bone china at several pounds a piece.

I. DOMESTIC POTTERY: GENERAL OUTLINE

Since 1958 production of domestic pottery has risen from £32·5 million to £42·9 million in 1966, a rise in value terms of 32 per cent. Tables 6.3 and 6.4 show the annual figures for home sales, exports and imports and the percentage year to year changes.

While home sales have progressed in nearly every year, though at times very slowly, exports were for a long time virtually unchanged and have only shown significant increases since 1963. Imports increased quite substantially from 1958 to 1962, but have not increased since, and they are still very small in relation to total production at home.

The percentage of production exported is very high, over 40 per

TABLE 6.3 *Domestic Pottery: Home and Export Sales and Imports*

	Home sales £m	*Export sales £m*	*Total production £m*	*Imports £m*	*Exports as percentage of total production*	*Imports as percentage of total production*	*Home sales and imports £m*
1958	18·4	14·1	32·5	1·73	43	5·3	20·1
1959	18·7	14·1	32·8	1·83	42	5·6	20·5
1960	20·3	14·1	34·4	2·17	41	6·3	22·5
1961	21·1	14·5	35·6	2·43	40	6·8	23·5
1962	21·4	14·5	35·6	2·43	40	7·5	23·8
1963	21·9	14·5	36·5	2·39	40	6·5	24·3
1964	23·3	16·1	39·4	2·80	41	7·1	26·1
1965	24·9	17·2	42·2	2·71	41	6·4	27·6
1966	24·1	18·8	42·9	2·62	44	6·1	26·7

cent, and the industry is proud of it. It is of particular interest that pottery contains almost no imported materials.

Too much should not be read into these tables, since annual figures are bound to be rather crude; and 'domestic pottery' figures, although considerably disaggregated already, cover a wide variety of products whose demand experiences may have differed in these years. At the crudest level of casual observation, however, there seems from Table 6.4 to be no obvious relation between movements in home and export sales. In the three years 1964-6, when exports showed the larger increases, two were years of relatively high rate of increase in home sales and one a year when, exceptionally, home sales fell.

TABLE 6.4 *Domestic Pottery: Changes on Previous Year (Percentages)*

	Home	*Export*	*Total*	*Imports*	*Imports plus home*
1959	+1·7	—	+0·9	+6·0	+2·0
1960	+8·7	—	+4·9	+18·5	+9·7
1961	+3·9	+2·7	+3·5	+12·2	+4·5
1962	+1·4	—	—	+10·3	+1·3
1963	+2·5	—	+1·7	−11·1	+2·1
1964	+6·4	+10·7	+7·9	+17·3	+7·3
1965	+6·9	+6·8	+6·9	−3·2	+5·8
1966	−3·2	+9·3	+1·7	−3·3	−3·2

Table 6.5 and the derived Table 6.6 below show the main pattern of international trade in domestic pottery. Table 6.5 is not comprehensive: basically it includes only those countries which report their commodity trade statistics to the United Nations but this includes U.K. manufacturers' main export markets, and their main rivals. Each row of Table 6.5 sets out the imports of individual countries broken down according to the major sources named across the head of the table. Hence each column relates to the exports of individual countries, but because the table is based upon import statistics it is not possible to add up the columns to give total country exports. Table 6.6 is based upon Table 6.5 and gives the percentage shares of each import market.

Looking at the columns of Table 6.5, it is evident that the world's

TABLE 6.5 *Domestic Pottery (S.I.T.C. 666) World Trade in $m, 1963*

	Sources of imports															
	U. Kingdom	Australia	N. Zealand	Canada	W. Germany	Italy	S. Africa	U.S.A.	Japan	France	Netherlands	Belg. Lux.	Switzerland	Sweden	Other	Total
Imports of U. Kingdom	/				1·7	1·3			0·6	0·4	0·3			0·1	2·3	6·7
Australia	4·0	/			0·3	0·1			3·4						0·2	8·0
N. Zealand	1·7		/						0·4						0·2	2·3
Canada	11·6			/	0·6	0·3		1·8	2·6	0·1					0·4	17·4
W. Germany	1·2				/	1·5			1·6	0·5	1·5	0·6	0·2	0·3	0·8	8·2
Italy	1·1				9·5	/			1·3	0·8					2·1	14·8
S. Africa*	(1·9)				(0·4)		/		(1·2)						(—)	(3·5)
U.S.A.	11·0				5·3	4·2		/	37·3	1·1	0·2		0·2	0·2	1·5	62·0
Japan									/						0·2	0·2
France	0·4				4·1	1·2			0·2	/	0·2	0·4			0·6	7·1
Netherlands	0·5				4·6	0·3		0·1	1·2		/	0·9		0·1	7·7	9·0
Belg. Lux.	0·1				2·8	0·5			0·9	1·0	1·4	/			0·8	7·5
Switzerland	0·6				3·1	0·3			0·2	0·4	0·1		/	0·1	1·1	5·9
Sweden	0·5				2·4	0·1			0·8					/	2.0	5·8

* South Africa's import statistics were not available, so these figures are taken from other countries' export statistics. As a result the figures for South African imports may not be complete, and are not comparable with other figures.

TABLE 6.6 *Domestic Pottery (S.I.T.C. 666) (Percentage Shares of Import Markets, 1963)*

Imports of	*Sources of imports*															
	U. Kingdom	Australia	N. Zealand	Canada	W. Germany	Italy	S. Africa	U.S.A.	Japan	France	Netherlands	Belg. Lux.	Switzerland	Sweden	Other	Total
U. Kingdom	/				26	19			9	6	4			1	35	100
Australia	50	/			4	1			43						2	100
N. Zealand	74		/						15						11	100
Canada	67			/	3	2		10	15						5	100
W. Germany	15				/	19			19	6	18	7	2	4	10	100
Italy	8				64	/			9	5					14	100
S. Africa*	(54)				(11)		/		(35)						(—)	(100)
U.S.A.	18				9	7		/	60	2					4	100
Japan									/						100	100
France	6				58	17			4	/	3	5			7	100
Netherlands	6				52	3		1	13		/	11		1	13	100
Belg. Lux.	2				37	7			12	13	18	/			11	100
Switzerland	10				53	5			3	7	2		/	2	18	100
Sweden	9				41	2			14					/	34	100

* South Africa's import statistics were not available, so these figures are taken from other countries' export statistics. As a result the figures for South African imports may not be complete, and are not comparable with other figures.

four leading exporters are the U.K., West Germany, Italy and Japan. The importance of Japan is underestimated by the tables since many of her Far Eastern markets are not included. No other country has more than 10 per cent of any important import market, except in a few isolated cases involving trade internal to the E.E.C.

The important point arising from these tables is the continuing strength of the U.K. in the older and richer Commonwealth markets (Australia, Canada, South Africa). This strength used to be even greater, particularly in Australia where the Japanese have made especially great inroads (partly corresponding to large Australian sales of wool to Japan and the consequent trade agreements). In the biggest and probably the most competitive import market, the U.S.A., the U.K. has not only maintained but slightly improved her share over the last eight or nine years (see Table 6.7 below).

TABLE 6.7 *Imports of Domestic Pottery by U.S.A.* *(Percentage Shares in Brackets)*

					U.S. $ million				
From	*1958*	*1959*	*1960*	*1961*	*1962*	*1963*	*1964*	*1965*	*1966*
United Kingdom	7·7	9·0	9·0	9·2	10·7	11·0	12·2	13·6	15·0
	(17)	(16)	(14)	(17)	(18)	(18)	(18)	(18)	(19)
Western Germany	5·1	6·5	7·0	5·7	5·7	5·3	5·5	5·6	6·0
	(11)	(11)	(11)	(11)	(10)	(9)	(8)	(7)	(7)
Japan	28·6	34·5	41·1	31·7	35·4	37·3	41·5	45·7	48·3
	(62)	(61)	(64)	(59)	(59)	(60)	(60)	(61)	(60)
Other	5·0	6·7	6·4	6·9	8·0	8·4	9·4	10·5	11·4
	(10)	(12)	(11)	(13)	(13)	(13)	(14)	(14)	(14)
Total	46·4	56·7	64·5	53·5	59·8	62·0	68·6	74·2	80·7

A further study of a very detailed breakdown of American imports of domestic pottery (in the American trade statistics) suggests at first sight that U.K. exporters are not really in very serious competition with the Japanese, since in very few commodity classes do both countries have significant shares of the market; in general, the Japanese dominate the cheaper sections and the U.K. is stronger in the expensive sections. But this may be because the U.K. industry is unable to compete in the manufacture of cheap products, and can only sell effectively when styling, pattern, colouring and so forth are more important than the price. Similar figures for the Canadian market show that the U.K. has managed to maintain its very high share of the import market in the last eight years. In Canada of course the U.K. enjoys a tariff advantage through Commonwealth Preference, and strongly enforced anti-dumping laws make it very difficult for exporters to the Candian market to quote low enough prices to overcome the tariff barrier.[1]

Employment in the pottery industry as a whole[2] has fallen fairly steadily from over 80,000 in 1951 and 1952 to about 65,000 in 1966. The greater part of this fall occurred, however, in the 1950s and was connected with, among other things, the introduction of continuous-firing ovens. The figures for employment, registered unemployed and the unemployment percentage are given below for the most recent years, with the national unemployment figure for comparison.

TABLE 6.8 *Employment in Pottery Industry*

Year	*Employees*	*Registered unemployed*	*Percentage unemployed*	*Percentage national unemployed*
1959	69,000	2,137	3·1	2·2
1960	68,000	935	1·4	1·6
1961	69,000	803	1·2	1·5
1962	70,000	1,097	1·6	2·0
1963	66,000	1,620	2·5	2·5
1964	65,200	984	1·5	1·6
1965	65,400	683	1·0	1·4
1966	64,600	759	1·2	1·4

For domestic pottery only, we have figures for employment and output so that it is possible to calculate output per employee. This is done below in Table 6.9 which also includes unfilled vacancies. The latter should be treated with caution, however, since the number of unfilled vacancies published by employers will depend on their production plans, and these in turn will depend on the number of employees that are thought to be available, or likely to be available, in the near future. Thus in a situation such as existed during the

[1] The U.K. share of the Canadian import market for pottery was 70 and 73 per cent in 1958 and 1959; and 73 and 75 per cent in 1965 and 1966, respectively.

[2] Breakdowns for the product categories within the total are not available on a comprehensive basis.

period of this research, where most firms are unable to get the labour they need to meet demand, production plans will be restricted by the general shortage of labour, and published unfilled vacancies will be considerably less than the underlying need for additional labour.

TABLE 6.9 *Domestic Pottery: Productivity*

	Employees	*Output (£m)*	*Output per employee (£)*	*Unfilled vacancies*
September 1958	30,014	32·5	1,083	1,169
September 1959	29,028	32·8	1,130	1,253
September 1960	28,776	34·4	1,195	1,401
September 1961	28,483	35·6	1,250	1,183
September 1962	28,703	35·9	1,251	801
September 1963	26,577	36·5	1,375	688
September 1964	27,306	39·4	1,443	1,012
September 1965	27,182	42·2	1,552	1,262
September 1966	26,807	42·9	1,600	1,354

II. DOMESTIC POTTERY: THE RESULT OF INTERVIEWS WITH FIRMS

In this section, we give an account of the interviews with managements of twenty-one domestic pottery firms. In Appendix A there is a detailed tabulation, firm by firm, of the responses to the main items of our firm questionnaire.

Size, Product and Exports

The apparent homogeneity of the domestic pottery sector of the industry conceals both a wide variation in type of product, and as a corollary to this, great variations in the degree of mechanization possible, the amount and quality of labour required and the sort of market situation existing both at home and overseas. As a result, the exporting problems facing firms vary quite markedly, and the degree to which they have been overcome depends on these external factors as well as on the firms themselves. For the firms in our survey it is possible to allocate them to more meaningful product categories than it is for the industry as a whole. Table 6.10 distinguishes the expensive and cheaper ends of the sector though such a division by product must be a little arbitrary since some firms make products from more than one category and even within categories products can be different. Nevertheless, Table 6.10 shows a clear relation between product type and the export proportion of total sales.

TABLE 6.10 *Exports and Type of Product**

Principal product	*Average proportion exports to sales*	*Range*	*No. of firms*
Fine china and fine earthenware	59	46–67	6
Medium earthenware	51	20–75	8
'Fancies'	16	8–30	3
Cheap earthenware	12	0–25	7

* This table and the following Table 6.11 include three firms which did not respond to the subsequent questions.

Amalgamation is reducing the number of firms and gradually increasing the relative importance and size of large firms. But there is still a large number of relatively small firms, many managed or controlled by members of the founding family. To a fairly remarkable degree the smaller firms are able to export successfully. The long history of exporting in the industry, with its accumulation of knowledge of export markets, long established commercial connections and consumer education in the virtues of British pottery continue to make this possible. There is no significant correlation in our sample as a whole between size of firm and success in exporting in the sense of proportion of output exported and some of the smaller firms have the highest ratios of exports to total sales. 'Size of firm' is here measured by the labour force as we found few firms willing to answer questions about the value of net assets of the firm.

The size of our sample makes it impossible to analyse with confidence size, export ratios and product category simultaneously.

TABLE 6.11 *Exports and Size*

No. of firms	*Size of firm by no. of employees*	*Average ratio of exports to sales*	*Highest and lowest ratio in category*
2	0–99	27	0–55
5	100–249	21	11–33
9	250–499	36	7–75
4	600–999	55	44–66
4	1,000 and over	48	8–75

Nevertheless it is interesting that, if firms in each category (excluding 'fancies' in which there are only three firms in the sample) are ranked according to size and proportion of output exported respectively, fine china and earthenware shows no significant coefficient whereas the rank correlation coefficient for medium earthenware of 0·78 is significant at the 5 per cent level. It would seem that size becomes more important for successful exporting where mass-production techniques play a larger part, and that lack of size need not be a handicap to a firm's exports if its products are very distinctive and contain a large amount of highly skilled labour. However, the cheap earthenware category shows no relation between size and export ratio. The reason may be that, of firms in our sample, two make hollow-ware (mugs, jugs, teapots and so on) and three of the remainder do not make the very cheapest product. In short, this product category is not very homogeneous. It is of interest that most of the manufacturers in this category themselves believed that the way to increasing exports was grading up, that is, moving into a more expensive product category, rather than more intensive mass-production techniques. Certainly with a relatively high ratio of bulk and weight to value, so that transport costs are substantial per unit of value, such firms need a substantial advantage in efficiency or a tariff advantage in order to compete abroad on price; and it is in the nature of their product that they cannot compete on anything else, such as pattern or styling. This last applies rather less to the hollow-ware manufacturers who do rather better abroad because of a fairly steady demand for English brown teapots. It is interesting that the only firm we saw which makes large quantities of plain white earthenware could only export in significant quantity to Canada where Commonwealth Preference gives it a tariff advantage.

The manufacturers of fine china emphasized the large amount of their production process which must be done by hand, such as the handling of bone china, and hand-decorating. This limits the potential benefits of economies of scale arising from mechanization. They also told us that for very expensive products like theirs, where a place setting can cost more than three figures (in pounds sterling), price is much less important than style, finish, and sometimes the waiting time for delivery. Even among the medium quality manufacturers selling success can depend much more on choosing a popular pattern than on price. These considerations reduce, although they do not by any means eliminate, the importance of being able to cut down manufacturing costs through mechanization, and therefore the importance of size which makes such mechanization possible.

Conversations with people in the industry gave a wide range of opinion as to the future importance of size of firm for exporting, biased, not surprisingly, by the size of the firm with which each person was concerned. In general, however, although it clearly helps to be in the right product category, there was quite wide agreement that size was going to become increasingly important.

Some further points arose in connection with size of firm. The two smallest firms could not afford to finance sales trips to their potential or existing export markets simply because of their small turnover – the risk of too small a resulting increase in sales was too great in relation to the cost of such trips. At this extreme, size is clearly a limiting factor. Another firm told us that it was too small to own its own overseas selling outlets, or to have agents who did not sell competing products; it could not rely on its existing agents to try hard enough. Significantly, this firm was taken over by a larger one soon after we had seen it. Only one firm that we saw used another firm's overseas selling facilities; they make non-competing products. One final point relating to size: one manufacturer was indignant at attempts to encourage small firms to export. He believed that small firms could do a great deal of harm to other U.K. exporters in markets they do not know since they do not have the resources to get to know them, nor to supply and service them adequately, and that this harm far outweighed any contribution to national exports. This view should be seen in the context of the pottery industry – the firm holding it had under 500 employees, which would be small in some other industries.

Allocative Decisions

Perhaps the most obvious reason why firms export is that they did last year, and things like that do not change very quickly, especially when a large investment is involved. Some firms also pointed out that the industry as a whole clearly could not sell the whole of its production on the home market, although this is not of course a reason for any particular firm to export. Answers like 'This firm has always been export minded', though plainly true and in a certain sense highly relevant, are not helpful analytically. In the interviews therefore we tried to establish further reasons for exporting, and particularly whether firms were trying to change their current balance between home and export sales. In describing answers to the questions in the questionnaire, it should be emphasized again that we tried, fairly successfully, to ask direct questions as little as possible and to fill in the answers as we thought they arose from the discussion. Our subjects only saw our assessment of their replies on the questionnaire when we sent it to them afterwards, and in only one or two cases did they see the questionnaire before or during the interview. With this in mind then, the responses to our enquiry about export policy aims are shown in Table 6.12.

TABLE 6.12 *Aims of Exports Policy*

	Frequency *
(*a*) To increase exports	15
(*b*) To prevent exports falling below some minimum proportion of sales	2
(*c*) To encourage exports as a way of diversifying markets	14
(*d*) To decrease exports as a proportion of sales	1
(*e*) To maintain exports at present proportion of sales	3
(*f*) To encourage exports as a way of spreading seasonal 'peaks' in sales	4
(*g*) To hold exports at present absolute level	1

* Some firms gave more than one aim.

The two firms giving answer (*b*) in Table 6.12 had very high export to total sales ratios, as did the firm answering (*d*) and two of the three firms answering (*e*). The single firm aiming to hold exports at the current absolute level (answer (*g*)) had the highest ratio in the sample.

Firms were asked to name the other benefits of exporting and the replies are tabulated in Table 6.13.

A majority of the firms were thus keen to increase exports and a large majority gave as a reason the need for security through diversification of markets. In other words, firms expect a variety of markets to provide a cushion against fluctuations of demand in any particular one. It might be thought therefore that they would not be likely to neglect export markets because of a rise in home demand, when one of the reasons for having export markets is to protect the firm against that rise proving to be temporary.

TABLE 6.13 *Benefits of Exporting*

	Frequency *
(*a*) Prestige, political or quasi-political benefit	5
(*b*) Security through diversification of markets	20
(*c*) Possibility of expansion which is harder (or impossible) to achieve at home	3
(*d*) Stimulus to introduce new products and/or new production techniques	8

* Some firms gave more than one category.

Firms' keenness to increase exports was confirmed when we asked if they wanted a different ratio of exports to total sales, if so what it would be, and what action they were taking to change it. Fourteen firms wanted a higher ratio. All four that wanted a lower ratio were currently exporting over 60 per cent of production, as were two out of the three which were content with their existing split.

When asked what action they were taking to change their current export ratio, firms gave the answers in Tables 6.14 and 6.15. We have added to these answers the replies given to our question on order priorities, where relevant; that is, whether firms gave first priority to either export or home sales.

TABLE 6.14 *Action to Increase Proportion of Exports to Total Sales*

(*a*) We are doing all we can already	6
(*b*) Changing mix of products to suit export markets	2
(*c*) Increasing selling effort overseas	1
(*d*) Looking for new markets	2
(*e*) Adding to productive capacity	1
(*f*) Giving priority to export orders	8

TABLE 6.15 *Action to Decrease Proportion of Exports to Total Sales*

Concentrating on the home market	2
No action	1
Some preference to *export* customers	2

There were some illogicalities in these replies. Two firms said they were doing all they could to increase exports, and yet were not giving priority to exports while in a position of being able to sell more than they could produce. Either they had not thought of favouring exports in this way, or believed that it would not be effective. A third possibility is that their desire for more exports was not enough to make them risk their home customers; any future increases in capacity would allow them to increase exports and keep their existing home customers.

Concerning order book priorities, there were thirteen firms altogether who gave export orders some sort of priority, of which eight are already accounted for above, as wanting higher export ratios. Three of the remainder were content with their existing export ratios, and were in the position of having to give priority to exports in order to *maintain* their export positions. It was suggested by several firms that exports might be more sensitive to delivery delays than home sales.

The remaining two firms which gave exports priority actually wanted lower export ratios; they were slightly unusual in that they had markets in the U.S.A. which were more profitable than home sales, but relatively static; and markets in Europe which were less profitable than home sales, but rapidly growing. They gave priority to U.S.A., home and European sales in that order.

Factors Preventing an Increase in Exports

In addition to asking firms why they export, and the related questions discussed above, we also asked firms what were the most important factors preventing an increase in their exports, or in the case of firms whose exports were increasing already, what was preventing an even faster increase. For firms who wanted a lower proportion of exports to total sales one answer to this question was clearly management policy, although in one or two cases no action was in fact being taken towards the ideal proportion. This apart, the answers were as in Table 6.16.

It should be emphasized once more that no answers to this question were suggested to businessmen, we simply recorded their remarks. Only answers (*a*) to (*g*) were printed on the questionnaire and so available as suggestions when the form was sent for checking. As

TABLE 6.16 *Hindrances to Exports*

	Frequency
(*a*) Prices of firm's products	6
(*b*) Quality and design of products	3
(*c*) Delivery dates	3
(*d*) Promotional effort	5
(*e*) Availability of finance	1
(*f*) Government policies (i.e. stop-go)	0
(*g*) Shortage of capacity	5
(*h*) Shortage of labour, skilled and unskilled	7
(*i*) Development of indigenous industry behind tariff barriers	4
(*j*) Lack of foreign currency in importing countries	3
(*k*) Technology, slow advance of	1
(*l*) Tariffs	5

a result, a number of answers may have been omitted as businessmen thought they were too obvious to mention, or completely outside their control and so not worth worrying about. Certainly the lack of foreign currency (*j*), tariff barriers (*l*) and development of local industry behind tariff barriers (*i*), which mainly concerned under-developed countries, are factors that must affect all exporting firms potentially; the firms which once had substantial exports to such countries tended to mention these factors, as did those managers who had been in the business for a long time and had long memories. There was surprisingly little feeling that the Government could have helped more by trying to bring pressure to reduce tariffs; managers seemed rather fatalistic about such problems. It may be that this is connected with the industry having so many firms that no one firm feels able to have any influence, although the trade association is extremely active. Perhaps even at the industry level the problem is thought to be too broad for even the trade association to have influence. Having said this, domestic pottery exports have not suffered as much in recent years from the imposition of tariff barriers as tiles and sanitary ware. The major losses to the domestic pottery industry were the pre-war South American markets which were extremely profitable in many cases. It should be added that although export markets can close down suddenly for political (e.g. Cuba, Rhodesia) or other reasons, in a way in which the home market is most unlikely to do, export markets, being sometimes the marginal requirements of a country above what indigenous industry can supply, can also *increase* very fast. Thus one firm, having related to us in great detail and at great length how one market after another had been closed to its products, appeared certain to have had decreasing exports in the last few years; on the contrary, it turned out that increased demand in its remaining markets had easily offset the closed markets, and exports had increased substantially.

Most of the firms mentioning prices as a hindrance to exports were manufacturing the cheaper products where the international competition is much fiercer and depends more on price. This is also the sector of the industry most likely to be affected by competition from indigenous industry – developing countries start with the manufacture of teapots and cheap cups and saucers and not with fine china. At the time of our interviews, the Japanese were reported to be entering the fine china field which could prove a future threat to this sector of the industry, in spite of its tremendous reputation.

Of the five firms who stressed lack of promotional effort, two were unable to do anything about it through their size – one could not afford a trip to America on his current turnover, the other could not even justify a trip to London. At this size level, a small firm is clearly at a disadvantage. Of the remaining three firms, one was trying to reduce its export to total sales ratio, one was unable to get labour to increase capacity so that the question of promotional effort was somewhat academic, which leaves only one firm that actually admitted its own shortcomings in this way, and in this firm a new manager was intending to change things as soon as possible. Of course, firms are naturally unlikely to admit their own weaknesses; and the very inflexible pricing policies described later in this chapter could be used as evidence of lack of promotional effort. But with so many firms able to sell more than they could produce, and unable or unwilling to expand capacity, the question of promotional effort appears unimportant.

On the supply side, shortage of capacity and shortage of labour were very widespread. In answer to the question 'Could you sell more if you could produce more?' only one firm answered in the negative, and one firm could have sold more of some products but not others. Of the remainder, all but two said it was because of shortage of labour or shortage of skilled labour. Both of the two exceptions were constrained by their factory sites in urban areas which they could not move for other reasons. A dilemma can arise in such a case, where a firm can get labour because of being near bus-stops, shops and so on, but in order to expand the factory would have to move somewhere where labour would be less easy to get. Four firms also mentioned finance as a constraint on expansion, for widely differing reasons.

Labour-saving technical advance, which would be one answer to this widespread labour shortage, is a potential solution of which most manufacturers are aware but progress is relatively slow, hindered in some cases by the size of firms, by lack of finance and by the inherent technical problems of the industry. In addition, as already mentioned above, the large female labour force is increasingly hard to keep.

The fact that no firm mentioned government stop-go policies as an export hindrance can be partially explained by the fact that the domestic industry is not severely hit by credit squeezes, hire purchase restrictions and the other paraphernalia of the stop part of the stop-go. Whatever are the short-run effects on export performance – and we return to this aspect below – firms did not take the view that its pressure of home demand variation was connected with long-run export performance.

The Profitability of Exports

What managements believe is the relative profitability of exports is sufficient up to a certain point in analysing the rationality of managements' choice between home and export sales, supposing they have such a choice. For this purpose our questioning was adequate. It is an interesting reflection on our preconceived ideas on this subject that our questionnaire provided for an analysis of why exports are less profitable than home sales, but none for explaining their superior profitability.

On the finer question of what constitutes profitability of one part of a firm's production our questions were inevitably inadequate – indeed a whole survey could be devoted to this question. There is a wide enough area of disagreement between economists and accountants and businessmen as to the nature of the total profits of a firm, and this area widens even further when one attempts to allocate profits to different products and/or market areas. In general most businessmen took our question to mean *gross profit*, that is selling price less direct costs, and also any additional costs or cost savings that could obviously be attributed to the market area, i.e. export as opposed to home sales. Some took into account, for example, the size of orders where this was relevant to costs and significantly different for export and home sales; some, however, did not. And not surprisingly cost saving, or profits increases, resulting from spreading seasonal peaks, or providing protection from the U.K. business cycle, were allocated in businessmen's minds to the unquantifiable benefits of exporting rather than to the calculation of direct profitability. The essential point remains that our survey is based on the hypothesis that firms' policies depend on what businessmen believe concerning relative profitability, and was thus devoted in the first place to enquiring about these beliefs; and in the second place to trying to discover their importance in export policy.

The answers to the question as to whether exports are more or less profitable than home sales are shown in Table 6.17. They are related to firms' desired changes in export to sales ratios.

TABLE 6.17 *Export and Home Sales Profitability*

Exports as compared with home sales described as	*Number of firms wanting exports to sales ratios*			
	Higher	*Same*	*Lower*	*Total*
(*a*) Less profitable	5	1	1	7
(*b*) Slightly less profitable	2	—	1	3
(*c*) No different	3	1	1	5
(*d*) Slightly more profitable	1	1	—	2
(*e*) More profitable	3	—	1	4

It is fairly clear from this table that there is no obvious connection between the relative profitability of exports and home sales, as seen by management, and desired export to total sales ratios. Clearly the non-quantifiable considerations, or those that are thought to be non-quantifiable,[1] frequently outweigh direct profitability. A general impression gained from the interviews was that many firms had not devoted very much thought to this question of relative profitability.

[1] Such as diversification of markets.

Overall policy on exports was fairly definite and unlikely to be changed while the broad general conditions under which that policy had been formed remained unchanged. Certainly many of the firms were too small to consider mounting elaborate statistical exercises on the question, even had they wanted to do so. A further reason why relative profitability was treated as a rather unimportant factor in the domestic pottery sector of the industry is that most firms quote the same prices for home and export markets most of the time. (This is in direct contrast to the tile-manufacturing sector where prices are generally substantially lower overseas, and therefore affect export policy, since the difference in profitability is of a much larger order of magnitude.) As a result, the answers given to why exports were more or less profitable than home sales in domestic pottery manufacturing are not complete in the sense that all the relevant factors may not have been specified. They only give the factors which managers consciously take into account. Thus the number of firms giving size of orders as a profitability factor for example does not necessarily include all firms for which this is important, but only those which take it into account, or which recognized it as a *possible* factor when presented with our questionnaire for checking.

We discussed with firms the contributory reasons why exports are less (or more) profitable. The responses are summarized in Table 6.18. Two firms gave reasons why exports were both more and less profitable than home sales; one of them thought the two influences cancelled, the other thought the factors making exports less profitable were stronger. All the other firms gave reasons on only one side or the other.

In the cases where exports are *more* profitable than home sales it is legitimate to enquire why firms continue to supply the home market. The answer is partly the same as for the reverse case, to provide security through having many markets. Additional reasons are that the home market is, in some non-quantifiable sense, 'easier' than export markets and to keep the firm's name before the public as a sort of long-term insurance premium.[1] An interesting special case is where most of 'home' sales are in fact to overseas visitors; in

[1] One firm told us that during one period when it did completely ignore the home market visiting Americans were greatly disturbed to find that few Englishmen had heard of their 'famous' dinner service.

TABLE 6.18 *Reasons for Differential Profitability*

	Frequency
(i) Exports less profitable than home sales because:	
(*a*) Lower prices, higher discounts, etc.	2
(*b*) Additional selling costs and paper work	10
(*c*) Small size of export orders	2
(*d*) Greater competition in export markets	4
(*e*) Longer period of payment for exports	5
(*f*) Variations in export products which add to production costs	5
(*g*) Export markets less stable	1
(ii) Exports more profitable:	
(*a*) Bigger orders from export markets	7
(*b*) Export rebate	4
(*c*) Better prices, lower discounts, etc.	1
(*d*) Products with higher margins go abroad	3

this case a 'real' home market must be maintained as well, in order to provide all-the-year-round demand for retailers, since tourist sales are concentrated in a few summer months.

A reason for maintaining both exports or home sales (which was only mentioned specifically by one domestic pottery manufacturer) is to achieve a larger scale of production. Where economies of scale exist and are significant, having additional markets can put a firm in a different cost category completely. To some extent this factor may be so basic (and obvious) that some firms did not mention it; on the other hand, size may have a limited importance in domestic pottery.

One manufacturer denied that additional paper work reduced the profitability of increased exports, because his firm had a department set up to deal with this problem anyway. Clearly this argument depends on how great the size of the increase and the time-period under discussion. A similar point applies to product variations for export: if a firm is geared up to supply these already, then the marginal cost of doing so may be very small. One manufacturer looked at this slightly differently. Product variations, he said, used up too much of his scarce skilled labour, and this was why he was favouring the home market with a more homogeneous product demand; this was of course another way of saying that he thought home sales were more profitable than exports.

The export rebate in operation at the time of the survey needs a special comment. We generally left it to businessmen to bring it up, and only mentioned it ourselves if they had failed to do so. Among the attitudes we met were: that it was a very nice contribution to profits, but that was all – in other words it had no influence on policy; that it was too small to be of any importance, though of course it was very pleasant to have; that it had enabled a price increase to be put off for a period, though this was a once-for-all possibility; that it was an offset to the lower profitability of exports, but not enough to change the overall picture. In only one case did the rebate appear to have influenced policy at all, and then so slightly that in the questionnaire this firm indicated it was still content with its current export/total sales ratio. Only one or two payments of the rebate had been made, however, and we were left with a fairly widespread impression of goodwill created towards the Government among businessmen. At least, they seemed to feel, the Government is trying. Few of the firms we saw seemed to have considered in detail the effect of the rebate on relative profitability – but since few of them allowed this to affect their export policy, this is not perhaps very surprising.

Pricing Policy

This survey was not intended as a contribution to the long methodological controversy on pricing of manufactures. Some discussion of prices, however, was inevitable, and in particular of export compared with home prices.[1] First, we asked how firms changed their prices, if and when it was necessary; the answers were as follows:

TABLE 6.19 *Methods of Changing Prices*

	Firms
(*a*) All prices changed by the same percentage simultaneously	9
(*b*) Each product treated separately	9
(*c*) Combination of (*a*) and (*b*), e.g. sometimes one, sometimes the other	3

Next we asked how the price of a new product was determined (Table 6.20).

1 See R. S. Edwards, 'The pricing of manufactured products', *Economica*, 1952, which contains an extract from a memorandum written by the chief accountant of a pottery firm on price fixing in the pottery industry.

TABLE 6.20 *Pricing of New Products*

	Firms *
(*a*) Solely on the basis of estimated cost	8
(*b*) Basically on a study of the market (subject of course to price being at least above direct cost)	1
(*c*) A mixture of (*a*) and (*b*)	11
(*d*) By fitting the price into existing product range	3

* Two of the answers to (*d*) were bracketed with answer (*a*).

Nearly all the firms involved were in a position where demand for their products was well above their capacity to supply it, so that they were able to exercise considerable control over their own prices. Yet most preferred to ration their production through order books, or through some other policy, rather than by price. And almost without exception they said they raised prices in answer to increased costs when they could not be absorbed, rather than in answer to demand conditions.

Perhaps not surprisingly in view of the basic situation outlined above, only two firms said their export prices ex-factory were different from home prices in general and one of these was trying to work back to equality of prices. In many cases export prices were modified in certain special circumstances. Thus, nine firms modified export prices for large customers, but of these, four said it was very rare to do so; and one or two firms occasionally modified export prices for new customers, orders placed at convenient times of year or for price changes of U.K. competitors.

It should be noted that the question specified ex-factory prices; the question of commissions to overseas agents where these differed from home sales, and other complications of this sort, were normally considered as part of selling costs. In many overseas markets price variation is severely constrained by anti-dumping laws, particularly in Canada where they are especially strict. One interesting way round this is to own your own selling subsidiary inside the export market, and then vary the mark-up.

The vexed question of selling exports at some price above direct cost but below average cost, on the grounds that a contribution to overheads is welcome in any form, did not really arise in this sector of the industry. One would not expect firms with a large proportion of their sales going overseas to be much impressed by this argument, but in spite of their clearly not needing to consider lowering export prices in any market in order to get business, the tone of businessmen's replies suggested that they would never even consider such action, and indeed many of them said as much. There seemed at times to be an almost moral feeling against differential pricing. Granted the constraints of anti-dumping laws, the comfortable demand conditions and many firms' high export to total sales ratio, such inflexibility on pricing in *all* markets was surprising. It was equally remarkable that the possibility of higher prices for exports as compared with home sales was not mentioned, given the general situation of buoyant export demand and capacity limitations.

Some firms, those selling the higher priced products, told us that within quite wide ranges price does not greatly affect sales, which are much more influenced by other factors such as design, delivery delays, and so forth. The same applies, though to a lesser extent, to those firms selling medium-priced products. We were also told that in the 'quality' markets there is a danger that low price or price-cutting will be associated with low quality,[1] so that in markets where the image of quality is so important, price-cutting can do more harm than good. This problem of very high priced goods, where the extra quality can only be seen by an expert (or in the price), can limit the markets in which fine china manufacturers are able to sell. Thus, many European markets have shown little interest in fine china, presumably either through a belief that French porcelain at a lower price is a better buy, or because of ignorance of the existence of the product. Such a situation can be changed, though only over a long period, and some firms claimed to have made the breakthrough in Europe, especially in West Germany.

Exports and Domestic Demand: The Pressure Hypothesis

In discussion we attempted to ask firms directly what effect they thought variations in home demand had on exports. The question is clearly a very difficult and sensitive one and also open to quasi-political replies; that is, firms might have been tempted to give the reply they wanted the outside world to hear, knowing that we were

1 See A. Gabor and C. Granger, 'Price as an indicator of quality, report of an inquiry', *Economica*, February 1966.

intending to publish the results. Our impression was very strong that in the pottery industry this was not so. Businessmen took great trouble over the questions, and went to great pains to make sure we had understood their position, and to tell us what they saw as the truth, or as near as one could reasonably get to it. It needs to be borne in mind that for some firms the question of falling home demand leading to a reduction in production was somewhat hypothetical since they had had long order books for home and export sales for a long period, some of them since the early 'thirties.

The answers we were given did not always fit exactly into the categories we had specified, and there were many reservations and qualifications. The results should therefore be treated as fairly broad generalizations; nevertheless we do not think they are misleading. Specifically, the answers to our question 'Which of the following statements is more appropriate for a period of peak demand for your products?' were:

TABLE 6.21 *Exports and Rising Home Demand*

	Firms
(*a*) Exports are helped because unit costs are lower	2
(*b*) Some exports are lost because of lengthening delivery dates	2
(*c*) Exports are adversely affected because home costs and prices are rising	—
(*d*) Exports are not significantly affected	13
(*e*) Category (*b*) above in the short run, (*a*) above in the long run	3
(*f*) Category (*d*) above in the short run, (*a*) above in the long run	1

The answers to the question 'Which of the following statements is more appropriate for a period of sharp deflation?' are shown in Table 6.22.

With reference to the discussion in Chapter 4, where it was suggested that the pressure of demand effect on exports might be related to a firm's exports to sales ratios, it is interesting to compare those giving answer (*d*), exports not significantly affected, and those giving the other answers, with their exports to total sales ratios (Table 6.23).

These results tend to support the hypothesis[1] that firms with high

[1] The number of observations are, however, too few to bear a statistical test of significance.

TABLE 6.22 *Exports and Falling Home Demand*

	Firms
(*a*) Exports are adversely affected because unit costs rise	3
(*b*) Exports benefit because, with lower home sales, more attention can be paid to exports	2*
(*c*) Exports will benefit from quicker delivery	3
(*d*) Exports are not significantly affected	10
(*e*) Category (*d*) above in the short term, (*a*) above in the long term	1
(*f*) Category (*c*) above in the short term, (*d*) above in the long term	2

* One of these firms said exports did not really benefit very much since overseas customers tended to know that the home market was weak and drive a harder bargain. As this firm claimed to have the same export and home prices, the remark should not perhaps be taken too seriously.

and low proportions of exports are little affected by changes in home demand as far as their export sales are concerned; whereas firms in intermediate positions, for whom exports and home sales are interchangeable in the statistical sense, that is for whom a change of demand or supply conditions in one market *could* be compensated for by a proportional change of the same magnitude in the other, tend to be more affected, although in several widely differing ways.

Those firms giving answers (*a*) and (*e*) to both the questions tabulated in Tables 6.21 and 6.22, that is those for whom the effect

TABLE 6.23 *Exports and Home Demand*

		Firms giving answer (d): 'no effect'	*Other firms*	*Total*
(i) Effect of rising home demand (Table 6.21)				
Export/sales ratio:	0–19	5	1	6
	20–39	2	2	4
	40–59	1	3	4
	60 and over	5	2	7
(ii) Effect of falling home demand (Table 6.22)				
Export/sales ratio:	0–19	4	2	6
	20–39	2	2	4
	40–59	0	4	4
	60 and over	7	0	7

on unit costs was most important, seemed to have no discernible characteristics in common. One might have expected them to have had spare capacity either currently or in the recent past, but this was not so. The only firm we saw with chronic spare capacity had exports which were too small a proportion of output (less than 10 per cent) to be affected.

The overall picture then is that the exports of more than half the firms in the sample are *affirmed* not to be affected by variations in home demand, either at all or in the long run. One of the reasons for this would appear to be very high or very low export to total sales ratios, and this was confirmed in many cases at interviews. Indeed there is something absurd in asking a firm which exports 75 per cent of its production whether it neglects exports when home demand is strong.

Another point which came out very clearly in the interviews is that building up an export market takes time and money, and usually a great deal of both. Agents must be found, or foreign selling subsidiaries, and distributions must be set up, production adapted to suit the markets and experience of dealing with the market's peculiarities painfully won. Such an investment is not willingly thrown away to gain a short-term profit at home, nor is it possible to make such an investment quickly enough to compensate for the sort of short-term slack which is the nearest the home market has come to recession since the war.

Firm after firm made this point to us; and many firms also pointed out to us that they had been exporting for a very long time (200 years in some cases) which meant that new, unexploited markets were not easy to find. Also, many of the markets in which the industry is *not* selling at the moment are very risky either politically or from the point of view of foreign currency availability (see the discussion of hindrances to exports above). With reference to the theoretical discussion in Chapter 4, on whether reduced home demand would induce firms to seek new export markets, the answer for the domestic pottery industry is that post-war history has not suggested to firms that falls in home demand are likely to be large enough or long enough; and that even if expectations on this point were to change, it is by no means certain that new overseas market investments are available.

Answer (*b*) of Table 6.21 – 'some exports are lost because of

H

lengthening delivery dates' – was surprisingly infrequent considering that only one firm said it could not sell more if it could produce more, and only three or four more were roughly able to match production to sales. Clearly it is possible for changes in the length of home order books to lead to changes in export order positions and it was agreed by a majority of firms that export customers are sensitive to quoted delivery times. Two main reasons emerged for the infrequency of answer (*b*). One was the priority given to export orders by many firms. Thirteen firms gave exports as their first priority in regulating orders; of the remainder, two gave first preference to big customers, who tended to be export customers in both cases, one worked entirely on a first in first out basis, and one gave preference to old customers, among whom were some overseas ones. The other firms had no queue to regulate. The other major reason for the small impact on exports of delivery dates was the number of firms who made different products for export, so that the two markets were largely insulated from each other, at any rate in the short term. Several firms said that this factor made answer (*d*) – 'exports are not significantly affected' – appropriate for part of their production, but gave us one of the other answers if it was applicable to the remainder. The question of flexibility of sales staff from home to export and back again arose less in this industry than in others because of the large number of small- to medium-sized firms which did not have specialized export sales staff.

There were some interesting comments arising out of discussion of these two questions. One or two firms said that if demand was generally strong it was the home market that suffered. This points to an interesting problem. If a firm is in the position of being able to sell much more than it can produce, then an increase in export sales must be at the expense of home sales, and vice versa. Capacity production is not a completely inflexible figure at any one moment, but a firm which has had long order books for a lengthy period will presumably be operating near or at normal limits of capacity. As a result, a relative increase in exports must be accompanied by a relative decrease in home sales, and while this may arise because home demand is falling, it could equally arise because of a deliberate policy of favouring exports.

Another firm said that its reaction to falling home demand was to stock up its distributors in North America, and that this had always been enough to tide it over lulls in the home market. While this would appear in any statistics as an increase in exports, and in a certain sense it would be correct to say that it was caused by reduced home demand, it represents no increase or decrease in exports in any real sense, since actual export sales to final consumers would not necessarily change at all. There would of course be a reverse effect when home demand revived.

The whole discussion of this question has so far been in terms of what businessmen said they do, rather than in terms of what actually happens. There are several drawbacks to this, some of which have already been suggested. Firms may be in the grip of forces over which they have no control, or less control than they themselves believe; some answers may have been 'politically' motivated; to some firms the questions were largely hypothetical, or appeared to be, since it is more difficult to discuss movements about a trend, for example, than absolute changes of direction. Nevertheless, two things emerge fairly clearly. Most firms believed that they have considerable control over where they sell their output, enough control, that is, to make our questions about policy relevant. Secondly, a very large majority rejected the thesis that movements in home demand, whether government induced or not, have a significant effect on the flow of goods to overseas customers. And, it was suggested, even when the two are connected in a causal way, either the relation is the opposite of that suggested by the normal pressure hypothesis, or the direction of causation is from exports to home sales, rather than the reverse.

Reactions to Falling Demand

We asked firms about their reactions to domestic deflation, though a number answered in terms of reactions to falling total demand for each firm's own products. The question was framed before we realized how loose in some cases the connection was between home demand in general, and the home sales of individual firms in the domestic pottery industry.

Thirteen firms said their first reaction, or joint first reaction, was production for stocks; several qualified this by saying this reaction was only temporary. Clearly there are severe limitations to large-scale stock-building for very long. Quite apart from the major financial problems, most firms make a large number of patterns and there is a big danger of stocking the wrong ones.

The incentives towards stock-building are strong. In any industry with fixed costs, reduction of output below a certain point (described by most businessmen as capacity) causes sharp rises in average cost, and this is greatly accentuated in pottery, for technical reasons. Pottery is fired in ovens which must be used continuously to justify their existence – the process is known as continuous firing – and they represent quite a heavy proportion of the costs of production. In addition to the obvious benefits of using them all the time, ovens with less than a full load may produce a higher proportion of second-quality items than with a full load. This technical factor gives an added incentive to pottery manufacturers to try to keep ovens going full blast if they possibly can; and incidentally makes them extremely reluctant to over-invest in productive capacity. (This latter point may be an explanation for the predominance of firms which have longish order books and delivery dates more or less indefinitely. The number of ovens in even quite large factories is small, so that another oven represents a very large proportional addition to capacity.) Additionally, the tightness of labour conditions in the area makes firms extremely reluctant to release labour unless every means of keeping them has been explored. Labour 'hoarding' is often much deplored but it may be a perfectly rational policy for a firm, especially if it has invested in training skilled labour. If a firm believes a fall in home demand for its products is only temporary, and wants to be able to supply the increase when it comes, and if it also knows that it may not be able to re-engage the same labour, or any other, it is sound policy to retain it as long as possible. Added to this are the loss of goodwill, and the high cost of settling new labour into the firm (or even the original labour) should labour be obtainable. Several firms had actually been through the experience of reducing their labour force and bitterly regretting it later. And many more were acutely aware of the problem. No firm gave increased sales effort abroad as its first reaction, and only one gave it as a reaction without mentioning sales effort at home as well. Two firms said they increased sales effort at home without mentioning overseas selling effort.

Given that many firms deliberately give exports priority, and pursue exports more than home sales as a matter of policy in spite of lower export profitability, it would be reasonable to expect that many firms would have scope for increasing home sales when necessary, or at least stopping a decline, and that few firms would have much scope for increased selling effort abroad since this was being maximized as a matter of policy. In addition there is the problem of the length of time needed to establish a new export market. In fact six firms said they increased sales effort at home and abroad, either as a first reaction, or subsequent to or simultaneously with making for stock. The only surprising thing about this result is the small number of firms who increase selling effort at home. It is possible that many firms were normally able to increase home sales before a critical point was reached, and so neglected to give this answer. Only a few firms said as much. Some also said that in a situation where everyone's (that is, all rival firms') home demand is falling, increased selling effort is not much use.

The rather hypothetical nature of the question for many firms who had not really been faced with this situation for many years, again made interpretation of the answers rather difficult.

Regarding price changes in response to falling demand, only one firm reckoned to change export prices, and only two reckoned to change home prices, none of them as a first reaction. Price-cutting as a policy is regarded by most firms in this industry not only as slightly shady practice, but as a policy extremely unlikely to bring any benefit, even in the short term. And many thought that a time of weak demand would be the worst time to indulge in it anyway. Only one firm gave as a sole answer to this question that it made no change in output, prices or sales effort. Such confidence deserves respect! The unwillingness of firms to cut prices was generally supported on the following lines. Price cuts must be greater than some minimum discreet amount partly because there are some costs involved (informing customers, for example) and partly because they must be big enough to make an impact on buyers. But if price cuts are big enough to make an impact they may induce competitive price cuts[1] and the final outcome for the firm's sales is extremely

[1] In spite of the apparently large number of firms in the pottery industry, there are so many product categories that each product market tends to be supplied by relatively few firms.

problematical. Moreover, if the fall in demand is not expected to last long, firms must consider whether they will be able to restore prices when demand recovers; several firms thought they would not.

The general impression which emerged from our interviews is that most firms thought that the impact of fluctuations in domestic demand upon exports was nil or minimal. We now proceed to examine how far the statistical data obtained from the domestic pottery firms supports this view.

III. DOMESTIC POTTERY: STATISTICAL AND ECONOMETRIC STUDY OF FIRMS' EXPORT AND HOME SALES PERFORMANCE

At the time of the interview with each firm, we explored the possibility of obtaining statistical data covering the period 1958-65, which would allow an *ex post* study of the relation between their exports and possible determining factors, particularly overseas demand and home demand. We had mixed success. Most of the firms were extremely co-operative, although they were put to some considerable trouble in assembling past data, some of it of a confidential nature. Out of twenty-one firms covered by the interview survey, fifteen responded to our request for the further statistical data. On the other hand, the data which firms in general could reasonably readily provide from their records was neither as detailed nor as comprehensive as we required for a fully adequate study of the empirical relation between export performance and home demand. There were two crucial deficiencies. First, nearly all firms' records were organized on an annual basis and quarterly data were not available. This was a disappointment, as statistics on a yearly basis are rather blunt weapons for the study of short-run relationships, relationships which might well operate with time-lags of a fraction of a year. And secondly, it was not in general possible to obtain export figures broken down by country of destination as these could not have been obtained from firms' records without an impossible amount of labour. We had to be content with estimated proportions of exports destined for the firms' main markets in key years.

Thus the basic statistical series which we obtained were annual value figures of home and export sales separately (normally for the period 1958-65) and the destination estimates just referred to.

Product prices in the home and export markets might, or might not, affect sales in the short run. However, only one firm interviewed calculated price indices of its home and export sales. Six other firms followed the practice of making across-the-board price changes with a common percentage increase for most products; we recorded the relevant data for these firms. The level of capacity working is an elusive thing to define, let alone measure, for the individual firm. We had little hope at the start of the survey of obtaining numerical data in this field and here at any rate expectations were satisfied. Nor, unfortunately, did it turn out to be a practical possibility to abstract any relevant data on the order book situation from firms' records and we had to be content with asking firms to categorize each year of the period we covered according to whether the firm was

(*a*) selling significantly below capacity, or
(*b*) selling at about capacity with no long order book, or
(*c*) with a long order book.

The answers to this question were perforce based mainly on the personal recollection of the respondents, hence their imprecise formulation.

Characteristics of Sample

Our sample accounted from roughly one-quarter to one-third of the domestic pottery industry in terms of sales value and employment. For the reasons explained in Section II above, the sample was not a random one but in fact the varying proportions exhibited in the final column of Table 6.24 are within the ranges which could have been ascribable to sampling error. The choice of firms to be included in the survey was, however, deliberately under-representative of the

TABLE 6.24 *Domestic Pottery: Sample Characteristics, 1964*

	Sample	*All industry*	*Sample as percentage of industry*
Home sales (£m)	5·8	23·3	25
Exports (£m)	4·9	16·1	30
Total sales (£m)	10·7	39·4	27
Exports as percentage of total sales	54	41	
Employment (thousands)	8·9	27·3	32

smaller firms. At the time of the survey there were nearly one hundred members of the British Pottery Manufacturers' Federation in the domestic pottery business. The sample of fifteen firms covers a little less than one-sixth of the number of firms.

Variability in Sales Performance

The most simple and striking property of the home and export sales figures of individual firms is the extreme degree of variability of performance both as regards individual firms from one year to another and, in any particular year, between one firm and another. Table 6.25 is based upon the percentage year-to-year changes in individual firms' values of home and export sales. Table 6.25 sets out for each firm the average and standard deviation of the year-to-year percentage changes in the home sales and export sales (generally relating to the period 1958-65).

The average growth rates for home sales range from 0·9 per cent p.a. (firm 7) to 37·9 per cent p.a. (firm 6) and for export sales from a fall of 7·6 per cent p.a. (firm 14) to a growth of 33·5 per cent p.a. (firm 7). Substantial differences of performance between firms are

TABLE 6.25 *Firms' Percentage Year-to-Year Changes in Home and Export Sales: Averages and Standard Deviations*

Percentages

	Home sales		*Export sales*	
Firm no.	*Average*	*Standard deviation*	*Average*	*Standard deviation*
1	5·3	7·3	4·5	9·3
2	2·4	5·0	0·5	30·5
3	8·9	11·1	6·2	20·0
4	3·0	13·7	−6·5	16·1
5	5·9	8·6	−3·7	10·2
6	37·9	14·5	14·0	21·1
7	0·9	6·5	33·5	35·2
8	4·6	8·8	1·3	31·8
9	2·7	6·1	1·7	9·1
10	8·6	14·9	3·2	16·5
11	7·8	8·4	2·9	11·7
12	4·9	11·8	−3·3	14·3
13	4·4	7·0	0·4	14·6
14	4·4	6·3	−7·6	14·4
15	7·9	10·2	3·5	7·3

of course to be expected. In the case of home sales, differences are likely to reflect in the main factors internal to the firm although, even here, there will be difference in the demand situation they face. In the case of exports no two firms of course have the same market composition of exports and, as we shall see, there are considerable variations from one overseas market to another in any year. It is interesting that there are generally higher standard deviations under the export sales head than the home sales head, that is, export sales fluctuate much more than home sales. One must be wary of concluding from this that firms' export demand is more variable: if a firm were to give priority to export sales and ration home sales by, say, the order book, it could well show a greater degree of fluctuation in its exports. In Table 6.26, similar measures of the fluctuations over the period 1958-65 are calculated for (*a*) total home sales of the domestic pottery industry, (*b*) total exports of the industry and (*c*) total imports of domestic pottery in three important markets – U.S.A., Canada and Australia.

TABLE 6.26 *National Statistics of Percentage Year-to-Year Changes in U.K. Home Sales, U.K. Exports, and Certain Overseas Countries' Imports: Averages and Standard Deviations over Period 1958-65.*

	Average	*Standard deviation*
U.K. home sales	4·5	2·6
U.K. exports	2·9	4·0
Total imports of		
United States	7·2	10·7
Canada	3·7	7·1
Australia	2·7	11·8

The relatively large standard deviations for imports of United States, Canada and Australia – and these are typical of other overseas country imports of domestic pottery – show how much more variable is overseas import demand of individual countries than home demand in this country. This is to be expected for, to a certain extent, imports meet excess demand at the margin which home production cannot satisfy. But it does mean that firms exporting to a very small number of overseas countries may face a much more variable demand situation than they would face in the home market.

To sum up so far, the relatively high variability of home sales of individual firms suggest that factors specific to the firm – and factors difficult to quantify – might play a dominant role in the short-run performance of the firm in the home market. There is no reason to expect this to be any different for export sales.

In the analysis so far we have not considered the time pattern of firms' sales in relation to each other and to national figures. This is done in Table 6.27.

TABLE 6.27 *Percentage Year-to-Year Changes of Firms' Home and Export Sales Compared to National Figures*

	Percentage change on previous year						
Firms in sample	*1959*	*1960*	*1961*	*1962*	*1963*	*1964*	*1965*
Home sales							
Average	3·3	11·1	4·1	5·0	2·4	10·3	7·1
Standard deviation	11·2	16·2	9·8	12·14	15·2	11·7	9·4
Export sales							
Average	−7·2	7·0	5·1	−3·5	18·1	10·4	5·7
Standard deviation	11·3	18·3	14·4	16·8	17·2	27·3	16·2
Industry home sales	1·7	8·7	3·9	1·4	2·5	6·4	6·8
Industry exports	−0·4	0·4	2·7	—	0·2	10·7	7·0
Imports of							
United States	22·2	14·1	−17·1	11·8	3·7	10·6	8·1
Canada	1·1	−2·2	3·4	—	−3·9	20·6	5·1
Australia	−12·4	14·1	−10·1	2·5	−2·4	3·8	...

Two points emerge from Table 6.27. The first is that in each of the years, the inter-firm variability as measured by the standard deviations of the individual firms' performances is greater for exports than for home sales. Thus, in 1960, the average rise for all sample firms in the value of home sales was 11·1 per cent and the standard deviation of the individual firm figures was a little over 16 per cent. For exports, the standard deviation was a little over 18 per cent around an average of 7 per cent. In the following year, the difference was greater: the percentage increase in home sales showed a standard deviation around the average of over 14 per cent compared with a standard deviation for home sales of less than 10 per cent. One possible reason for this large variability in export experience is suggested by the overseas import figures for three important domestic pottery markets set out at the bottom of Table 6.27. Taking the same two years 1960 and 1961 again as fairly typical examples, in 1960, the imports of the United States and Australia each increased by 14 per cent, whereas those of Canada fell by 2 per cent. In the following year, United States imports fell by 17 per cent, Australia by 10 per cent, while Canadian imports rose by nearly 3½ per cent. Whatever else exporting offers domestic pottery firms in comparison with the home market it does not appear to be greater stability in sales from one year to the next. A situation where different markets perform in very different ways offers the possibility of short-run stability to the firm which is in a position of exporting to many countries. But this might not be a possibility for smaller firms without running the risk of over-extending themselves in too many markets and failing to prosecute individual markets sufficiently.

Table 6.27 shows that there is a similar considerable degree of variation between the performance of firms in the home market. As a whole, the sample firms showed a similar performance in the home market over the period 1958-65 as did the industry as a whole. Both for the sample firms and for the whole industry the years 1960, 1964 and 1965 were the ones which showed the greatest growth in value terms. In 1960, industry home sales rose by 8·7 per cent (11·1 per cent for the sample firms); in 1964, the comparable increases were 6·4 per cent for the industry (10·3 per cent for the sample) and in 1965, 6·8 per cent for the industry (7·1 per cent for the sample). But the experience of individual firms was very different. In 1960, the standard deviation of the firm figures around the average of 11·1 per cent was as high as 16·2 per cent. In fact, one-half of the firms showed a *fall* in the value of home sales between 1959 and 1960. In 1964, when the sample firms on average showed a 10·3 per cent rise, only one firm's sales fell, a very little. But the magnitude of the increases varied very much; even excluding the four most extreme values, the percentage increase in the value of home sales of the remaining eleven firms varied between 1·5 and 17·7 per cent.

Too much must not be read into a simple analysis such as this of sales value figures. For example, it would be wrong to make an equation between large proportionate value increases in sales and a rise in the pressure on a firm's productive capacity. Increases in sales value can arise from a number of causes – price increases, running down of stocks, additions to capacity – which do not necessarily imply that the pressure on capacity has risen. Nevertheless, these inter-firm comparisons suggest that it would be quite wrong to assume that total industry figures necessarily give an adequate picture of the performance and situation of the majority of individual firms in that industry.

Exports, Overseas Demand and Home Demand

In this section we describe the results of an econometric study of the relationship between the exports of the domestic pottery firms in our sample and possible determinants of exports, particularly the overseas demand facing the firm and the pressure of home demand. This study is founded upon the statistical data obtained from firms, upon relevant U.K. industry figures and upon statistics of overseas country imports of domestic pottery.

For the reasons explained in Chapter 5, where we discussed the problem of setting up a testable relation at firm level, we have not set up a model directly in terms of the value of firms' sales figures. The basic variables in the estimations are either percentage year-to-year changes in value figures or percentage deviations from linear trend of value figures. As to the latter, it will be clear from the discussion earlier in this section that the fitting of a linear trend to the export and home sales value data cannot be well supported in view of the large variable year-to-year fluctuations in these figures. But since the basic data are on an annual basis and with a small number of observations (normally eight) per firm, there could be little justification for any curvilinear trend fitting.

The constructed variables used in the estimated equations are as follows:

Exports $DX(t)$ proportionate change on previous year in value of firm exports

$X\%(t)$ proportionate deviation from linear trend of value of firm exports.

Home sales $DHS(t)$ proportionate change on previous year in value of firm home sales

$HS\%(t)$ proportionate deviation from linear trend of value of firm home sales.

Overseas demand Index numbers of value of imports of domestic pottery by the major importing countries were constructed. For each firm, these index numbers were weighted according to the average proportion of exports of the firm going to these markets. (Because of the limited information from firms about their export markets the weights were generally based upon the export destinations of a proportion of export sales.) These weighted index numbers formed our basic measure of overseas demand, thus:

- $DM(t)$ proportionate change in weighted import index (weights specific to each firm)
- $M\%(t)$ proportionate deviation from linear trend of weighted import index.

Home demand As the main measure of the home demand situation facing the firm we used the sales value figures of the domestic pottery industry as a whole:

- $HD\%(t)$ proportionate deviation from trend of industry value figures.

Other variables entering particular equations are described below.

The construction of a satisfactory overseas demand variable presents conceptual as well as statistical problems and certainly the one used in this analysis is not ideal. It has statistical deficiencies arising from the limited amount of destination of exports data obtained from firms. It can also be argued that imports of domestic pottery into an individual overseas market is not a wholly adequate measure of the demand facing the industry as a whole, even less the individual firm. For it is known from the interviews with firms that different sub-sectors within 'domestic pottery' can face very different situations. Similarly, overseas markets are not homogeneous. Imports of domestic pottery into the United States cannot be relied upon to reflect, say, the American demand for British fine china. Nor, for that matter, would the variation of total U.S. imports measure the demand for U.K. exports of domestic pottery as the product mixes are different. But whether or not further disaggregation might be desirable, it is not practicable on the basis of the available international trade statistics.

The Results

In general, the estimated equations do not lead to conclusive results, almost certainly for two reasons: first, the high degree of variability of firm performance and second, though probably less important, the deficiencies of the destination of firm exports data. The R^2 values are low though this is not unusual in cross-section analysis. $R^2 = 0{\cdot}15$ is a high value among the equations below. This of course reflects the large role played in a firm's performance by factors strictly specific to the firm. A low value for R^2 can, in principle, be consistent with significant or at least informative estimates of parameter coefficients as indeed is the case for some of the results below.

As a preliminary we examined on the basis of percentage year-to-year changes the relation between exports, $DX(t)$ as defined above, overseas demand, $DM(t)$, and home sales of the firms, $DHS(t)$. The coefficients of both the explanatory variables failed to be significant and the R^2 was virtually zero.

$$DX(t) = 0{\cdot}45 + \underset{(0{\cdot}31)}{0{\cdot}03\,DM(t)} + \underset{(0{\cdot}17)}{0{\cdot}19\,DHS(t)} \qquad R^2 = 0{\cdot}01.$$

It is surprising that the overseas demand variable failed to perform, though interesting that the confidence interval estimate for its coefficient excludes the value of 1 which would imply a unit elasticity of demand. One possible explanation could be the unreliability of the estimates of the destination of exports data for a number of the firms. However, the equation was also estimated for those firms (half of the sample) for which we had destination of exports data for at least two-thirds of their total exports. The outcome was not substantially different.

We then proceeded to test models based upon deviations from trend variables discussed in Chapter 5 above. The export determination equation in the case of the additive model was (Equation 1.1):

$$X\%(t) = \alpha M\%(t) - \alpha\beta . kM\%(t) - \gamma\beta . (1-k)HD\%(t)$$

where $X\%(t)$ is proportionate deviation from trend of exports

$M\%(t)$ is proportionate deviation from trend of relevant overseas imports

and $HD\%(t)$ is proportionate deviation from trend of industry home demand.

Verbally, the model suggests that the short-run pattern of export fluctuations is dependent upon three exogenous variables: overseas demand, home demand and the relative importance of exports and home sales in individual firms' total production. A regression of $X\%(t)$ on $M\%(t)$, $kM\%(t)$ and $(1-k)HD\%(t)$ would lead to estimates of the model parameters α, β and γ.

However, this model proved not to be estimatable due to the multicollinearity between the variables $kM\%(t)$ and $(1-k)HD\%(t)$; the k values dominated these two variables and the least squares regression in effect treated the values for each firm as roughly equal to k and $(1-k)$ and yielded coefficients of the two almost equal and opposite in sign. This problem was evaded, rather than solved, by omitting the variable $kM\%(t)$ with the following result

$$X\%(t) = \underset{(0{\cdot}207)}{0{\cdot}703} + \underset{(0{\cdot}208)}{0{\cdot}300}M\%(t) + \underset{(0{\cdot}955)}{0{\cdot}195}(1-k)HD\%(t) \qquad R^2 = 0{\cdot}037.$$

The value of R^2 of course is not significant. It is interesting that, as for the regression based upon year-to-year percentage changes, the coefficient of the overseas demand variable is significantly less than unity with a 95 per cent confidence interval range of $-0{\cdot}1$ to $0{\cdot}7$. The estimate of the partial effect of home demand is inconclusive. As an alternative approach, two separate equations were estimated on the basis of pooled data for (i) the four years 1959, 1962, 1963, 1964 when the pressure of home demand on the industry was the lower and (ii) the remaining years 1958, 1960, 1961, 1965 when it was higher. The respective R^2 were insignificant. The overseas demand coefficient was higher for the years of lower pressure of demand, 0·345 compared to 0·181 but the standard errors were large and the difference is not significant.

Various export-determination equations were also estimated including the firm home sales variable $HS\%(t)$ among the explanatory variables. There is a difficult identification problem here. If there were a partial negative correlation between home sales and export sales, it could not be concluded that the pressure of home demand has an adverse effect on export performance, for a statistical relation of this nature could arise from a deliberate policy of favouring exports at the expense of home sales at times of high capacity utilization arising from buoyant exports. In fact, the coefficient of home sales was not significant, thus:

$$X\%(t) = \underset{(0{\cdot}261)}{0{\cdot}675} + \underset{(0{\cdot}203)}{0{\cdot}307}M\%(t) + \underset{(0{\cdot}183)}{0{\cdot}020}HS\%(t) \qquad R^2 = 0{\cdot}037.$$

In general, the data support the hypothesis of no relation between fluctuations in export sales and home sales, whether fluctuations are measured in terms of year-to-year changes or deviations from trend. One particularly interesting and apparently perverse result came out of a study of the export performance of a sub-group of the sample firms, namely the manufacturers of fine china. This is a group of firms which, as is known from the interviews, is relatively homogeneous: there is a considerable overlap in their overseas markets, the home demand situation can be expected to be much the same for them all and they all experienced through the period under study long order books and full capacity utilization. For these firms, a regression of export fluctuations upon fluctuation in overseas demand and home demand on the industry showed no significant coefficients. On the other hand, a substitution of the home sales variable specific to the firm or the industry home demand variable gave:

$$DX(t) = \underset{(0{\cdot}412)}{-1{\cdot}36} - \underset{(0{\cdot}412)}{0{\cdot}024}DM(t) + \underset{(0{\cdot}181)}{0{\cdot}346}DHS(t) \qquad R^2 = 0{\cdot}15$$

where the variables here are based on year-to-year percentage changes. The coefficient of home sales, $DHS(t)$ is positive and significantly so at a little higher than the 5 per cent level. It is not possible to interpret with confidence this positive coefficient of home sales. One plausible explanation is that, in a situation where firms are rationing both export and home sales over a long period by the order book, additions to capacity will be immediately reflected by increased sales in the short run. And if a firm does not discriminate between home and export sales, they will both rise in such circumstances, and their fluctuations will be positively correlated.

It only remains to record that a number of other explanatory variables were tested for marginal association with export fluctuations with no significant results. These included the rough price and capacity utilization measures described at the beginning of this section, and dummy variables representing the size of firm and proportion of output exported. Share models were also estimated but, as might be expected, were also inconclusive; the R^2 values were small and the confidence interval for the coefficient of home demand invariably well-straddled positive and negative values.

The results can be briefly summed up: aggregate home and overseas demand factors play a small part in accounting for the variability between domestic pottery firms over time in their short-run export sales performance. Factors specific to the firm are dominant. The estimated equations are consistent with a demand elasticity for exports of substantially less than unity. No clear effect on exports one way or the other is shown by the pressure of home demand. In conclusion, though this analysis is rather tentative, results so far as they go are in line with the picture given by the interviews with firms. In particular, the demand elasticity of exports can well be expected to be less than unity in a situation where many of the firms have experienced over a number of years consistently long export order books.

IV. DOMESTIC POTTERY: AN ECONOMETRIC ANALYSIS FOR THE INDUSTRY

In this section, we present the results of a market study of the determination of the exports of the domestic pottery industry over the period 1958-65, using quarterly data. The two major overseas markets are the United States and Canada (see Table 6.5 above) and United Kingdom exports to each of these countries were investigated. However, in the case of Canada, the analysis threw up inconclusive pressure of demand effects and since this could be the consequence of a discontinuity in the Canadian trade statistics during the period analysed, the results for Canada are not given. For the United States, as usual, a number of single-equation models were estimated. The dependent variable X_t, was U.S. imports of domestic pottery from the United Kingdom (thousand dollars). The proxy variable for overseas demand, M_t, was total U.S. imports of domestic pottery (thousand dollars). Three measures of domestic demand pressure were tested: (i) Great Britain unemployment rate, U_t, (ii) employment in the pottery industry, E_t and (iii) domestic pottery production for the home market, HS_t (£ thousand). In the absence of suitable price deflators the value figures are all in current price terms. Seasonal adjustment was effected by dummy variables; their coefficients are not included in the results set out below.

In a regression of X_t upon M_t and the various home demand variables (unlagged and lagged up to two quarters) the only demand variable which proved significant was home production lagged two quarters (HS_{t-2}). A typical estimated equation was

$$X_t = \underset{}{72{\cdot}4} - \underset{(3{\cdot}65)}{1{\cdot}21t} + \underset{(0{\cdot}299)}{0{\cdot}794t^2} + \underset{(0{\cdot}025)}{0{\cdot}077M_t} + \underset{(90{\cdot}9)}{79{\cdot}4U_t} - \underset{(0{\cdot}170)}{0{\cdot}093HS_t}$$

$$+\underset{(0{\cdot}135)}{0{\cdot}271HS_{t-2}} \qquad R^2 = 0{\cdot}92 \quad d = 1{\cdot}94.$$

With only the lagged production variable present, and a linear instead of a quadratic trend fitted, the result was:

$$X_t = -1{\cdot}770 + \underset{(0{\cdot}38)}{1{\cdot}44t} + \underset{(0{\cdot}023)}{0{\cdot}107M_t} + \underset{(0{\cdot}106)}{0{\cdot}484HS_{t-2}}$$

$$R^2 = 0{\cdot}90 \quad d = 1{\cdot}43.$$

The coefficient of HS_{t-2} is significant at nearly the 5 per cent level in the first equation; it is significant at the 1 per cent level in the second equation where, however, the Durbin-Watson statistics drops to a significant level. The sign of the coefficient of the home demand variable is, from the point of view of the pressure hypothesis, perversely positive.

Regressions were also estimated using the logarithmic values of X_t and M_t; HS_t was replaced by the logarithm of its deviations from linear trend, log DHD_t. The estimated equations corresponding to the two above were:

$$\log X_t = 3{\cdot}36 + \underset{(0{\cdot}0020)}{0{\cdot}0050t} + \underset{(0{\cdot}0001)}{0{\cdot}0002t^2} + \underset{(0{\cdot}127)}{0{\cdot}436 \log M_t}$$

$$+\underset{(0{\cdot}031)}{0{\cdot}058U_t} + \underset{(0{\cdot}225)}{0{\cdot}609 \log DHS_{t-2}} \quad R^2 = 0{\cdot}92 \quad d = 1{\cdot}73$$

and

$$\log X_t = 1{\cdot}781 + \underset{(0{\cdot}0017)}{0{\cdot}0094t} + \underset{(0{\cdot}129)}{0{\cdot}612 \log M_t} + \underset{(0{\cdot}220)}{0{\cdot}998 \log DHS_{t-2}}$$

$$R^2 = 0{\cdot}90 \quad d = 1{\cdot}51.$$

As is to be expected, the sign of the coefficient of the measure of the pressure of home demand on the industry, that is the coefficient of log DHS_{t-2}, is again positive (in both equations at the 5 per cent level of significance) suggesting that exports are favourably affected by a high pressure of home demand. On the other hand, the coefficient of U_t is positive – the 'right' sign for the pressure hypothesis – but is significant at only the 8 per cent level. The coefficient of log M_t, equal to 0·612, measuring the short-run elasticity of exports with respect to demand, is significantly less than unity.

Domestic Pottery: Conclusion

We have studied the relation between exports and the pressure of home demand for the domestic pottery industry from three points of view: interviews with senior managements, and econometric analyses of the performance of individual firms and of the industry as a whole. In two important respects, these different approaches are at least consistent. First, they provided little or no support for the hypothesis that domestic pottery exports are adversely affected by high pressure of demand and benefited by relatively low pressure of demand. Second, the econometric studies at firm and industry level, so far as they go, both suggest that the short-run elasticity of demand for exports is less than unity, not a surprising result in view of the enduring nature of the export order books revealed by many of the firms from the interviews.

V. TILES AND SANITARY WARE: FIRM INTERVIEWS

In this section we review the interviews with firms manufacturing tiles and sanitary ware. These two product groups depend very heavily on the building trade, which in turn tends to be much more quickly and seriously affected by government measures to change home demand than the domestic pottery side of the industry. Another major difference is that tiles and sanitary ware firms make a much smaller range of products than domestic pottery firms, and these products are in general less elaborately decorated and thus more susceptible to mass-production methods. Thus the average labour cost as a percentage of total costs was only 36 per cent as compared with 51 per cent in domestic pottery.[1] (The range in each case was quite small, 30 to 43 per cent and 42 to 64 per cent respectively.)

We saw only seven firms in this branch of the industry so that the account of their answers to the questionnaire and of the interviews is largely descriptive, and much less susceptible to statistical analysis or generalization.

Size and Exports

In domestic pottery it was found that the proportion of output exported tended to increase with size as the product became less distinctive and more easily mass-produced. One would therefore expect a fairly high correlation between size and percentage of exports to total sales in tiles and sanitary ware, and this is supported by our sample in which the rank correlation between the two is 0·86,[2] even higher than for medium-grade earthenware.

Allocative Decisions

All the firms said their export policy was 'to increase exports' and all mentioned as a reason for this 'security through diversification of markets'. Other benefits of exporting mentioned were the possibility of expansion which is harder (or impossible) to achieve at home (two firms) and the stimulus to introduce new products and production techniques (three firms).

Firms were not, however, keen to export a higher proportion of output. Only two firms gave this as a definite policy objective, and four were content with the present division. The remaining firm only wanted to export more of output if exports could be made more profitable (an answer which most firms would have given, we suspect, if they had had it suggested to them).

Rather curiously, one tile manufacturer stipulated lack of capacity and finance as a hindrance to exporting, yet was unable at the time to sell his whole output. The answer to this paradox lies, partly at least, in North America. As he put it, if your product is 'in' there, the orders come in thick and fast, too fast very often for a firm of

1 The average was calculated by adding the percentage of labour to total costs for each firm and dividing by the number of firms, so that the average is not weighted by size.

2 This figure is significant at the 5 per cent level.

his size to cope. The firm was therefore unwilling to go for new parts of the North American market until it had a better chance of meeting demand, hence the importance of finance and capacity. Finance was especially important at a time when home sales were down and a lot of money was tied up in stocks ready to meet the expected resurgence in home demand. Because the manufacturer believed the short fall in home demand to be temporary (this was before July 1966) there was not time to launch a campaign in a new North American market and risk losing it, or his home customers, almost immediately. Building is to some extent a seasonal trade, and this affects the manufacture of tiles and sanitary ware. The geographical distribution of wealthy countries is a hindrance here, because most of them are in the northern hemisphere, and thus have similar seasonal demand patterns.

The Profitability of Exports and Pricing Policy

The whole question of prices, profitability and export ratios appeared to be closely linked, especially when compared with domestic pottery manufacture. All the tile manufacturers in our sample had export prices substantially lower than home prices, and none of the three wished to increase their existing export ratio. Perhaps surprisingly, in view of what they said about overseas competition, two out of the four sanitary ware manufacturers said that export prices were the same as home prices, although one was prepared to modify export prices for large customers and price changes of competitors. Of the other two firms, one could obtain the same prices as for the home market in U.S.A. and Canada, but not elsewhere; and the other had not applied the previous year's increase in all prices to exports because of the export rebate, but regarded this as a once-for-all move. This last firm was also, however, willing to modify export prices for big customers, or for changes in competitors' prices. Of the four, only the two which could get the same price in some at least of their export markets wanted higher export ratios. The 'ideal' figures mentioned were only 25 and 40 per cent: while too much significance should not be attached to these hypothetical figures, they were significantly lower than the figures mentioned by most domestic pottery firms.

Basically, with a given capacity output, firms which believe exports to be less profitable than home sales are, among other things, balancing the benefits of spreading their sales in many markets against the loss in profitability. If this analysis is correct, then there is presumably some degree of reduced profitability for exports which is so great that it might begin to outweigh the (uncertain) benefits from further market-spreading; and the tile manufacturers might have reached such a point. They appear not to have gone past it since none of the three that we saw actually wanted to *reduce* its export ratio. Sanitary ware manufacturers were on the margin. They wanted more exports at prices the same as or near to home prices, but not at anything much less. Domestic potters, in general, were still at the point where further gains were to be had from increasing their export ratios.

Exports and Domestic Demand: The Pressure Hypothesis

Five out of the seven firms said that exports were not significantly affected by fluctuations in home demand, either at all, or in the long run. One of these five thought that exports would suffer in the short run from lengthening delivery dates at a time of rising home demand, and three thought that exports would benefit in the short run from shortening delivery dates when home demand was falling. Of the two remaining firms, one also quoted this short-term effect through delivery dates, but thought the long-term effect was that exports were helped by rising home demand, and hindered by falling home demand, because of the effect on unit costs. The other firm also quoted this effect, but did not confine it to the short term. This was also the only firm in the whole pottery industry which thought that rising home demand was 'bad' for exports because of rising costs and prices.

The sample was really too small for significant comparisons between answers to these questions and the proportion of output going to export. Nevertheless, the firms with the three lowest and the two highest export to total sales ratios were those which answered that exports were not significantly affected by home demand. But the two highest exported less than 50 per cent of output so this result is not really comparable with the equivalent finding in the domestic pottery branch of the industry. The explanation is more likely to be that the firms with high export ratios were protecting their investment in export markets.

Like the domestic potters at a time of falling demand, all the firms were desperately keen to maintain capacity production, for much the same reasons. They did not have the same technical problem of lower quality when the ovens were not full, but having lower direct costs and higher overheads (in other words more mass-production techniques) were heavily committed by their cost structure to maintaining output. The problem of which product to stock was relatively minor as the firms have a much smaller range of products than domestic pottery firms, in some cases only two or three that sold in any significant quantities.

As a result, all firms said that their initial response to falling demand was to make for stock, for some firms accompanied by extra selling effort at home and overseas. The limitations on this policy are obvious: apart from those of finance, space is a real problem, especially in sanitary ware which is very bulky. In fact, in some factories we saw there were stocks everywhere, and one firm was employing labour, which it did not want to lose permanently, in building more storage space. This particular manufacturer explained that in his experience the firm suffered an accelerated form of stocks cycle, as wholesalers (builders' merchants) unwound and rebuilt their stock positions. It was essential therefore to have sufficient supplies available when the build-up began. Substantial stock-building involves considerable faith in the existence of the next upturn in demand, and a big risk in forecasting how long it is likely to be delayed.

Conclusions

In comparison with the domestic pottery sector, one can make a few generalizations about the tiles and sanitary ware manufacturers. Overseas competition appears tougher in general and more price-competitive in particular. Largely as a result of this, exports are markedly less profitable than home sales. Firms are thus in general less able to export such large proportions of their output as domestic potters, and less willing to increase those proportions.

The firms thought their exports were largely unaffected by changes in home demand; either because maximum sales effort was being used already to overcome considerable export difficulties (tariffs, local production, price competition, the quality problem) or because the time schedule of home demand changes was not expected to be large enough to attain a new overseas market which could be supplied in the long term. There is a further possibility that some firms, especially those with the lowest relative amount of exports, were unaffected by changes in home demand simply because of the relative sizes of their home and export sales being too different. This last conclusion is only tentative because of the small size of the sample.

Chapter 7

THE U.K. MOTOR CYCLE INDUSTRY

INTRODUCTION

According to the Census of Production, the U.K. motor cycle and cycle industry consists of those firms '. . . which are involved in the production of motor cycles, three wheel vehicles, bicycles, tricycles, sidecars and parts and accessories for such vehicles'. This definition is similar to that used by the industry's trade association.

For the period 1958-66, the labour force and output volume figures show that this has been a declining industry and in this context we were particularly interested in the export performance of such an industry. Table 7.1 shows the industry's labour force and export records for the period and it can be seen that the decline in employment between 1960 and 1966 has been associated with a long-run increase in the proportion of output exported.

TABLE 7.1 *U.K. Motor Cycle and Cycle Industry*

Year	*No. of employees ** *(June)*	*Total value of exports*	*Proportion of output exported †*
		(£000s)	%
1958	n.a.	16,991	45·8
1959	36,670	17,000	35·6
1960	41,870	18,464	39·9
1961	33,920	15,020	41·8
1962	30,210	14,794	48·6
1963	29,600	16,914	54·1
1964	26,290	15,544	50·5
1965	25,800	17,377	52·3
1966	25,916	21,667	63·0

* Employees figure includes unemployed.
† Proportions are based on value figures.

For the purposes of our survey, we divided the industry into its motor cycle and cycle sectors and each was considered separately. This chapter is concerned with the motor cycle industry and it contains four major parts. In the first section, we undertake a general review of the U.K. motor cycle market with the aim of identifying any trends which are relevant for an understanding of the relationship between the domestic demand for motor cycles and exports. The review indicates that during the period 1958-66 there were major changes in the U.K. motor cycle market. In addition, our general analysis of the motor cycle market indicated that the British industry might have been experiencing a long-run decline in its competitiveness. This point seemed to occur so frequently that we felt obliged to allocate the second section of the chapter to considering the industry's competitiveness. We appreciate that this hypothesis, which is more of a long-run explanation, differs from the one which originally formed the basis for our study but, as we shall show later, it required some consideration in view of its relevance to our understanding of the industry's export performance, and hence for our subsequent tests of the pressure hypothesis which is essentially a short-run hypothesis. In addition, our analysis of competitiveness is especially useful for showing the limitations of aggregate data and the need for even further disaggregation: a point which is also apparent from our analysis in the first section. The results of our empirical work and especially the tests of the pressure hypothesis applied to the motor cycle industry are presented in Sections III and IV of this chapter.

I. THE U.K. MOTOR CYCLE MARKET

The changes which occurred in the U.K. motor cycle market between 1958 and 1966 can be understood from an examination of the trends in domestic demand, imports and the output of the U.K. industry. One point, with obvious implications for the pressure hypothesis, will soon become apparent, namely, that a single-product group generally classified as 'motor cycles' consists of a number of sub-markets. With the existence of such sub-markets, it will be seen that the U.K. industry's home and export sales are not perfect substitutes.

The Domestic Demand for Motor Cycles

Figures of vehicle registration provide one indicator of U.K. domestic demand during this period. The figures show two basic trends. First, there has been a decline in the proportion of motor cycles within the total motor cycle and private car population.[1] New motor cycle registrations as a proportion of total new registrations of motor cycles and private cars declined from an average of 22·7 per cent for the period 1958-62 to 13·7 per cent for 1962-6. Similar trends were evident in the absolute numbers of current motor cycle licences. Although annual increases occurred between 1958 and 1961, a peak of almost 1·9 million current motor cycle licences was reached in 1961 and since then numbers have declined annually to about 1·5 million in 1966. For industrial countries with rising real incomes and changing relative prices within the vehicle market, such a decline is not surprising. In fact, evidence suggests that income is a major determinant of ownership and that the proportion of people owning motor cycles tends to fall after a certain level of income is reached since consumers can afford to purchase a superior product.[2]

The second basic trend revealed by the registration figures is concerned with changes in the domestic demand for new motor cycles. A detailed analysis of new registrations for 1958-66 provided an indication of both the size and the changing composition of domestic demand. The evidence is shown in Table 7.2.

From Table 7.2, it can be seen that new registrations reached a peak for the period in 1959, followed by fluctuations around a declining trend with a trough in 1962, a smaller peak in 1964 and a low point for the period in 1966. Within the total of new registrations there was an increase in the proportion of machines in the under 250 cc. class and a corresponding decline in the proportion of larger machines. In fact, between 1963 and 1966, new registrations of large solo machines averaged less than a mere 8,000 per annum or about 5 per cent of total new registrations compared with the corresponding figures of 26,500 and 14·7 per cent in 1958. Once again,

1 For both current licences and new registrations. In this section, motor cycles consist of two-wheel vehicles and comprise mopeds, scooters and conventional machines.

2 See A. Maizels, *Industrial Growth and World Trade*, Cambridge: Cambridge University Press, 1963. Similar evidence applies to bicycles.

such a decline can be readily explained in terms of income and substitution effects, especially when it is remembered that the prices of new large motor cycles are similar to those of small, relatively new cars in the used-vehicle market. In addition, rising insurance rates for both learner drivers and large machines have probably contributed to the decline.

TABLE 7.2 *New Registrations of Motor Cycles – G.B. (Sept. Quarter)*

	1958	*1959*	*1960*	*1961*	*1962*	*1963*	*1964*	*1965*	*1966*
Under 250 cc.									
Number (000)	152·8	293·5	226·1	187·1	126·2	156·4	196·1	142·8	102·5
Proportion (%)	85·2	89·7	89·4	89·4	91·1	95·1	96·0	94·6	93·3
Over 250 cc.									
Number (000)	26·5	33·4	26·7	22·0	12·1	7·9	8·0	8·1	7·3
Proportion (%)	14·7	10·3	10·6	10·6	8·9	4·9	4·0	5·4	6·7

Notes: (1) Figures exclude motor cycles with sidecars or trailers. Since such machines are usually in the 'over 250 cc.' class, their inclusion increases the proportions in this class by a maximum 2 per cent points for 1958-66. Three-wheelers are also excluded.
(2) Small machines are defined as motor cycles of less than 250 cc.; large machines are 250 cc. and over.

Source: Ministry of Tranport, *Highway Statistics.*

Within the small machines market, motor cycles of less than 50 c.c., including mopeds, have become increasingly popular. Between 1958 and 1962, such machines accounted for an average of 32·4 per cent of new registrations, but the share increased to 45·6 per cent for 1962-6. In fact, for 1963 and 1964, machines in the under 50 c.c. size range accounted for over 50 per cent of new registrations. In addition to reflecting significant shifts in demand within the motor cycle market some of the increased demand for small machines must have resulted from the higher real income of the traditional domestic consumers of bicycles. Having outlined the major changes in demand, an analysis of imports and the output of the U.K. industry will enable us to identify the sources of supply.

The Supply of Motor Cycles in the U.K. Market: Imports

The annual value of motor cycle deliveries to the U.K. market consists of the total output of the U.K. industry plus imports but minus exports. Between 1958 and 1966, imports averaged 33 per cent of the value of sales of complete motor cycles in the U.K. market. The peak year for imports was 1959, with a smaller peak occurring in 1964. Imports have been dominated by the smaller motor cycles, especially scooters, mini-motor cycles and mopeds, the relevant data being shown in Table 7.3:

TABLE 7.3 *Motor Cycle Imports: Percentage Analysis by Value of Product*

Product (*% of total imports*)	*1958*	*1959*	*1960*	*1961*	*1962*	*1963*	*1964*	*1965*	*1966*
Mopeds	10·5	17·6	18·5	29·8	22·9	26·9	14·7	13·5	6·6
Scooters	87·9	82·3	81·4	59·4	60·4	24·1	23·2	38·1	44·0
Other motor cycles	1·6	0·1	0·1	10·8	16·7	49·0	62·1	48·4	49·3
Total imports: (£000s)	4,732	10,171	7,305	3,721	3,325	5,694	8,461	4,398	3,419
Imports as percentage of domestic demand (value)	30·4	33·0	28·4	24·5	26·6	43·3	50·2	34·4	29·4

Notes: (1) U.K. domestic demand is defined as domestic output plus imports minus exports of complete machines (excluding parts). This definition was not used in the econometric analysis of Section IV of this chapter.

(2) Owing to classification change in 1961, it has been assumed that under 60 cc. = mopeds, 60-250 cc. = scooters. After 1961, motor cycles are all classes other than mopeds and scooters.

Sources: (1) Board of Trade, *Business Monitor: Motor Cycles, Three-Wheel Vehicles, Pedal Cycles and Parts.*

(2) British Cycle and Motor Cycle Industries Association Ltd.

(3) U.K. trade statistics.

Table 7.3 shows quite clearly the changing product composition of motor cycle imports. In fact between 1958 and 1966, imports can be divided into two periods each of which reflected the domestic market's response to new product innovations originating amongst foreign suppliers. First, the period 1958-62, which was the era of scooter imports from Italy together with the imports of machines in the less than 50-60 c.c. class, mainly mopeds, from France and

West Germany. During this period, Italian scooter imports accounted for an average of 57 per cent of the value of U.K. motor cycle imports. Second, the period 1963-6 which was dominated by the import of mini-motor cycles from Japan.[1] In Table 7.3, these machines of less than 250 cc. dominate the 'other motor cycles' group. Between 1963 and 1966, other motor cycles, consisting mainly of small Japanese machines, accounted for an average of 52·2 per cent of the total value of U.K. motor cycle imports, with scooters averaging a further 29 per cent.[2]

Figures for import volume are even more impressive than those for value and they can be compared with the domestic deliveries of the U.K. industry to provide an indication of the annual total number of units supplied to the U.K. market: the results are shown in Table 7.4.

TABLE 7.4 *Total Number of Units Supplied to the U.K. Domestic Market*

Year	*Imports (units 000s)*	*Domestic deliveries of U.K. industry (units 000s)*	*Total (000s)*	*Imports as a percentage of total number of units*
1958	82·6	104·0	186·6	44·2
1959	171·5	206·0	377·5	45·4
1960	134·0	160·9	294·9	45·4
1961	77·5	116·9	194·4	39·8
1962	59·0	76·3	135·3	43·6
1963	146·9	74·6	221·5	66·3
1964	185·8	75·6	261·4	71·0
1965	81·0	64·5	145·5	55·6
1966	58·7	43·8	102·5	57·2

Sources: Board of Trade, *Business Monitor*.
British Cycle and Motor Cycle Industries Association Ltd.

By relating the figures of new registrations to the total domestic deliveries of the British industry and to an analysis of the product composition of imports, it soon becomes apparent that imports are supplying a substantial proportion of U.K. domestic demand and

1 See Appendix B2, *The Japanese Motor Cycle Industry.*
2 The Anglo-Japanese trade liberalization agreement was concluded in 1962.

especially the market for small machines.[1] In general, motor cycle imports have reflected the introduction of new products and the associated shifts in consumer tastes and preferences within the market: hence the Italian scooter boom which was followed by another product innovation in the domestic market, namely the Japanese mini-motor cycles. Thus, it seems reasonable to suggest that the relatively high proportion of imports in domestic demand and their changing product composition are a reflection of shifts in consumer demand induced by such factors as income changes, basic product innovations from overseas suppliers and the development of mass-produced foreign substitutes resulting in the availability of models at lower relative prices.[2] Finally, the importance of imports and the fact that product innovations have originated from foreign sources of supply immediately raises the problem of the U.K. motor cycle industry's position in the domestic and world markets and its associated competitiveness: this issue will be discussed after we have presented an outline of the U.K. industry's output and export record. For the present, it is sufficient to observe that a substantial market demand exists in the U.K., much of which has been supplied by imports, a fact which suggests that the U.K. motor cycle industry has in some sense 'failed' to adjust to satisfy the preferences of its home market consumers.

The Supply of Motor Cycles: The U.K. Motor Cycle Industry

The U.K. industry's sales (deliveries) and export record during the period 1958-66 is shown in Table 7.5.

Table 7.5 shows that since the peak in 1959, the industry's total volume of output and its deliveries to the home market have both followed a declining trend, reaching a low point in 1966. This decline in the total volume of output suggests that excess capacity might exist in the industry. Unfortunately, since we have no data on long-run capacity output and short-run capacity utilization, we can only suggest this as a possibility. In the short run, if such excess capacity exists, then the immediate effect of a reduction in the

[1] See Appendix B1, *The Product Composition of U.K. Motor Cycle Imports and Exports, 1961-6*.

[2] New consumers can enter the market – e.g. under-twenty age group; low income adults who might replace bicycles with mopeds.

TABLE 7.5 *The U.K. Motor Cycle Industry, 1958-66*

	Value			*Volume*			
Year	*Total (£000s)*	*For export (£000s)*	*Exports as percentage of total value*	*Total (000s)*	*Domestic market (000s)*	*For export (000s)*	*Exports as percentage of total volume*
1958	16,032	4,548	28·4	139·7	104·0	35·7	25·5
1959	25,577	5,047	19·7	248·9	206·0	42·9	17·2
1960	24,486	5,252	21·4	203·2	160·6	42·6	20·4
1961	17,022	3,862	22·7	145·7	116·9	28·8	19·7
1962	13,124	4,044	30·8	106·0	76·3	29·7	28·0
1963	12,330	4,900	39·8	107·1	74·6	32·5	30·3
1964	14,272	5,906	41·4	111·6	75·6	36·0	32·2
1965	16,512	8,307	50·3	108·0	64·4	43·5	40·3
1966	20,097	13,803	68·6	105·0	53·8	61·2	58·2

Notes: (1) Value figures have not been adjusted for price changes. Also, figures include three-wheel vehicles.
(2) Figures are based on deliveries.

Source: Board of Trade, *Business Monitor*.

domestic demand for a firm's products will simply be an increase in spare capacity, with no change in export sales. Similarly, with excess capacity, an increase in a firm's domestic sales is unlikely to be at the expense of exports until excess demand arises. In fact, with excess capacity in the U.K. motor cycle industry and given the significance of imports in domestic demand, it seems likely that limited variations in domestic demand will affect imports rather than exports.[1] We recognize that in the absence of capacity data and prior to testing the pressure hypothesis, these can only be tentative suggestions. At the most, if the reasoning is valid, it indicates that there might be no significant negative relationship between the exports of motor cycles and the pressure of domestic demand.

Despite the decline in the industry's domestic sales, Table 7.5 shows that since 1959 the export market has been absorbing a rising proportion of deliveries, and by 1966 the industry was exporting

1 The years of peak imports in 1959-60 and 1963-4 were periods when the U.K. *economy* was either experiencing reductions in, or had reached a minimum level of, spare capacity.

over 50 per cent of its output. In the event of a given decline in the volume of domestic sales, such an export-orientated industry can maintain output by achieving a less than proportionate increase in export volume. However, only in 1966 did the industry export more than 50 per cent of its output volume and consequently in earlier years to offset a given decline in domestic sales required a more than proportionate increase in export volume. An analysis of output between 1959 and 1966 shows that the decline in annual total volume of some 144,000 units comprised a decrease in domestic sales of over 162,000 units and a rise in export volume of more than 18,000 units per annum. Thus, the industry's declining volume has been the result of a decrease in its home market sales which was not offset by a sufficiently large increase in export volume. The industry's sales performance in the home market raises yet again the issue of its competitiveness. Nonetheless, the industry's export performance was extremely impressive when it is realized that between 1958 and 1966 the growth in value of motor cycle exports exceeded the national average for both total exports and the exports of manufactures. But the crucial question still remains: would motor cycle exports have been even higher if the pressure of domestic demand had been lower?

A product analysis of the industry's volume of output revealed that conventional motor cycles accounted for more than 50 per cent of output and at least 87 per cent of export volume for every year during the period. In view of the product composition of U.K. imports, it was not surprising that the industry's exports were dominated by large conventional machines in the over 250 cc. size range.[1] Moreover, for each year between 1962 and 1966, the export of large motor cycles exceeded the number of new registrations of such machines in the U.K. domestic market. It seems that in the absence of a relatively large home market for high-powered machines the U.K. industry has to export in order to achieve a substantial volume of output. The British industry's specialization in conventional motor cycles is further confirmed by the brief outline of moped and scooter output and exports shown in Table 7.6.

[1] See Appendix B1, *The Product Composition of U.K. Motor Cycle Imports and Exports, 1961-6.*

TABLE 7.6 *U.K. Motor Cycle Industry: Product Composition of Output and Exports*

	Mopeds		*Scooters*		*Other motor cycles*	
Year	*Total output (000s)*	*Moped exports as percentage of total exports*	*Total output (000s)*	*Scooter exports as percentage of total exports*	*Total output (000s)*	*Other motor cycle exports as percentage of total exports*
1958	20·5	n.a.	19·7	4·0	94·7	96·0
1959	78·8	n.a.	29·2	4·9	127·5	95·1
1960	33·8	9·0	29·9	3·5	130·4	87·3
1961	24·4	5·9	25·9	5·4	88·0	88·5
1962	16·1	7·0	25·2	5·5	55·5	87·3
1963	32·1	1·7	15·8	4·8	50·9	93·3
1964	36·6	3·4	7·8	2·5	55·2	94·0
1965	28·6	7·7	3·8	0·9	62·8	91·3
1966	15·1	2·6	2·4	0·1	77·2	97·2

Notes: (1) Figures are based on volume of output. See also Appendix B1, *The Product Composition of U.K. Motor Cycle Imports and Exports.*
(2) Prior to 1960, moped export figures were not separately listed.
(3) Three-wheelers are excluded.
(4) Other motor cycles consist of all conventional motor cycles, excluding mopeds and scooters.

Sources: (1) Board of Trade, *Business Monitor*.
(2) British Cycle and Motor Cycle Industries Association Ltd.

Table 7.6 shows the importance of conventional motor cycles in the total volume of output and exports. The share of moped production in total volume fluctuated between 15 and 30 per cent but its contribution to export volume was relatively small. Scooter production has been even less significant. Even during its peak years between 1959 and 1962, scooter output never accounted for more than 26·0 per cent of the industry's total volume and by 1966 its share was 2·5 per cent. This was a period in which scooter imports declined but not to the same drastic extent as the U.K. industry's deliveries. At the same time U.K. scooter exports never exceeded 2,000 units and in 1966 a mere ninety scooters were exported. The decline in scooter production after 1962 probably resulted from the change in U.K. consumer demand associated with the product innovation, at lower relative prices, of the Japanese mini-motor cycles, the shift in demand being especially severe for U.K. scooters. This explanation requires a detailed analysis of relative product prices in order to show that the U.K. industry was at a competitive disadvantage in the domestic scooter market: we shall undertake such an analysis in a later section.

Finally, to complete this survey of the U.K. industry's output and export record, an analysis of the country distribution of exports is required. One of the most outstanding features of the period 1958-1966 has been the spectacular rise in the proportion of U.K. motor cycle exports allocated to the United States market. In 1958, the U.S. market received about 31 per cent of the total export value of U.K. motor cycles and parts; by 1964, this proportion had increased to 61 per cent and in 1966 it was over 80 per cent. Furthermore, a product breakdown of U.K. motor cycle exports showed that in 1966, not only did large conventional machines over 250 cc. account for most of the total but the export of these machines to the U.S. market accounted for 75 per cent of total export volume. Thus, by 1966, the U.K. industry specialized in the export of a single product range, namely large conventional machines, which were mostly allocated to one market, the United States.

Authorities in the industry have suggested a number of factors which might explain the rise in exports to the U.S.A. At the outset, it must be recognized that U.K. exports have only formed one component of a much larger increase in total U.S. motor cycle imports during the period 1958-66. In general terms, there has been a foreign supply response to satisfy U.S. consumer demand. Some of the excess U.S. demand for large machines from its own domestic industry was transferred to the U.K. which had traditionally specialized in large motor cycles: apparently the British products were both lighter and relatively cheaper than those of their U.S. rivals. At the same time, it must be remembered that since 1959 the U.K. industry's total domestic market and especially its home market for large machines had been declining so that the supply capacity for satisfying any foreign consumer demand for such motor cycles was available. However, this only explains the U.K. industry's supply response to market opportunities: the actual causes of the increase in the U.S. demand for motor cycles are more fascinating. Some authorities believe that this rise in demand for motor cycles reflects road congestion, the pursuit of health[1] and the desire to 'reach the countryside' with all the advantages offered by powerful motor cycles in terms of speed, mobility and access to remote areas. In addition, the American demand for large machines probably reflected both rising real income levels[2] and the geographically large U.S. market which requires high-powered motor cycles for long-distance journeys.

II. THE COMPETITIVENESS OF THE U.K. MOTOR CYCLE INDUSTRY

At various points in our outline of the major changes in the motor cycle market, we raised the question of the U.K. industry's competitiveness. Evidence from the previous sections suggests the hypothesis that the industry has a competitive advantage in the production of its traditional specialism, namely conventional motor cycles, especially large machines, and that it is at a competitive disadvantage in the production of smaller machines such as mopeds, scooters and mini-motor cycles. In this section, we shall attempt to test this hypothesis.

Initially, we had to determine the appropriate measures of competitiveness. We considered competitiveness in terms of prices and types of product. Given this framework, we considered such indicators as unit values, imports, the ratio of exports to imports and trends in market shares.[3] Whilst these are extremely crude measures, when taken together they presented prima facie support for the hypothesis. We do, of course, appreciate that this section is concerned with a different hypothesis from the one which initially inspired our research. Applied to the motor cycle industry, the

1 For example, President Kennedy actively campaigned for a 'healthier' U.S.A. Road congestion and the pursuit of health have also been suggested as explanations of the increased U.S. demand for bicycles.

2 More information is required on the relationship between motor cycle ownership and rising real incomes. As one possible hypothesis, motor cycle ownership might increase within relatively low income ranges so that motor cycles are normal goods. For increased income levels, motor cycles might become inferior type goods after which U.S. experience suggests that for some people motor cycles, probably of a different type, might return to normal type goods.

3 See, I. B. Kravis, R. E. Lipsey, and P. Bourque, *Measuring International Price Competitiveness: A Preliminary Report*, Occasional Paper 94, N.B.E.R., 1965.

hypothesis about competitiveness would state that the U.K. industry's long-run export performance and its share in the world market can be explained by a decline in competitiveness. Our task is merely to identify any lack of competitiveness without attempting to quantify the significance of this variable in explaining long-run trends in the U.K.'s share of world motor cycle trade. However, we felt that if we could identify any lack of competitiveness, it would at least provide a basis for explaining any long-run decline in market shares whilst the pressure hypothesis might provide a possible explanation of short-run fluctuations around the declining trend.

As a first step in measuring competitiveness, we compared the unit values of the U.K. motor cycle industry's exports, its domestic deliveries and imports. The unit value figures were obtained by dividing value figures by volume and consequently they are based upon motor cycles as a group with no distinction between various types and they do not take account of product changes during the period 1958-66. At the most, the unit value figures are only useful as a means of determining relative price movements and the size ranges of motor cycles in various markets. The results are shown in Table 7.7.

A number of general points emerged from Table 7.7. First, in commenting on the export performance of the U.K. economy in recent years, some authorities have noted that domestic wholesale prices have tended to rise faster than the prices obtainable on the export market and this might have had the effect of directing marginal supplies from exports to the home market.[1] The evidence from Table 7.7 suggests that for motor cycles there is no relationship between movements in the industry's domestic and export unit values. Whilst domestic prices have fluctuated, tending to rise and fall in alternate years, export unit values have followed a rising trend. Throughout the period, export unit values have exceeded those for domestic sales by the U.K. industry. Secondly, during this same period, import unit values have been below the prices of the U.K. industry's domestic sales. To some extent, competition from imports must have caused both a change in the product composition of the U.K. industry's domestic sales and the fluctuations in its domestic unit values. Thirdly, since there tends to be a positive relationship between

[1] See, e.g. S. J. Wells, *British Export Performance*, Cambridge, 1964, p. 63f.

the size of a motor cycle and its unit value,[1] the evidence of Table 7.7 simply confirms the heterogeneity of the motor cycle market. The differences between import unit values and the domestic and export prices for the U.K. industry's products, tend to reflect differences in the product composition of the various markets. As a result, the

TABLE 7.7 *The Unit Values of Motor Cycles*

	Unit values (£)				*Relative unit values*	
Year	*Domestic sales of U.K. industry*	*U.K. exports*	*U.K. imports excluding tariff*	*U.K. imports including tariff*	*Domestic sales ÷imports*	*Exports ÷imports*
(1)	(2)	(3)	(4)	(5)	(6)	(7)
1958	110·4	127·4	65·6	80·4	137·3	194·2
1959	99·6	117·6	61·4	75·2	132·4	191·5
1960	119·7	123·4	61·3	75·1	159·3	201·3
1961	112·5	134·1	50·5	61·9	181·7	265·5
1962	119·0	136·1	48·9	59·0	201·6	278·3
1963	99·5	150·8	38·8	47·5	209·4	388·6
1964	110·6	164·5	45·3	55·5	199·2	363·1
1965	127·2	190·9	54·0	71·6	177·6	353·5
1966	143·6	225·5	58·2	77·1	186·2	387·4

Notes: (1) The import unit values in column (5) and the relative unit values of domestic sales and imports (column 6) are based on import prices including a tariff rate of 22½ per cent *ad valorem* plus the import surcharge for 1964-6. The relative unit values of exports and imports (column 7) excludes tariff rates from import prices: this achieves some consistency, since U.K. exports will be subjected to tariffs in the importing countries. The inversion of the relative prices of exports and imports will give the terms of trade.

(2) The domestic sales and U.K. exports include a limited number of three-wheelers.

(3) All unit values are in current prices, reflecting the lack of a suitable and readily available price deflator.

Sources: Board of Trade, *Business Monitor*.
U.K. trade statistics.
British Cycle and Motor Cycle Industries Association Ltd.

1 See, e.g. Appendix B1, *Product Composition of U.K. Motor Cycle Imports and Exports, 1961-6*.

U.K. industry has been supplying the more expensive sector of the domestic market whilst U.K. exports and imports have been dominated by large and small machines, respectively.

Some insight into the unit value and volume components of the changing value of motor cycle sales can be obtained with the aid of a basic index number calculation. Price and volume indexes were calculated for the domestic sales and exports of the U.K. industry and for imports, the results being shown in Table 7.8. It must be stressed, however, that the table is no more than a guide since the data were not adjusted for changes in the product mix during the period.

Table 7.8 shows that the decline in the value of the industry's domestic sales between 1958 and 1966 comprised a 30 per cent rise in unit values and nearly a 60 per cent decline in the volume of

TABLE 7.8 *Price and Volume Movements, 1958-66*

Index 1966 (1958 = 100)

	Domestic sales of U.K. industry	*U.K. exports*	*U.K. imports*
Price index	130·0	177·0	95·8
Volume index	42·1	171·4	77·8

Notes: Import figures include tariffs and import surcharge.
Sources: Ibid.

output. The decline is not difficult to understand when it is realized that during these years not only did incomes rise but the relative unit values of domestic and imported motor cycles changed in favour of the latter group. The rise in the value of export sales was attributable to an almost identical increase in both unit values and volume: such increases reflected the greater importance of large motor cycles in total exports. Finally, the value of imports declined, this decrease consisting of a reduction in unit values and a larger decline in volume.

A further simple indicator of the relative competitiveness of the U.K. motor cycle industry was obtained by comparing exports by product group with the *product* composition of the domestic industry's output and imports. Indeed, the motor cycle products which the U.K. industry did *not* export in substantial quantities provided one useful indication of its international competitive position in such product markets. For this purpose motor cycle products were classified into mopeds, scooters and 'other motor cycles' (i.e. 50-500 cc.).

During the period 1960-6[1] scooter exports never exceeded 2,000 units and failed to reach a total value of £200,000 in any one year, whilst moped exports reached a maximum figure of 4,011 and a total value of £141,610. These are small quantities on any criterion, especially when they are related to total U.K. motor cycle exports (See Table 7.5). In addition, for most of the period, the annual volume of imports of each of these products exceeded both the total and the domestic output of the U.K. industry,[2] the data being given in Table 7.9. In total, this sort of evidence suggests that the U.K.

TABLE 7.9 *The U.K. Domestic Market: A Product Analysis*

	Mopeds			*Scooters*			*Motor cycles*		
Year	*U.K. industry's output for domestic market*	*Imports*	*U.K. industry's % of domestic demand*	*U.K. industry's output for domestic market*	*Imports*	*U.K. industry's % of domestic demand*	*U.K. industry's output for domestic market*	*Imports*	*U.K. industry's % of domestic demand*
1960	24,989	48,141	34.1	27,437	85,330	24.3	91,863	n.a.	n.a.
1961	22,455	42,411	34.6	28,204	34,923	44.6	60,035	4,789	92.6
1962	14,074	28,524	33.0	26,597	33,316	44.3	30,337	7,453	80.2
1963	31,529	68,114	31.6	16,731	20,647	44.7	20,814	57,970	26.4
1964	34,815	55,809	38.4	6,935	28,536	19.5	22,966	102,340	18.3
1965	25,158	19,830	55.9	3,398	23,514	12.6	22,454	38,042	37.1
1966	13,518	7,654	63.8	2,310	20,879	9.9	18,329	30,141	37.8

Notes: (1) Volume figures: these obviously distort the 'other motor cycles' section which consists of both large and small motor cycles, excluding mopeds and scooters

(2) Domestic demand consists of the U.K. industry's volume of output for the domestic market plus import volume.

Source: British Cycle and Motor Cycle Industries Association Ltd.

industry has been at a competitive disadvantage in the manufacture of mopeds and scooters.

The competitive disadvantage of the U.K. industry in mopeds and scooters was reflected in an annual deficit on the balance of trade

1 The trade association provided detailed statistics for this period. For 1960, scooter imports have been estimated.

2 With the exception of mopeds in 1965-6.

for each of these products during the period 1960-6. For any trading country with such a deficit, it might be concluded that its costs and prices were out of line with those in the rest of the world. Although there are data problems, including difficulties of product differences, some limited evidence of the British industry's competitive position in the world moped and scooter market can be obtained from the U.K. export and import unit values for these products with the latter figures being regarded as an indicator of foreign prices. The evidence is presented in Table 7.10 where, under 'heroic' assumptions about the similarity of products, it will be seen that in terms of prices, the U.K. industry appears to be far from competitive in both these product groups.

TABLE 7.10 *Unit Values: Mopeds and Scooters*

	Mopeds			*Scooters*		
Year	*U.K. export unit values*	*U.K. import unit values*	*Relative unit values: exports ÷imports*	*U.K. export unit values*	*U.K. import unit values*	*Relative unit values: exports ÷imports*
	£	£	£	£	£	£
1960	35·3	21·7	162·6	107·7	n.a.	n.a.
1961	38·5	26·1	147·5	97·3	63·3	154·0
1962	29·5	26·7	110·4	80·3	60·3	133·0
1963	45·2	22·5	200·8	84·6	66·5	127·0
1964	36·5	22·3	163·6	76·4	68·8	111·0
1965	34·3	30·1	113·9	87·8	71·3	123·1
1966	35·5	29·5	120·3	82·6	72·1	114·5

Note: Export and import unit values *both* exclude tariffs.

Source: British Cycle and Motor Cycle Industries Association Ltd.

It was not possible to obtain data on the unit values for the domestic sales of the U.K. industry's scooters and mopeds and so it was necessary to use export unit values as indicators of home price movements. A comparison of export and import unit values for scooters indicated that during the period, relative price differentials narrowed and, if such movements also occurred for the domestic sales of U.K. scooters, then the especially severe decline in U.K. scooter sales appears even more surprising. In addition to price differentials, this decline might have been partially attributable to differences in type and quality of product, with the U.K. being at a further competitive disadvantage in this sphere. For mopeds, the price differential between exports and imports declined during the period and if this also occurred for the industry's domestic sales, it might help to explain the rise in the industry's share of home market sales.

Further simple indicators of competitiveness provide supporting evidence for the hypothesis that the U.K. industry has generally been at a competitive disadvantage in all but large conventional motor cycles. A ratio of the value of exports to imports expressed as a percentage can be used to reflect the industry's competitive position in its home and export markets. Here, the use of such a ratio might be supported on the plausible reasoning that if an industry's products can compete in the export market, it will be able to compete in the home market.[1] Table 7.11 presents the record for the U.K. motor cycle industry for the period 1958-66.

TABLE 7.11 *Ratio of Exports to Imports: U.K. Motor Cycle Industry*

Year	*Ratio*
	(%)
1958	106·4
1959	72·5
1960	74·8
1961	115·4
1962	133·1
1963	96·8
1964	77·0
1965	183·1
1966	358·0

Note: The ratio is simply the value of U.K. motor cycle exports to imports expressed as a percentage.

In connection with Table 7.11, two points seem worth mentioning. First, there was a substantial rise in the ratio between 1964 and 1966 and here it would be interesting to discover the extent to which this rise reflected such factors as changes in tastes, the effect of the import

1 See, e.g. S. J. Wells, *Trade Policies for Britain*, London: Oxford University Press, 1966.

surcharge and export rebate during these years and/or a possible belated 'shock-effect' resulting in an improvement in the competitiveness of the U.K. industry. Second, an industry ratio conceals significant product differences which tend to support much of our earlier analysis. A product approach shows that for the period 1961-6, the average percentage ratio of exports to imports was 6·9 for mopeds and 5·0 for scooters: these relatively low figures are not surprising in view of the previous analysis of unit values and the composition of U.K. imports. For the other motor cycles group, the percentage ratio was 392 which, together with previous evidence, might be used to support the view that the U.K. industry has a competitive advantage in conventional motor cycles. We can be even more specific. From an analysis of the product composition of U.K. imports and exports, we know that small motor cycles in the under 250 cc. class have dominated the imports of conventional machines and that larger motor cycles have accounted for most of the value of U.K. exports: this tends to indicate that the U.K. has been at a competitive disadvantage in small machines and a competitive advantage in large motor cycles.[1] The ratio of exports to imports for each of these groups for the period 1961-6 supports this conclusion, the average percentage ratio being a mere 47 for the small machines in the other motor cycles group and greatly in excess of 8,000 for large conventional motor cycles.[2]

As a final indicator of competitiveness, we considered trends in the U.K. industry's share of imports into the United States' motor cycle market. The U.S. market was selected for more detailed consideration because of its leading position as an importer in the world motor cycle market and its relative importance for the U.K. industry's export trade. The U.K.'s share of motor cycle imports into the U.S. market was also used in some of our subsequent tests of the pressure hypothesis. Data on the U.K.'s share are shown in Table 7.12 below.

Table 7.12 shows quite clearly that since the peak year of 1959, the U.K.'s share of U.S. motor cycle imports has followed a

[1] See Appendix B1, *Product Composition of U.K. Motor Cycle Imports and Exports, 1961-6*.

[2] Each ratio was based on the other motor cycles group (conventional machines) and excluded mopeds and scooters.

long-run declining trend. Although the above figures refer to both motor cycles and parts, a similar trend is evident when complete motor cycles only are considered. It is also apparent from Table 7.12 that the declining share has been experienced in a market which in the period 1961-5 was rapidly expanding. In fact, by failing to maintain its 1958 share of U.S. imports, the U.K. industry experienced a total 'loss' in exports to the U.S.A. of £16·7 million for complete motor cycles and a further £3·1 million in parts during the

TABLE 7.12 *U.S. Motor Cycle Imports*

Year	*Total value of U.S. imports of motor cycles and parts*	*U.K. share of U.S. imports*
	(*$ million*)	(%)
1958	14·9	36·2
1959	14·9	46·0
1960	16·0	43·0
1961	17·1	30·0
1962	29·0	22·0
1963	45·7	20·0
1964	72·8	17·0
1965	141·5	13·6
1966 *	162·3	14·1

* Based on data for first three quarters only.

Source: U.S. Imports of Merchandise for Consumption. All value figures are in U.S. $.

period 1958-65.[1] However, a more detailed analysis of the U.S. imports for the period showed that the U.K. was not the only country to have experienced a decline in share in this market. Table 7.13 shows that with one exception each of the world's major motor cycle manufacturing countries encountered declining shares.

From this description of the U.S. market together with an analysis of the trade statistics, it is possible to make a number of tentative suggestions. First, the U.S.A. has some claim to being classified as a growth market in the world motor cycle trade. During the period 1958-65 the U.S.A. became both the world's major importer

[1] It should be remembered that these 'losses' refer to *one* product group, namely motor cycles, in *one* overseas market.

of motor cycles and, of the large import markets, it apparently grew at the fastest rate. Moreover, the British industry allocated an increasing proportion of its export value to the U.S.A. and hence it was exporting its output to one of the world's major growth markets. Second, an analysis of the product composition of U.S. imports suggests, prima facie, that the U.K. industry lacked product competitiveness during the period 1958-65. For example, in 1965, small motor cycles under 250 cc. and mainly from Japan, accounted for about 70 per cent of the total value of U.S. imports, with the U.K. failing to obtain any significant proportion of this trade.[1]

TABLE 7.13 *Country Distribution of U.S. Motor Cycle Imports*

Country	*Share of U.S. motor cycle imports* 1958	1965
	%	%
U.K.	34·0	12·7
Italy	30·9	9·0
W. Germany	14·8	1·6
Austria	13·6	1·7
Japan	2·9	67·4
France	1·6	0·5

Note: Figures are based on value of *complete* motor cycles, excluding parts.

Source: Ibid.

In addition, the limited data available suggested that during the 1960s, small conventional motor cycles were a major growth product in both the U.S. and world markets.[2] Thus, the limited evidence in this section suggests that the U.K. motor cycle industry allocated a substantial proportion of its exports to a growth market in the world motor cycle trade but that it was only catering for one section and certainly not the fastest-growing section of this market. It must, however, be stressed that these results are only tentative and, owing to the difficulties of obtaining data on world motor cycle trade, they do not represent a satisfactory test of the hypothesis which explains

1 This is consistent with events in the U.K. motor cycle market.

2 See Appendix B2, *The Japanese Motor Cycle Industry*.

the U.K.'s export performance in terms of the geographical and commodity composition of its overseas trade.[1]

Our results can now be summarized. The various measures of competitiveness suggested that over the long run, the U.K. motor cycle industry has experienced a lack of price and product competitiveness and this was especially evident for mopeds, scooters and motor cycles under 250 cc. Having identified a lack of competitiveness it seems relevant to enquire into its possible causes. Although a variety of hypotheses can be suggested,[2] we shall be concerned with two, namely, a failure to innovate with its implications for product competition and the length of production runs with its effects on unit costs.

With the benefit of hindsight, it might be argued that the industry's lack of competitiveness, especially product-wise, was due to a failure to innovate and adapt to changing market requirements. In reply to the criticism of a failure to transform, representatives of the industry argue that in the immediate post-war period the British industry did in fact introduce a variety of product innovations of the type which were later introduced by foreign manufacturers. It is argued that these product innovations were rejected by the British consumer and consequently the industry lost some of its more unorthodox designers as firms continued to sell established conventional machines. The point about this argument is that at one time the industry possessed the technical ability to innovate but the absence of consumer demand for new types of product in the period after 1945 resulted in the continued emphasis upon orthodox designs. It is, however, admitted by some representatives in the industry that after their immediate post-war experiences, there was a tendency for British firms to neglect market research with the inevitable failure of domestic suppliers to recognize and respond to the market changes which occurred in the late 1950s.[3] Even if such explanations are included within the failure to innovate hypothesis, a number of fundamental problems nonetheless remain.

1 See Chapter 1.

2 See Chapter 1. Also, L. T. Wells Jnr., 'Tests of a Product Cycle Model of International Trade: U.S. Exports of Consumer Durables', *Quarterly Journal of Economics*, February 1969.

3 For example, with scooters the British industry's supply response was too late, coming after the peak of the domestic market's scooter boom.

First, in its present form the hypothesis tends to be an all-embracing descriptive statement capable of describing everything and of explaining very little. A more satisfactory approach would be to attempt to measure the U.K. industry's innovatory and market research potential and performance and compare the results with similar evidence from the motor cycle industries of Japan, Italy and France.[1] Here, comparative data at the firm level on such variables as expenditure on market research and research and development, the number of qualified scientists and technologists and the skill composition of the labour force would be a useful starting-point for testing the hypothesis. In the absence of such data, we have confined ourselves to more qualitative and general remarks.

Second, if, as the evidence indicates, the U.K. industry has a competitive advantage in the manufacture of large machines, it would seem a rational response for profit-maximizing firms to continue specializing in and producing those products in which they have the greatest competitive advantage.[2] In this context, firms will continue in production as long as they can cover their supply prices. Third,[3] even if it is concluded that the U.K. industry has failed to innovate, it is still necessary to ask whether the industry could actually be competitive not only in development but also in the manufacture of mopeds, scooters and mini-motor cycles. This takes us from the research and development stage in a product's life-cycle to the production point and it brings us to a second possible explanation of the industry's lack of competitiveness.

The annual volume of production with the associated opportunities for economies of scale and decreasing costs might provide the basis for an explanation of the U.K. industry's lack of competitiveness and its long-run export performance. In effect, such an explanation is based upon relative production costs with their implications for price competitiveness. We attempted to obtain quantitative evidence on the extent of economies of scale in motor cycle production

1 We prefer the more realistic assumption that innovations are not a monopoly of U.K. industry and that the 'failure' hypothesis needs to show that an industry has 'failed' in relation both to its potential and to the performance of rivals.

2 Even so, questions might be raised about the time horizon applied to the objectives of these firms and their associated attitude towards risk-taking: here, the experiences of the immediate post-war period might have been formative influences.

3 Points two and three are associated.

but we were not very successful. However, one representative from the U.K. industry stated that, 'The unit costs of producers of 250,000 to 1½ million units per annum are . . . vastly different to the costs of the manufacturer producing 4,000-5,000 units per annum. As I have no experience of the costs involved with the larger volume production, I am afraid that I am unable to give you accurate information on the reduction of cost, except to say that it would be very substantial. Not only would manufacturing methods be different with the latest automatic machinery but also materials would be bought at considerable discounts.' It was suggested that an indication of the possible economies of scale which typically result from mass-production activities could be obtained from the U.K. car industry: an industry in which such economies are indeed 'substantial'.[1]

Ideally, for an analysis of the quantitative significance of economies of scale in motor cycle manufacture, unit cost and volume figures at the firm level are required but these were not available. In the absence of more accurate data, we proceeded on the assumption that scale economies are substantial and, since the major motor cycle industries in Japan, Italy and the U.K. are each dominated by a small number of relatively large firms, we used industry figures to obtain a broad indication of volume differences and hence of the extent to which firms in these industries might be reaping economies of scale. Initially, some simple tests of the relationship between an industry's domestic sales, its total production and export volume for all machines gave results which might be partially explained by the fact that motor cycle manufacture is a decreasing cost activity.[2] The available evidence indicated that for motor cycle manufacture as a whole, large-scale competitive exporting is associated with both volume production for the domestic market and large-scale total production. More interestingly, it appears that with increasing

1 G. Maxcy and A. Silberston, *The Motor Industry*, London: Allen and Unwin, 1959.

2 The regression equations, based upon data from the motor cycle industries of the U.K., E.E.C. and Japan for 1965 were:

$$(a)\ X = -10{,}196 + 0.38\,P \qquad r = 0{\cdot}985$$
$$(b)\ X = -658 + 0{\cdot}58D \qquad r = 0{\cdot}958$$

where X = total volume of exports,
P = total volume of production,
D = total volume of an industry's domestic market sales.

Both correlation coefficients were significant at the 0·1 per cent level.

domestic and total production, the *proportion* of output exported by an industry increases. Here, the size of an industry's domestic market and the extent to which it provides an opportunity for firms to reap most of the worthwhile economies of scale might be crucial. Certainly, with the aid of such relationships it becomes possible to understand the competitiveness of the Japanese motor cycle industry and its successful export performance with small motor cycles. In both 1964 and 1965, the Japanese industry produced an annual total of more than 2 million units of which 1·6 to 1·7 million were for the domestic market compared with the corresponding figures for the U.K. industry of under 110,000 and less than 75,000 units per annum, respectively. Even more convincing evidence on volume production in the Japanese industry can be seen by considering Table 7.14 which shows motor cycle output for the three largest firms in 1965.

TABLE 7.14 *Japanese Motor Cycle Production, 1965*

	Motor cycle production (units)					
Company	*Under 50 cc.*	*51–125 cc.*	*126–250 cc.*	*Over 250 cc.*	*Total*	*Percentage of total industry output*
Honda	457,220	791,383	119,309	97,850	1,465,762	66·2
Suzuki	110,403	218,749	12,215	—	341,367	15·4
Yamaha	46,304	164,777	27,525	5,452	244,058	11·0

Source: Midget Motor Manufacturers' Association of Japan.

Each of the three major firms shown in Table 7.14 achieved an annual volume which exceeded the output of the U.K. industry in 1965. Even if the U.K. industry had possessed a monopoly of U.K. domestic market sales during the period 1964-6, its annual average output for the domestic market would have only represented one-tenth of the Japanese industry's domestic sales.[1]

1 See Appendix B2, *The Japanese Motor Cycle Industry*. It must also be remembered that in selling its machines in the U.K. market, the Japanese industry incurs transport costs from Japan, and U.K. import duties. For some more general points on the relationship between exports and the size of the home market see, e.g. S. B. Linder, *An Essay on Trade and Transformation*, New York: Wiley, 1961; also, E. J. Mishan, *Twenty-One Popular Economic Fallacies*, London: Allen Lane, 1969.

Disaggregation of the motor cycle data into mopeds and scooters tended to confirm the relationship between an industry's domestic sales, its total production and the export volume of the product:[1] once again, a relationship which might be partly explained by the existence of scale economies. For mopeds, France[2] is the world's leading producer, with annual production exceeding 1·1 million units for 1964-6 and the industry's domestic sales being in excess of 800,000 for these years. During this same period, U.K. total moped production was about 3 per cent of the French figure. The French industry's large domestic market has resulted partially from the low price of mopeds relative to bicycles and also partially from legislative factors. Compared with the U.K. French legislation permits younger people to drive mopeds without the need for a licence. For scooters Italy is the world's leading manufacturer and the available evidence shows that the Italian scooter industry's annual output exceeded 300,000 units between 1964 and 1966,[3] with the industry's domestic sales varying between 120,000 and 290,000 units per annum for these years: such figures are considerably in excess of British scooter output.

To summarize, the evidence suggests the existence of substantial scale economies in motor cycle manufacture and these might explain why exports are associated with large-scale total production and volume production for an industry's home market. We do, of course, appreciate that more evidence is required not only on the quantitative significance of economies of scale but also on their contribution to explaining the U.K. industry's long-run export performance. Moreover, there still remains the outstanding question of how the firms in a nation's motor cycle industry actually achieve the scale of production to obtain most of the worthwhile economies of scale: the size of the domestic market might provide one explanation

1 For example, for mopeds, the regression equations based on data from E.E.C. and the U.K. for 1965 were:

$$(a)\ X = -3{,}886 + 0{\cdot}28\,P \qquad r = 0{\cdot}96$$
$$(b)\ X = -1{,}592 + 0{\cdot}37\,D \qquad r = 0{\cdot}92.$$

Variables as in previous equations. Both correlation coefficients were significant at the 0·1 per cent level.

2 The industry is dominated by one major moped manufacturer.

3 A period after the scooter boom of the late 1950s. Two firms dominate Italian scooter production.

but here more evidence is required on such factors as comparative advantage, *per capita* incomes, the degree of tariff protection, managerial performance and sales effort in the home and overseas markets. Our own exercise has simply established that motor cycle exports can probably be related to a scale effect such that given a level of demand sufficient to achieve capacity-working then, as a result of economies of scale, a firm's unit costs will tend to be lower the larger the scale of output; costs will, in turn, be one of the determinants of product prices and hence of profitability and competitiveness. This long-run relationship differs from the pressure hypothesis which predicts that the short-run export performance of both large- and small-scale producers will be subject to short-run variations in the pressure of domestic demand. Thus, the pressure hypothesis is essentially short run and applies at any given scale of production but in the long run, other things being equal, unit costs decrease as output increases to a larger scale with consequent favourable long-run effects on exports.

Conclusion

Motor cycles within the U.K. provide a useful study of the workings of a market. In response to changing tastes and preferences, new products, mainly of foreign origin, were introduced into the domestic market. In other words, there was a foreign supply response to changing tastes and preferences in the U.K. market. Whilst the introduction of new foreign sources of supply into the home market probably 'shocked' the British industry into increased efficiency and into an attempt to increase the overseas sales of its existing product range, there was still some reduction in the domestic resources allocated to the U.K. motor cycle industry as both domestic and world consumers demanded Italian, French and Japanese machines. In the first two sections of this chapter we have shown that the U.K. industry's domestic sales and its exports are not perfect substitutes. We have also shown that the industry's export volume has increased, despite a decline in its volume of home market sales. For the U.K. industry, the rank correlation coefficient between exports and domestic volume for the period 1959-66 was $r = -0{\cdot}48$ but this was not significant. Finally, our analysis of the U.K. industry's competitiveness simply confirmed the degree of specialization in the world motor cycle market with France producing mopeds, Italy specializing in scooters, Japan concerned with small conventional motor cycles and the U.K. being most successful with large machines. With this general understanding of developments in the motor cycle market, we shall proceed to present the results of our empirical work on the pressure hypothesis, beginning with our interview and questionnaire results.

III. INTERVIEW AND QUESTIONNAIRE RESULTS

Introduction

Our tests of the pressure hypothesis can be divided into two distinct parts. This section contains the results from our interviews and questionnaire and includes evidence not only on the pressure hypothesis but also on a number of related aspects of the export behaviour of motor cycle firms. Unfortunately, since firms in both the motor cycle and cycle industries were reluctant to provide statistical data, we were unable to test each individual firm's reply to our questions on the pressure hypothesis. In these circumstances, our econometric analysis of the pressure hypothesis was confined to the industry level, the results of which are presented in the final section of this chapter.

Although the results of the motor cycle questionnaire are based on a numerically small sample of four firms, two large and two small, these enterprises accounted for over 90 per cent of the motor cycle industry's volume of output. The interviewing of firms was undertaken in 1966: three firms were interviewed and a fourth replied to a postal questionnaire. The detailed questionnaire evidence is presented in Appendix A. In this section, we shall simply state some of the more significant results and these will be grouped under the general headings of allocative decisions, the profitability of exports, pricing and excess demand and the pressure hypothesis.

Allocative Decisions

In 1965-6, the larger firms in our sample exported a larger proportion of their motor cycle output than the smaller firms, the relevant percentages being 65 to 70 per cent and 50 to 55 per cent, respectively. Table 7.15 shows some additional evidence on the proportion of factory production exported for three firms. From the table, it will be seen that Triumph and Norton machines are especially 'export-orientated'.

TABLE 7.15 *The Proportion of Output Exported* (*Volume*)

Firm		*1962-3*	*1963-4*	*1964-5*	*1966 (6 months)*
		%	%	%	%
B.S.A.	B.S.A.	64·3	57·8	61·8	58·6
Triumph	B.S.A.	68·7	73·2	80·0	82·1
Norton	A.M.C.	68·5	65·7	74·2	79·1
Matchless/A.J.S.	A.M.C.	71·1	52·7	66·3	47·8
Greeves		54·3	58·3	55·8	64·2

Notes: (1) Triumph is part of the B.S.A. group.
(2) Norton, Matchless and A.J.S. formed Associated Motor Cycles Ltd, which since our interviews has been acquired by Manganese Bronze Ltd.

Not surprisingly, for the firms in the sample, the U.S.A. was a dominant export market and this merely confirmed the industry's statistics which indicated that by the mid-1960s over 80 per cent of motor cycle exports went to this market. For one of the larger firms, sales to the U.S. market were both more important and more profitable than in the home market. Similarly, one of the smaller firms allocated 80 per cent of its exports to the U.S.A. Other motor cycle export markets for our sample firms included E.E.C., E.F.T.A., Australia and South Africa.

Both the larger firms stated that they would prefer a different proportionate division of exports and domestic sales, with an increased proportion of the latter. In relation to this desired change, one firm anticipated that with future increases in its labour force, it would be able to increase its home deliveries. The remaining firm tended to be more pessimistic and maintained that only marginal home gains could be achieved and these were generally at the expense of competitors. Moreover, this pessimism was reinforced by the view that the home market was no longer a substantial source of sales for large machines. It seems, then, that both large firms, exporting 65 to 70 per cent of their 1965 output, were not achieving an 'ideal' allocation of output between home and export markets.[1] By comparison, the two smaller firms with exports accounting for 50 to 55 per cent of their output desired no further change in the proportionate division of sales between exports and the domestic market.

The attitude of firms towards the proportionate division of sales between home and export markets might have some interesting implications for the pressure hypothesis. In so far as firms do not wish to increase the proportion of output exported, then such an attitude might place a constraint on the export effect of a domestic deflation. Certainly in the motor cycle industry sample during 1965-6, it seems that there was no desire for a higher proportion of exports within total output. Of course, other things being equal, if the motor cycle firms maintain proportions and increase output or increase their proportion of domestic sales for a given output, the result will favour the balance of payments through either exports and/or import substitution. In this context of the relationship between the national interest and firms' attitudes, it is rather illuminating to quote one authority from the industry: 'Although it is often policy to subscribe to the national interest, etc. . . . refraining from more matter of fact commercial reactions, it is my experience that companies trade where the appropriate volume and/or lucrativeness is most readily or easily obtained. Personal survival or profit, in terms of companies, is much more real . . . than the more remote national economic survival.' The reference to company survival is consistent with the ways in which firms described their export policies. Obviously, in order to survive, companies require profits and exports form one source of revenue for this purpose.[2] In our questionnaire, we attempted to obtain some additional information on the attitude of firms towards exports.

Each firm in the sample stated that it wished to encourage exports as a method of diversifying markets. In fact, the larger firms emphasized the need to diversify in markets other than the U.S.A., despite the fact that for one of the firms, the U.S. market was more

[1] In this context, 'ideal' requires further analysis and needs to be assessed against a statement of a firm's objective function.

[2] See, e.g. F. Machlup, 'Theories of the Firm: Marginalist, Behavioural, Managerial', *American Economic Review*, March 1967.

profitable than the home market. For one of the small companies, a decision to enter the export market was made in the late 1950s as an 'insurance' against '. . . collapse of the home market'. Two firms, one large and one small, expressed a desire to increase exports but in each case this was compatible with the aim of diversification. Although it is not possible to be more precise without a detailed statement of a firm's objectives, it seems reasonable to regard diversification as a means of reducing the range of fluctuations in net receipts. For the motor cycle industry, the emphasis upon diversification must, to some extent, reflect the competitive conditions in both the home and world markets.

Against this background of attitudes towards exports, all firms in the sample reported a rising trend in both the value and volume of overseas sales for the years 1961-6, although for one respondent, the increase had only applied to the larger machines. These trends were consistent with the industry's data for the same period. However, all firms felt that there existed a number of factors preventing a further increase in exports. For three enterprises, labour shortages were regarded as an important short- or long-run constraint on exports. For such firms, it might be reasonable to expect that a domestic deflation which released geographically- and occupationally-mobile labour resources for alternative uses might result in a favourable effect on exports. In general, however, this proposition received little support from the evidence which is presented below. Within the sample, only one firm stated that prices were both a short- and long-run constraint: this firm also listed capacity, delivery dates and export finance as further short-run factors preventing an increase in its exports. None of the firms indicated that government policies were an important constraint.

The firms used a variety of selling methods for their exports, ranging from wholly-owned U.S. distributors to export sales representatives. Three of the firms in the sample, including the largest, used both the Board of Trade export services and the E.C.G.D. The interesting feature of this variety was that the larger firms used a greater range of selling methods than the smaller concerns but there was no one method which was common to all companies. One firm explained the variety of its selling methods as a response to the individual and different characteristics of each country's market: 'There is no conformity of method: each country, the agent, etc. requires its own treatment. . . .'

The Profitability of Exports

In answer to the profitability question, firms generally agreed that exports were less profitable than home sales. There was one exception. One firm regarded the U.S. market as *more* profitable than the domestic market and this greater profitability was apparently due to the fact that it was a market for the larger, high unit-value machines which included a greater margin: the firm stated that its remaining export markets were slightly less profitable than domestic sales. In general, the motor cycle firms attributed the lower profitability of exports to the greater competition which existed in overseas markets. Higher selling costs, the greater risk of less and lower export prices were given as additional but subsidiary factors.

Given that firms regarded exports as less profitable than home sales, we returned to the question of why do firms export. The firms in our sample were exporting 50 per cent or more of their output and this was justified in terms of obtaining security through market diversification and through the fact that exports provided the possibility of expansion which was harder or impossible to achieve at home. Here, it must be remembered that the U.K. domestic market has been dominated by the demand for small machines, many of which were imported. The U.K. industry has been more successful with large motor cycles, but the domestic market for these machines has far from substantial. Thus, if the more profitable home market, especially for the British industry's products is relatively small and declining, then in order to increase or even maintain the sales of a given product range, it becomes necessary to obtain overseas orders. As one firm explained, 'The development of high-performance motor cycles requires a substantial outlet to justify costs: the only substantial outlets are export markets'.

The lower profitability of motor cycle exports might be used to support the hypothesis that in the years prior to 1966, the U.K.'s export performance might have been improved if overseas sales had been more profitable. The fact of lower profitability for motor cycle exports might have meant that manufacturers '. . . found it less worth their while to devote their energies to exporting and this may have affected design, quality, delivery and salesmanship'.[1] Against this view, there is apparently the superficial evidence that our sample of firms exported at least half their output and that such a performance could not have been achieved if such variables as quality and salesmanship had been neglected. Here, the emphasis must be on the words 'apparently' and 'superficial', since such evidence does not refute the proposition that, other things being equal, with increased profitability, motor cycle exports might have been even higher in the years up to 1966.

Pricing and Excess Demand

In the field of pricing, firms generally agreed that price changes for existing products were made on a selective basis and that the prices of new products were established by considering estimated costs and modifying the resulting 'cost-plus' price according to market conditions (e.g. competition; prices of existing products). No firm determined new product prices solely on the basis of estimated costs.[2] In explaining its pricing policy, one firm maintained that overheads were recovered on motor cycles and profits were earned on spares, whilst a second firm stated that though it aimed to make a profit on large machines, it might agree to a marginal transaction with small machines.

For two firms, export prices 'ex factory' were not identical to home prices for the same products. For these companies, one stated that export prices were determined by competition, whilst the other relied upon 'individual negotiation'. In some cases, export prices were modified for large customers, new customers for existing products and (rarely) the price changes of foreign competitors. From the two remaining firms, one stated that its home and export prices 'ex factory' were identical, whilst the other maintained that these prices were identical for the U.S. market but not for other overseas markets.

1 N.E.D.C., *Export Trends.* H.M.S.O., London, 1963.

2 This was an especially interesting result in view of the fact that '. . . most, if not all, of the investigations which have led to the suggestion that full-cost pricing might be the rule, have relied entirely upon the method of the questionnaire', I. F. Pearce, 'A Study of Price Policy', *Economica*, vol. 23, 1956.

Firms which are reluctant to vary prices in response to an increase in demand might attempt to 'ration' their existing output through variations in the length of their order books, and consequently, in the delivery dates for motor cycles. For example, one of the relatively smaller firms revealed that the time interval between the receipt of an order and its despatch had varied between twelve months or more in 1959-60, two weeks in 1961 and four to five months in 1966. A similar-sized firm stated that its delivery dates had varied from six to nine months during the years 1961-6. One of the larger firms revealed that it worked to a 'season' and did not accept orders beyond the current season: about two-thirds of the year's production was usually accounted for by firm orders.

In a period of increasing demand, with order books lengthening, firms differed in their methods of allocating their available output between home and export markets. All our evidence suggested that rather than increase prices in such situations, queues are allowed to form and the motor cycle firms determined a customer's ranking in the queue by giving preference to export or large customers, to new customers or to the 'first-in' (such a policy was regarded as beneficial to long-term export orders). It was rather interesting to observe that two firms specifically gave preference to export customers, but in one case this appeared to be a rational response since overseas sales accounted for 70 per cent of its output and its U.S. exports were more profitable than domestic sales. All the firms suggested the existence of an excess demand for motor cycles in 1966 by maintaining that production and not sales was the constraint on output. In this context, there was unanimous agreement that labour shortages were the major restriction on production although two firms mentioned a shortage of capital and one suggested a shortage of suitable land, as further restrictive factors. The shortage of labour was perhaps not surprising since the firms in the sample were located in the Midlands and South-East.

Exports and Domestic Demand: The Pressure Hypothesis

Three of the firms felt that exports were not significantly affected during a period of peak domestic demand for their products. A variety of plausible explanations can be suggested for this reaction and many of these have already been given in our earlier, more theoretical treatment of firms and the pressure hypothesis. At this stage, we shall simply adopt the position that an assessment of the characteristics of the respondents to this question might be informative in suggesting further hypotheses. One feature which was common to the three firms was that they exported between 55 and 70 per cent of their output. For these firms, the home market tended to be a 'residual' and, in a situation of excess demand and labour shortages, it seems reasonable to expect them to give priority to their much larger overseas sales.[1] We obtained some evidence suggesting that, either directly or indirectly, export orders received such priority. The remaining firm in our sample, company *M*, stated that during a period of peak domestic demand some exports were lost due to lengthening delivery dates and the lack of capacity: this reply was consistent with the predicted effects of the pressure hypothesis.

During a period of sharp domestic deflation the firms generally agreed that exports were not significantly affected. However, two firms qualified their replies. One large company maintained that in export markets other than the U.S.A., small machines tended to benefit from a deflation since, with lower home sales, greater attention could be paid to these exports. By comparison, this company's exports to the U.S.A. – its major market – were not significantly affected by a deflation. Such a reply suggests that the export effects of a deflation might differ between geographical markets for different products, the differences reflecting the priority given by a firm to particular export markets. In addition, a smaller firm stated that in a deflation, exports benefited from quicker delivery in the short run, but in the long run, exports were not significantly affected. Both these qualifications can be regarded as providing some support for the pressure hypothesis.

Company *M*, which exported 50 per cent of output and which had replied that in a period of peak demand some exports were lost, now suggested that in a deflation its exports were not significantly affected. It explained that a large proportion of its domestic sales were to local authorities and apparently the demands from this source tended to remain unaffected by a domestic deflation, so

[1] Especially in view of the limited size of the domestic market for large motor cycles.

providing the firm with what it regarded as a 'guaranteed' home market. In fact, in 1966, company *M* felt that, at a maximum, a domestic deflation would only affect about 20 per cent of its volume of output and, in practice, it was expected that the figure would be much smaller.

For the sample as a whole, the general conclusion seems to be that firms felt that exports were not significantly affected by a domestic deflation. Once again, this might be partially explained by the fact that for the sample, domestic sales accounted for between 30 and 50 per cent of a firm's output so that, to a large extent, export markets might be regarded as 'insulating' a firm from some of the major effects of a decline in domestic sales. Furthermore, for a firm producing at capacity and allocating say 70 per cent of its output to exports, a 10 per cent decrease in home market sales could be exactly 'offset' by a much smaller percentage increase in exports and in these circumstances, it is conceivable that the absolute and percentage magnitudes of any rise in exports might be so small as to lead a businessman to conclude that 'exports were not significantly affected'. At the same time, it will be remembered that the U.K. industry's domestic sales have consisted of mopeds, scooters and conventional machines but with exports it has been most successful with large motor cycles so that in a deflation, some of the products which cannot be sold on the home market are not likely to be the ones which will be most competitive in overseas markets. Finally, there might be some significance in the fact that no firm stated that in a period of peak demand, exports were assisted because of lower unit costs and during a deflation, no company indicated that exports were adversely affected because of a rise in unit costs. It is possible that with batch production techniques together with the large proportion of output exported, changes in domestic demand were not associated with substantial changes in unit costs: such a proposition can be regarded as no more than extremely tentative.

All the firms responded to a domestic deflation by an increased sales effort in the home and/or overseas markets but, if these replies are to be consistent with the relationship between exports and domestic deflation it can only be assumed that an increased sales effort overseas leads to a marginal rise in exports. In fact, one firm qualified its reply by stating that with its overseas sales effort, 'everything or nearly everything was being done already'. These replies provided some support for the view that the export market is not a 'sink' into which surplus production capacity can be speedily redeployed. In addition to an increased sales effort, three firms indicated that they would respond to a domestic deflation by reducing total output but this response was given a low ranking. Two firms indicated that they might change their product prices in either the home or overseas market and, rather surprisingly, only one firm stated that it would produce for stocks.

Conclusions

Of the many interesting points which emerged from our field work, one merits some further emphasis. In making a policy choice between home and export sales, the attitude of at least one firm was that '. . . this is where cold-blooded appraisal in terms of profitability or losses takes charge of the individual company, for . . . neither it nor its shareholders are willing to risk commercial suicide in the interests of national well-being'. It was, in fact, noticeable that not one firm gave 'prestige' as one of the benefits of exporting. Such attitudes suggest that the objective functions of the motor cycle firms are such that simple governmental appeals to firms to increase exports will be relatively ineffective.

To conclude our analysis of the interviews and questionnaires, we can state that the evidence suggested that the majority of motor cycle firms felt that exports were not significantly affected by the pressure of domestic demand. However, this was a majority and not a unanimous reply, a fact which indicates that the export effect of pressure varies between firms within an industry. For periods of both peak demand and deflation, we obtained some limited support for the pressure hypothesis at the level of the individual firm: in each phase of the cycle, at least one firm in the sample reacted in the way predicted by the pressure hypothesis. Furthermore, whilst firms were quite specific in their replies to questions on the relationship between exports and domestic demand, it must also be pointed out that in answering other questions, some firms referred to the problem of labour shortages as a constraint on exports! In these circumstances, qualitative tests of the pressure hypothesis are not very satisfactory:

ideally, data are required to test the hypothesis for the individual firm. In the absence of such data, we proceeded to test the hypothesis at the industry level. At least our industry analysis had one great advantage over the qualitative tests at the firm level: the latter were only able to analyse reactions by numbers of firms and, where reactions were indeterminate,[1] and in the absence of an adequate weighting system, it was not possible to aggregate questionnaire replies and make predictions for the whole industry.

IV. AN ECONOMETRIC ANALYSIS FOR THE INDUSTRY

In the absence of data from individual motor cycle firms, we were obliged to test the pressure hypothesis at the industry level. We constructed a series of multiple regression equations in which, as dependent variables, we analysed both variations in the level of U.K. motor cycle exports to the U.S. and Canadian markets and the U.K. industry's share of total motor cycle imports into each of these markets.[2] The choice of markets was determined by data availability and by the fact that the U.S.A. was the major market for U.K. motor cycle exports. In addition, since they are adjacent markets, we felt that it might be interesting to compare the U.S.A. and Canada. The analysis of these markets was based on quarterly data for the period 1958-66. Dummy variables were included in the regressions in order to account for the seasonal variation and a time-trend was also incorporated into the equations.

For the pressure of domestic demand variable, we employed two basic measures. First, we considered those measures which might be regarded as directly reflecting the pressure of domestic demand on the motor cycle industry, namely the total value of the U.K. industry's domestic sales and the unemployment rate for the motor cycle and cycle industry.[3] Second, we considered measures which reflect the general pressure of domestic demand at the economy level, namely

1 For example, where the firms' reactions differed between markets or where the reply was 'exports are not significantly affected'.

2 Both the level of exports and market shares were based on value figures for motor cycles and parts. Owing to the absence of a suitable index, these and all other value figures in this section are in current prices.

3 It was not possible to separate the motor cycle sector from the rest of the industry.

the unemployment rates for Great Britain and the Midlands region.[1] We appreciate that these various measures are not immune from criticism: for example, our measure of the motor cycle industry's domestic sales excluded imports and this choice represented an attempt to obtain an indicator of domestic demand which reflected pressure on the U.K. industry's resources. Nevertheless, given their limitations, we obtained some interesting and significant results from our level of exports and shares models, and we shall proceed by reporting on each of these models in turn.

In Table 7.16 below, we present some of the data for the Canadian market which simply provides a general background for our analysis:[2] the corresponding data for the U.S. market has already been presented in Table 7.12. Table 7.16 clearly shows a long-run declining trend in the U.K. share of imports into the Canadian market, a decline which also occurred in the adjacent U.S. market. In such circumstances, our shares model was concerned with explaining the deviations of import share from its declining trend.

TABLE 7.16 *Canadian Motor Cycle Imports, 1958-66*

Year	*Total imports*	*U.K. share of imports*
	($000)†	(%)
1958	1,454	42·5
1959	1,575	35·4
1960	1,701	31·0
1961	1,592	29·3
1962	1,466	30·7
1963	1,796	24·0
1964	4,230	10·0
1965	10,369	7·6
1966*	12,668	11·0

* Based on data for first three quarters only.
† Imports are in Canadian $.

In order to explain variations in the level of U.K. motor cycle exports to particular markets, we constructed a number of log-linear regressions with overseas and domestic demand as independent

[1] There is some concentration of motor cycle firms in this region.
[2] Our regressions used quarterly data.

variables.[1] As an indicator of overseas demand, we used the foreign market's imports and our measures of domestic demand were based on the value of the industry's domestic sales and the national unemployment rate. The results of the analysis suggested that for all equations for both the U.S. and Canadian markets, the overseas demand measure made a significant and positive contribution to explaining variations in the level of U.K. motor cycle exports to each market. For all equations, the estimated coefficients were in the range 0·56 to 0·73 which, as a log-linear relationship, indicated that the partial elasticity of U.K. motor cycle exports to the U.S.A. and Canada with respect to overseas demand in these markets was substantially less than unity. Since we have already commented upon the general relevance of this partial elasticity,[2] we shall merely state the result and remind the reader of its implications for our shares model. As for the domestic demand variable in our equations, only in the case of the U.S. market and only when using a measure based on the industry's domestic sales, was it possible to obtain a significant relationship with exports, but the sign of the pressure coefficient was positive. For exports to the Canadian market, we did not succeed in estimating a statistically significant coefficient for the pressure variable. Some examples of our results are presented in Table 7.17.

In view of the relative lack of success with the pressure variable in the level of exports model, we shall proceed to examine its performance in a shares model. In such a model, the results will depend upon the assumptions made about the partial elasticity of U.K. exports with respect to overseas demand: we shall assume an elasticity of unity. Having stated the assumption of unit elasticity, it can only be stressed that to the extent that the true elasticity is less than one – and the above evidence, if accepted, suggests that this might be the case – then a shares model will tend to overestimate the magnitude of any negative pressure effect.[3] It was, however, felt that a comparison of the results of the level of exports and shares models might be interesting: in fact, there was no inconsistency between the results from the two models.

1 The basic model was: $X = aD^{\alpha} M^{\beta} e^{kt}$.

2 See Chapter 2 and also R. J. Ball *et al.*, 'Export Performance and The Internal Pressure of Demand', *Economic Journal*, September 1966.

3 See Chapters 2 and 5.

TABLE 7.17 *The Level of U.K. Motor Cycle Exports to the U.S.A. and Canada*

	Coefficients of					
Exports	log *HS*	log *U*	log *M*	*t*	$\bar{R}^2$	*d*
1. log X_{US}	0·29** (0·09)	...	0·66** (0·11)	−0·007 (0·01)	0·892	1·94
2. log X_{US}	...	−0·30 (0·20)	0·73** (0·12)	−0·02 (0·01)	0·863	1·62
3. log X_C	0·08 (0·15)	...	0·56** (0·11)	−0·02 (0·01)	0·852	1·95
4. log X_C	...	0·23 (0·29)	0·63** (0·11)	−0·02 (0·008)	0·854	1·96

Notes: (1) log X_{US} and log X_C are logs of value of U.K. motor cycle exports to the U.S.A. and Canada, expressed in U.S. and Canadian dollars, respectively.
(2) log *HS* = log of deviations from trend of value of U.K. motor cycle industry's domestic sales.
(3) log *U* = log of unemployment rate for Great Britain.
(4) log *M* = log of value of motor cycle imports. In Equations 1 and 2, log *M* refers to U.S. motor cycle imports (U.S. $) whilst in 3 and 4 it refers to Canadian imports (Canadian $).
(5) Dummy variables were used for seasonal adjustment.
(6) *t* = time-trend, 1958 I to 1966 II.
(8) $\bar{R}^2$ is coefficient of multiple determination adjusted for degrees of freedom.
(9) *d* is Durbin-Watson statistic.
(10) ** significant at the 1 per cent level.
* significant at the 5 per cent level.

To explain the U.K.'s share of a market's motor cycle imports, we constructed a number of linear and log-linear equations using all our various measures of domestic demand as independent variables, each equation incorporating a time-trend and dummy variables for seasonal adjustment.[1] For the U.K. industry's share of total U.S. motor cycle imports, the only internal pressure variable which proved to be statistically significant was based upon the value of the industry's

[1] The basic models subject to seasonal adjustment were:

$$S = \alpha_0 + \alpha_1 D + \alpha_2 t$$
$$S = \alpha_0 D^{\alpha_1} e^{kt}$$

domestic sales but, as in the level of exports model, the sign of the estimated coefficient was positive: this is not consistent with the predictions of the pressure hypothesis. The introduction into a linear regression of a two quarterly lag for the value of the industry's domestic sales reduced both the statistical significance of the pressure coefficient and the amount of explanation offered by the whole equation. Further linear regressions, using the industry, regional and national unemployment rates, provided some support for the estimated positive relationship between internal demand pressure and deviations of market share in the U.S. from its trend, but none of the unemployment variables were significant at the 5 per cent level. The construction of log-linear regressions incorporating measures of pressure based on the value of the motor cycle industry's domestic sales and the national unemployment rate simply confirmed the previous analysis. Table 7.18 presents some examples of our results.

TABLE 7.18 *The U.K. Industry's Share of U.S. Motor Cycle Imports, 1958-66*

Share of U.S. market	*Coefficients of* HS	log HS	U	log U	t	$\bar{R}^2$	d
1. S_{US}	0·0029** (0·0011)	...	...	...	−0·99 (0·13)	0·792	1·81
2. S_{US}	...	...	−5·05 (3·52)	...	−1·25 (0·15)	0·753	1·55
3. log S_{US}	...	0·22* (0·10)	...	...	−0·04 (0·004)	0·813	1·74
4. log S_{US}	...	...	...	−0·26 (0·22)	−0·05 (0·005)	0·792	1·62

Notes: (1) Share figures are based on percentages.
(2) HS = value of U.K. motor cycle industry's domestic sales (£000).
(3) U = unemployment rate for Great Britain.
(4) Remaining details as for Table 7.17.

The results suggest that for the U.S. market, the pressure hypothesis is not consistent with the facts and that for motor cycles in this market an increase in the domestic demand for the product in Britain has had favourable effects on short-run movements in the U.K.'s share of U.S. imports.[1] In fact, by using Model 1 in Table 7.18, it was estimated that if domestic demand for the British industry's motor cycles in 1960 had been maintained at the peak level of the first quarter of that year, then, other things being equal, British motor cycle exports to the U.S.A. for 1960 would have been some £170,000 greater or about 7 per cent higher than the level actually achieved. These figures are, however, simply illustrative, their purpose being to indicate some orders of magnitude which might be placed upon the 'loss' of exports to the U.S. associated with a *decline* in the value of the U.K. motor cycle industry's domestic sales. Before commenting further on these results, we need to consider the evidence from the adjacent Canadian market.

For the Canadian market, we performed similar tests to those undertaken for the U.S.A., but with completely contrasting results. For the linear and log-linear shares models applied to the Canadian market, we found that the only measure of the pressure of internal demand which gave statistically significant results was the national unemployment rate and, in contrast with the U.S.A., the signs of the coefficients were consistent with the predictions of the pressure hypothesis. The remaining indicators of pressure when applied in linear and log-linear form tended to provide further supporting evidence but none of the coefficients for the various pressure indicators were significant at the 5 per cent level. Here, the interesting point was that such indicators as the value of domestic sales and the industry's unemployment rate, both of which might be regarded as directly reflecting pressure on the motor cycle industry, failed to provide any statistically significant relationship with deviations of share from its trend in the Canadian market. The introduction into a linear regression of a two quarterly lag for the value of the industry's domestic sales did not result in any improvement. Some examples of our results from the Canadian market are shown in Table 7.19 below.

Table 7.19 shows that the unemployment rate for Great Britain is positively associated with deviations from trend for the U.K.'s share of Canadian motor cycle imports. Since national unemploy-

[1] Deviations from trend. Table 7.18 indicates that the U.K.'s share of U.S. imports has fluctuated around a long-run declining trend.

TABLE 7.19 *The U.K. Motor Cycle Industry's Share of Canadian Imports, 1958-66*

Share of Canadian market	Coefficients of *HS*	log *HS*	*U*	*t*	$\bar{R}^2$	*d*
1. *Sc*	−0·0015 (0·0009)	...	...	−1·08 (0·12)	0·767	2·00
2. *Sc*	...	...	6·01* (2·78)	0·90 (0·11)	0·783	2·01
3. log *Sc*	...	−0·24 (0·16)	...	−0·06 (0·006)	0·708	1·43

Notes: Details are the same as for Tables 7.17 and 7.18.

ment rates increase as the pressure of domestic demand at the economy level decreases, the sign of the coefficient for the unemployment variable in Table 7.19 is consistent with the predictions of the pressure hypothesis. By using Model 2 in Table 7.19, together with some additional assumptions, it is possible to estimate the 'loss' of U.K. motor cycle exports to the Canadian market which resulted from maintaining a relatively high pressure of internal demand. Assuming other things remain equal, and taking 2 per cent as a 'target' rate of unemployment for Great Britain, we can assess the effects on motor cycle exports to Canada of allowing domestic demand in the economy to rise, so giving national unemployment rates of less than 2 per cent. In 1964, the national unemployment rate varied between 1·4 and 1·9 per cent and we estimated that at such relatively high pressures of demand U.K. motor cycle exports to the Canadian market were some £40,000, or about 30 per cent, below the level which would have resulted if unemployment had been maintained at 2 per cent. A similar calculation for the following year, 1965, resulted in an export 'loss' to the Canadian market of some £130,000 worth of motor cycles and parts, equivalent to about 50 per cent of U.K. motor cycle exports to Canada for that year. Little attention should be given to the rather spurious degree of accuracy shown by these figures: as previously suggested, they are merely meant to provide some general orders of magnitude and they are sensitive to the assumption about the partial elasticity of U.K.

motor cycle exports with respect to overseas demand. Where this elasticity is substantially less than one, then the size of the pressure coefficient in the Canadian shares model will be correspondingly reduced. Moreover, it might be argued that attempts to maintain permanently a higher national unemployment rate might result in a major change in the basic structural relationships in the economy, so invalidating estimates of export 'loss' based on a completely different set of relationships. However, given these limitations, it is relevant to observe that the estimates are by no means insignificant when it is remembered that they refer to one U.K. export product and one export market.

The fact that changes in demand pressure in the U.K. appear to have different and opposite results on the U.S. and Canadian markets requires some further explanation.[1] The interesting point lies in the *opposite* direction of the pressure effect as between adjacent markets. Here, the evidence appears to suggest that the movements of motor cycle imports into both markets and the choice of measures of domestic demand pressure do not provide the basis for an explanation.[2] Furthermore, the positive pressure effect for the U.S. market is the one which is perhaps more intriguing since it cannot be easily explained away by biases in the estimation procedure. The basis for a plausible explanation of our results might be derived from the attitudes of motor cycle firms towards the U.S. and Canadian markets, the former being regarded as 'more attractive' because of its relative importance in the U.K. industry's total sales and its profitability resulting from the substantial market for the U.K. industry's traditional specialism, namely large motor cycles. The questionnaire provided some support for this explanation of our regression results, one major motor cycle firm stating that its U.S. exports, consisting mainly of large machines, were not significantly affected in a domestic deflation, whilst its exports to other markets, especially of small machines, apparently benefited from lower home

[1] The results are, of course, sensitive to the assumptions made about the partial elasticity of U.K. motor cycle exports with respect to overseas demand.

[2] Movements in U.S. and Canadian motor cycle imports were positively associated. Also, an examination of the relationship between the U.K. industry's domestic sales and the national unemployment rate showed that whilst they moved in similar directions during 1958 and early 1960, the period 1958-66 as a whole was dominated by the indicators moving in opposite directions.

sales: for this firm, U.S. exports were more profitable than its home sales, and, in periods of excess demand, the firm gave preference to its export customers. We realize, of course, that this explanation of our regression results is far from complete and that more information is required not only on the objective functions of firms and their attitudes to various export markets but also on the product composition of U.K. domestic demand and exports to the U.S.A. and Canada, together with an assessment of the degree of capacity-utilization for each of the relevant product lines.[1] An analysis of capacity-utilization needs to be included since it will determine a firm's position on its short-run marginal cost curve and, in Chapter 4, it was found that for a profit maximizer under imperfect competition, a given change in domestic demand will result in opposite effects on exports, depending on whether the marginal cost curve is rising or falling. Thus, one explanation of our contrasting regression results as between the U.S. and Canadian markets is based upon differences in the attitudes of firms towards these markets and upon possible differences in the product composition of exports and the degree of capacity-utilization between the various products exported to the markets.

Conclusions

From our interviewing and questionnaire results, with all the problems of holding 'other things constant', the majority of firms suggested that total exports were not significantly affected by the pressure of domestic demand. At the industry level, our regression results of share of particular markets as distinct from the level of exports found that short-run movements in shares were a function of the pressure of domestic demand but that the relationship was positive for the U.S. and negative for Canada. We found that our questionnaire results had anticipated that the effect of changes in the pressure of internal demand might differ between geographical markets, the difference partly reflecting the fact that motor cycles are not a homogeneous product group. Of course, where the pressure

1 From our limited study, we obtained some support for the hypothesis that the U.K. industry's domestic sales and its exports to the U.S. and Canada consisted of different product groups. Also, see Section I of this chapter, where our analysis of the U.K. industry's total output and its exports indicated excess capacity for large conventional motor cycles.

effect has opposite results in different overseas markets then, at the disaggregated level, rational public policy decisions need to be based upon considerations of the relative size of each foreign market and hence the 'net export-effect' of any given change in the pressure of internal demand. Also, it is perhaps relevant to stress that our regression results have shown that the U.K. motor cycle industry's share of U.S. and Canadian imports has fluctuated around a declining trend. It is possible that this might have been a factor which dominated our questionnaire results, especially in view of the difficulty of 'holding other things constant' in any questionnaire. We appreciate that time-trends conceal a 'multitude of sins' but it seems plausible to suggest that the long-run declining trend in share reflects the U.K. motor cycle industry's declining competitiveness. We have already presented some evidence on competitiveness and we must stress that this is only offered as a possible hypothesis and one which certainly requires more rigorous testing: such tests are beyond the scope of this project which is concerned with short-run movements in share and hence with fluctuations around its trend. For the motor cycle industry, we can only reiterate our major results, namely that the pressure effect differs between geographical markets, with the Canadian market providing support for the basic pressure hypothesis.

Chapter 8

THE U.K. PEDAL CYCLE INDUSTRY

Our analysis of the U.K. cycle industry has been divided into three sections, the first of which will provide general factual information on some of the significant trends in the bicycle market prior to the presentation of the results of our field work and statistical analysis. In order to simplify the analysis, bicycles are defined as pedal cycles: mopeds, some of which are manufactured by the cycle industry, are included in the analysis of the motor cycle market.[1]

I. THE U.K. CYCLE MARKET

The U.K. industry's sales and export record in complete cycles for the period 1958-66 is shown in Table 8.1.

Table 8.1 reveals a number of significant points. First, throughout the period, the industry exported more than 50 per cent of its output so that its export sales exceeded those in the domestic market. Secondly, the volume figures reveal a substantial decline in output. In fact, annual output fell by over 700,000 units between 1958 and 1966, with export sales accounting for over 60 per cent of the decline. However, in spite of this decline, the proportion of the industry's output exported was virtually unchanged for the years 1958 and 1966 and, between these years, the proportion generally reached 65 to 70 per cent. The decline in the industry's output, which has been evident since the early 1950s, can be explained by a combination of factors.

Evidence suggests that once a certain level of income has been

1 See, Board of Trade, *Business Monitor*, Production Series: *Motor Cycles, Three-Wheel Vehicles, Pedal Cycles and Parts*, London: H.M.S.O., December 1966.

TABLE 8.1 *The U.K. Cycle Industry*

Year	*Value (£000s)* *Total*	*For export*	*Exports as percentage of total value*	*Volume (000)* *Total*	*For export*	*Exports as percentage of total volume*
1958	21,047	12,443	59·0	2,156	1,361	63·1
1959	22,174	11,953	53·9	2,213	1,288	58·2
1960	21,741	13,212	60·8	2,278	1,508	66·1
1961	18,901	11,158	59·0	1,980	1,320	66·6
1962	17,312	10,750	62·0	1,927	1,347	69·9
1963	18,913	12,014	63·6	2,050	1,446	70·5
1964	16,507	9,638	58·4	1,740	1,134	65·1
1965	16,654	9,070	58·3	1,683	1,048	62·2
1966	14,258	7,864	55·1	1,423	895	62·8

Source: Board of Trade, *Business Monitor*. Figures exclude parts.

reached, bicycles tend to be 'inferior' goods, so that further rises in income will result in consumers substituting such 'superior' products as motor cycles and subsequently cars, as well as other forms of leisure activity for pedal cycles.[1] In addition, cycle production is relatively simple to organize in the under-developed nations and in the post-war period there has been a rise in the proportion of bicycle production outside the main industrial countries with a consequent effect on the U.K.'s cycle exports. The growth of local cycle production in overseas markets together with increased tariff protection has resulted in import-substitution and this has been evident in such nations as Brazil, India, Mexico and South Africa.[2] These, then, are some of the major factors which have contributed to the long-run decline in the U.K. industry's volume of domestic and export sales. However, within this long-run decline, the U.K. industry's exports of *complete* cycles has become increasingly dependent upon the U.S.A. In 1958, the U.S.A. accounted for almost 19 per cent (by value) of complete cycle exports, but by 1966, this figure was 27 per cent. Data on the country distribution of the U.K.'s exports of complete cycles and the magnitude of decline in a number of markets are shown in Table 8.2.

[1] See, A. Maizels, *Industrial Growth and World Trade*, Cambridge: Cambridge University Press, 1963, pp. 308-16.

[2] Ibid., pp. 316-33; also, M. C. Wyatt 'The Bicycle Industry', *Westminster Bank Review*, May 1966.

TABLE 8.2 *U.K. Cycle Exports, 1958 and 1966*

Country	*Percentage distribution of U.K. exports (value figures)* 1958	1966	*Change in annual volume of U.K. exports: 1958 compared with 1966*
Canada	6·7	6·4	−50,473
Central Africa	7·6	5·9	−64,172
Iran	7·6	4·7	−58,996
Malaysia }	6·1	1·7	−29,393
Singapore }		1·0	−27,691
New Zealand	1·9	0·7	−20,283
Nigeria	10·6	10·3	−56,500
U.S.A.	18·6	27·2	−31,112
Others	40·9	42·1	−238,336

Notes: (1) Percentage distribution figures are based on value totals, complete cycles only.
(2) Volume figures are complete cycles only.
(3) Central Africa is defined as Malawi, Rhodesia and Zambia.
(4) The export figures obtained in the trade accounts do not correspond with those supplied by the Board of Trade.

Source: U.K. trade statistics.

Table 8.2 shows the increase in the relative importance of the U.S.A. as a market for U.K. exports and the decline in the position of Iran, Malaysia and Singapore. In terms of export volumes, the losses sustained in Canada, Central Africa, Nigeria, Iran, Malaysia and Singapore accounted for about 50 per cent of the decline in the *annual* volume of U.K. complete cycle exports for 1958-66: these losses can be partially explained by some of the factors stated above. In addition to the export of complete cycles, there is a substantial trade in the export of cycle parts. During the period 1958-66, the export of complete cycles accounted for between 66 and 73 per cent of the total value of cycle exports, with parts accounting for the remaining proportion. Throughout the period, the major markets for the exports of parts have consisted of the U.S.A., South Africa, the Netherlands and Canada. In the case of countries such as South Africa, Ceylon, India and Ireland, the existence of U.K.-owned overseas subsidiary companies accounted for a large part of the export trade in cycle parts to these nations. In addition, the U.K.

exports a large number of frames to Holland and smaller quantities to several other European countries.

Table 8.1 showed that the figures for exports as a proportion of total output are generally higher when expressed in volume terms than for the corresponding value percentages. This suggests at least two possibilities: first, that different prices exist for a given product mix in both home and export markets or second, a difference in the composition of export sales compared with the home market. In the latter case, the limited data available shows that orthodox adult bicycles accounted for 85 per cent of exports with juvenile bicycles accounting for a further 10 per cent; in the domestic market the corresponding figures were 35 and 29 per cent respectively.[1] Thus, there is some evidence of a difference in the product mix of home and export sales: a fact which, during a domestic deflation, is relevant to the possibilities of allocating domestic production to the export market.

An analysis of the unit value figures for pedal cycles, given in Table 8.3, shows that in current prices for every year between 1958 and 1966, the domestic unit values of the U.K. industry exceeded its export unit values and the difference between the unit values tended to increase during the period. It must also be stressed that in terms of current prices, the trend during the period has been towards increasing domestic unit values. These differences in the home and export unit values might reflect differences in the product mix or, to the extent that products are similar, the higher unit values for the U.K. industry's domestic sales might partially explain the greater profitability of such sales compared with the export market:[2] in the latter, competitive pressures in the world cycle market are a major determinant of prices. Morcover, except for duty-free Commonwealth and E.F.T.A. cycles, the domestic industry was protected from foreign competition by a 20 per cent *ad valorem* tariff during the period 1958-64 and, between 1964 and 1966, the degree of protection was increased with the introduction of the import surcharge.

[1] Data based on the period January to June 1967: the data show that pedal cycles are a heterogeneous group, a point which is frequently concealed in aggregative studies. The U.K. industry produces juvenile bicycles, orthodox adult bicycles, small-wheel machines, sports models and trader's cycles.

[2] See questionnaire results for cycle industry.

TABLE 8.3 *Unit Values for Cycles*

Year	*U.K. industry's domestic unit values*	*U.K. export unit values*	*U.K. import unit values Excluding tariffs*	*Including tariffs*
	£	£	£	£
1958	10·8	9·1	8·8	10·5
1959	11·0	8·3	8·1	9·7
1960	11·0	8·8	6·8	8·1
1961	11·7	8·5	10·4	12·4
1962	11·3	8·0	10·6	12·7
1963	11·4	8·3	10·7	12·8
1964	11·3	8·5	8·9	10·9
1965	11·9	8·6	8·2	10·8
1966	12·1	8·7	9·2	12·1

Notes: (1) Unit value figures are in current prices.
(2) The tariff rate for cycle imports was 20 per cent. *ad valorem* plus an import surcharge for 1964-6. These figures are not an average tariff rate since they exclude the Commonwealth and E.F.T.A. preference rates.

Sources: Board of Trade, *Business Monitor*.
U.K. trade statistics.

Using index numbers, the U.K. cycle industry's sales performance in the domestic and export markets can be analysed in terms of the relevant price and volume changes: the results are summarized in Table 8.4. However, at the most, these figures are only a rough guide since they are based on volume data, without any distinction between different products within the cycle group and, during this period, it is possible that the product mix might have varied.

Between 1958 and 1966, the value of the U.K. industry's domestic sales for complete cycles declined from £8·6 to £6·4 million: price increases accounted for some 12 per cent of this change whilst the volume of sales declined by 34 per cent. In the export market during the same period, the value of exports declined from £12·4 to £7·9 million: price changes were relatively small (a 5 per cent decline) but the volume of exports declined by 35 per cent. Income effects, industrialization and tariff protection might have combined to produce this decline. As for the effect of relative costs and prices, the available evidence on unit values failed to provide conclusive support for the existence of an unfavourable relative price position

TABLE 8.4 *Price and Volume Index Numbers, 1959-66*

	Index 1966 (1958 = 100)	
	U.K. industry's domestic market sales	*U.K. export sales*
Price index	111·8	95·1
Volume index	66·2	65·4

Note: Figures are based on complete cycles only.
Source: Board of trade, *Business Monitor*.

for U.K. cycle exports in the world market. However, a more satisfactory test, which is beyond the scope of this enquiry, requires an analysis of relative price movements for clearly-defined product groups of close substitutes in the world cycle market.

Within the U.K. market, sales consist of domestically-produced and imported cycles. During the period 1958-66, U.K. imports of complete cycles were insignificant and the relevant facts are shown in Table 8.5.

TABLE 8.5 *U.K. Home Market, 1958-66*

Year	*Sales by U.K. industry in domestic market (units)*	*U.K. imports (units)*	*Total (000)*	*Imports as percentage of total*
1958	795,000	9,495	804·5	0·1
1959	925,000	13,418	938·4	1·4
1960	770,000	16,814	786·8	2·1
1961	660,000	8,529	668·5	1·2
1962	580,000	9,040	589·0	1·5
1963	604,000	9,040	613·0	1·4
1964	606,000	9,821	615·8	1·5
1965	635,000	9,356	644·4	1·4
1966	673,000	6,130	679·1	0·9

Note: Figures are volume of complete cycles only.
Sources: Board of Trade, *Business Monitor*.
U.K. trade statistics.

From the Table, it can be seen that annual total domestic demand never reached 1 million units with imports accounting for less than 3 per cent of this demand. As expected with such import figures, the cycle industry earned a substantial surplus on its balance of trade but in current prices, the size of this surplus declined between 1958 and 1966.

In the world cycle market, the U.K., together with West Germany, Italy, France, the Netherlands and Japan are major exporting nations, whilst the U.S.A. is a major importer. During the period 1958-66, the U.K.'s share of the U.S. cycle imports declined from 37·1 per cent in 1958 to 23·3 per cent in 1966. However, these figures conceal the fact that the U.K.'s share of the market declined from 1958 to 1960, after which there was an increase until 1963 when a peak share of 47 per cent was reached, followed by a return to a declining trend.[1] The U.K. was not the only country to experience a declining share of the U.S. market. In fact, amongst the major cycle exporters, only Japan showed a substantial increase in the share of the U.S. market: this share increased in a somewhat erratic manner from a small base of 4 per cent in the late 1950s to 21 per cent by the mid-1960s. Throughout the period, U.S. imports of complete cycles consisted largely of bicycles with wheels over 25 inches.

Within the world cycle market, the export performance of countries varies and part of this variation might possibly be explained by the extent to which firms are reaping economies of scale with their effects on unit costs and hence on product prices and profitability. Here, we only wish to comment on the existence of such economies without specifying their contribution to the U.K. cycle industry's long-run export performance, nor do we attempt to explain the fundamental issue of how the firms in an industry reach a level of output to achieve most of the worthwhile economies of scale. Although we obtained little evidence on the quantitative significance of scale economies in cycle production, it was suggested that these are 'substantial'. In our field work, the view was given that at the firm level, there are few economies that cannot be realized at an annual output of 500,000 units, but to obtain the maximum benefits from scale economies, a firm probably requires an annual production of more than 1 million cycles. The relevance of the home market for economies of scale was emphasized by one authority in the industry who distinguished between '. . . companies which rely on exports for a large proportion of their business and those which rely

[1] See Table 8.6.

primarily on the home market, exporting only small quantities. Export prices . . . are generally lower than those obtainable at home. If the home demand is sufficiently large to enable economies of scale to be achieved and to support the fixed costs of the organization, then a company can profitably export at marginal costs and hence at prices which appear very attractive by the side of the manufacturer who depends upon exports as part of his base load.' Of course, economies of scale provide a possible explanation of long-run export performance as distinct from the short-run explanation offered by the pressure hypothesis.

This completes our brief survey of the bicycle industry. By way of summary, two of the points derived from the survey are relevant to the pressure hypothesis. First, the heterogeneity of products means that domestic sales and exports might not be perfect substitutes. Second, evidence shows that the U.K. cycle industry is a declining industry and, if there are lags in the adjustment of production facilities to decreased demand, excess capacity will exist. For at least one U.K. firm in 1966, production capacity could have been extended without any substantial investment in additional plant, output simply being expanded by increasing employment. Presumably, with excess capacity, together with a given and unchanged world market price and downward-sloping demand curves, a decline in the firm's domestic sales will, in its 'impact' effect, leave exports unchanged: the subsequent response of the firm depends upon factors which have already been considered. It is also interesting to observe that whilst both the U.K. bicycle and motor cycle industries have each been experiencing a decline in output, the latter actually achieved an increase in its export volume. For our purposes, these general points provide a useful basis for presenting the results of our questionnaire and econometric work.

II. INTERVIEW AND QUESTIONNAIRE RESULTS

Introduction

The interviewing and questionnaire results are based on a sample of three firms interviewed during 1966. The sample included one large manufacturer and two small firms, both of which had a labour force of less than 100: at the time of the survey, one of the small firms was a manufacturer of a relatively new product, the other being an established manufacturer. Although this was a numerically small sample in an industry consisting of about eighteen firms in 1966, we were assured that it represented over 90 per cent of the industry's output. Once again, it must be emphasized that some of the results of the questionnaire, since they are only first impressions which lack statistical data for verification, must be interpreted with caution. Moreover, owing to the need to preserve the identity of individual firms, our results can only be revealed in a generalized form and this explains why, for the purposes of presenting a summary of the questionnaire data in the Appendix, we have found it necessary to combine the evidence from both the motor cycle and cycle industries. For the purposes of exposition, we shall as before divide the interview and questionnaire results into the general headings of allocative decisions, profitability, pricing and the pressure hypothesis.

Allocative Decisions

Evidence on employment trends for each of the firms between 1961 and 1966 indicated that employment in the cycle industry declined during the period.[1] Against this background, the firms in the sample exported between 10 and 55 per cent of total output, with the small firms accounting for the 10 per cent figure. The U.S.A. was a dominant export market for each of the firms, but other markets included New Zealand for juvenile cycles, Africa and Malaysia. The dominant position of the U.S.A. is, of course, reflected in total cycle exports.

The firms suggested that import barriers and intense competition, especially from Japan and locally-protected cycle industries were important factors preventing an increase in their exports. One firm had responded to these developments, especially import barriers, by establishing, and purchasing shares in, overseas cycle companies whilst, at the same time, efforts had been made to diversify the company's activities. In addition, two firms stated that product

[1] For the three firms in the sample, labour costs as a percentage of total costs varied between 12 and 30 per cent, a difference which reflected the proportion of bought-out equipment and materials and the degree of vertical integration between firms.

prices were a short-run constraint on exports (one felt that prices were *also* a long-run constraint).

The firms' statements about export trends during the five-year period 1961-5 varied, with one firm experiencing a decline in both the volume and value of bicycle exports, although the export of components has risen slightly, whilst one of the small firms stated that its exports had been 'steady' until 1965, when they began to rise. The remaining small firm, company *C*, informed us that, in general, exports were only temporary. This was a most unusual reply but it was subsequently explained that exports were being used to establish licensed manufacturers in a number of countries which will then continue to manufacture *C*'s product under licence. The owner of company *C* argued that since he was primarily a designer-engineer rather than an entrepreneur-manufacturer, licensing arrangements were attractive since they resulted in foreign manufacturers bearing the risks and problems of overseas sales. In effect, it was intended that this company's future exports would be small and confined mainly to those areas without any indigenous cycle industries and hence, in which there are no possibilities of licensing arrangements. Because of firm *C*'s attitude towards export sales, the question on the ideal proportion of export to domestic sales was not regarded as applicable. The remaining firms both stated that they would prefer a different proportionate division of sales, but one firm qualified its reply by stating that it would only prefer a larger proportion of exports if these were profitable. The remaining small firm expressed a preference for a larger proportion of exports: the company suggested an ideal split of 20 to 30 per cent for exports and 70 to 80 per cent for home sales and stated that it was attempting to obtain the new markets through exhibitions, trade missions and special promotional pricing policies.

Two firms stated that their policy was to increase exports and a small firm wished to encourage exports as a way of diversifying markets. For firm *C* mentioned above, its export policy was simply one of exporting until a foreign manufacturing licensee was established and could relieve the company of its exporting activities. As in the motor cycle industry, firms used a variety of selling methods for their exports, including both the E.C.G.D. and Board of Trade export services. However, a small firm maintained that whilst it sometimes used the Board of Trade services, its products required specialist consideration which was not available at the Board of Trade.

Profitability of Exports

All the firms agreed that exports were generally less profitable than home sales due to greater competition in export markets and the additional selling costs and paper work in exports. When asked to indicate any other benefits of exporting, two firms stated that it resulted in security through diversification of markets. In addition, one company suggested that exports permitted quantity production and consequently lower unit costs and prices which it would otherwise be impossible to achieve in the home market alone. Firm *C* replied that other benefits of exporting included prestige and '. . . the establishment of the technical revolution of the company's product all over the world'. For such a company, it is tempting to suggest 'prestige' as part of its maximizing behaviour. Finally, the remaining small firm felt that one of the future benefits of exporting would be the stimulus to the introduction of new products and/or new production techniques but in 1966, it had to admit that these benefits hadn't yet been obtained!

Pricing

The price changes of *established* products are normally made selectively. In the field of *new* products, prices are generally determined on the basis of an estimate of costs (i.e. labour, materials, overheads plus a profit 'mark-up') and a 'guesstimate' of market conditions. In this context, it was interesting to observe that two firms of different sizes stated that export prices 'ex factory' were not identical to home prices. For the large firm, export prices were determined by competition and, to this extent, this firm, despite its size in the domestic market, must be regarded as a price-taker in the export market: such a conclusion is, of course, consistent with our earlier observation that prices are one of the factors preventing an increase in exports. At the same time, the firm maintained that '. . . you never increase prices when the market is declining', a statement which reflected the relationship between prices and market trends. For the small firm, in this case company *C*, export prices were based on '. . . anything you can get above works cost'. All the firms made modifications in export prices for large customers. Other export price modifications were made for the price changes of foreign competitors and for orders placed at convenient times of the year.

Only one small firm replied to the question on the determination of order priorities in a situation of excess demand: it stated that preference would be given to 'first-in' and to export customers. For this small firm, the normal lapse of time between the receipt of an order and its despatch during the period 1961-6 had varied between four to six weeks in the export markets and under four weeks to three months in the home market, so that the pressure of excess demand appears to have been concentrated upon domestic orders. This evidence, together with the firm's statement that it has tried to maintain export delivery dates in the region of four to six weeks, confirms its stated preference given to export customers. In such a situation, it was inevitable that the firm should reply that it could sell more if it could produce more but that a shortage of labour, especially over the peak season, prevented an increase in output. The remaining two firms were not experiencing excess demand for their products and this explains their lack of replies to the questions on delivery and order priorities. In fact, both these firms stated that sales (demand) and not production was a major limitation on their activities: both maintained that they could not sell more even though in one case, output could be increased.[1]

Exports and Domestic Demand: The Pressure Hypothesis

Both small firms stated that exports were not significantly affected during a period of 'peak domestic demand' for bicycles. In one of these cases, however, it was explained that due to labour shortages, exports could not be raised, so that there was the suggestion that if labour were available to the firm, exports might increase. In comparison, the large volume-producer felt that during a period of peak demand for cycles, exports were helped because of the lower unit costs associated with a greater output.

During a period of sharp domestic deflation, the small firms maintained that exports were not significantly affected. In fact, one

[1] Further evidence on the existence of excess capacity in the cycle industry: a point already referred to in Section I of this chapter.

small firm maintained that it manufactured a specialized, relatively high unit-value bicycle (e.g. racing cycles) and, since its customers were prepared to 'forego other consumption expenditure', it was insulated from changes in domestic demand; this firm also maintained that domestic recessions are generally too short to permit an increase in exports. As in the previous situation, the volume cycle producer stated that for a period of sharp deflation, exports were adversely affected because of the rise in unit costs associated with the decline in domestic sales. For this firm, it must be emphasized that in the years up to 1966, in both peak demand and deflation periods, excess capacity had been available. However, such statements about the relationship between unit costs and domestic sales are consistent with this firm's earlier statement that exports permit quantity production and hence lower unit costs. This is, of course, the argument about short-run behaviour which is frequently used by the motor car industry and presumably it might be characteristic of firms using volume production techniques and selling a substantial part of their output to the domestic market. For this type of argument to be valid, so that exports are adversely affected in the competitive world cycle market, it can only be assumed that the rise in unit costs due to the decline in home sales will, at a given price determined by international competition, result in a further reduction in the profitability of exports. In other words, for the price-taking volume producer in the world market, the adverse effect on cycle exports of a domestic deflation must be presumed to operate through a decline in profitability.[1]

During a period of domestic deflation, firms responded with an increased sales effort in the home market. One firm suggested that it would increase publicity in an attempt to try and increase the *total* size of the home market for cycles, rather than attempt to increase its own, already large, share of this market. Other responses included an increased sales effort in overseas markets, production for stocks, a reduction in total output and one small firm indicated that it might introduce a new model. Although both selling and output reactions were evident, no firm stated that it would change its home or export prices.

[1] Assuming given factor prices, but a deflation might be expected to favourably affect the movement of such prices.

Summary

The interviews and questionnaire results provided evidence on the export behaviour of firms and the relationship between exports and domestic demand in a declining industry dominated by a volume producer.[1] For our sample, both small firms maintained that exports were not significantly affected by the pressure of domestic demand, although for one of these, there was the suggestion that labour shortages had acted as a constraint on exports. From the volume producer's evidence, there was no support for the pressure hypothesis. In total, our qualitative tests provided little support for the hypothesis at the level of the individual firm and these results might be a reflection of the declining nature of the industry and the associated existence of excess capacity. We turn now to the results of our econometric tests of the pressure hypothesis.

III. AN ECONOMETRIC ANALYSIS FOR THE INDUSTRY

As with motor cycles, our tests of the pressure hypothesis for bicycles were undertaken at the industry level. In general, our approach, including the choice of the U.S. and Canadian markets[2] was identical with that used for motor cycles and, to avoid repetition, we shall proceed to outline in turn the results of our level of exports and shares models.

Table 8.6 shows annual cycle imports and U.K. share figures for the U.S. and Canadian markets between 1958 and 1966.[3] It can be seen that in 1958, the U.K.'s share of Canadian cycle imports was considerably higher than the corresponding figure for the U.S.A. However, whilst the Canadian share figures show a clear downward trend throughout the period, this is not the case in the U.S. market. For the U.S.A., the apparent downward trend revealed when comparing 1958 and 1966, conceals an upward turn in the share figures for the years 1961-3: a feature which greatly affected the econometric results.

To explain variations in the level of U.K. cycle exports to the U.S. and Canadian markets, we used log-linear regressions with

1 For evidence, see Appendix.
2 The U.S. market being the major U.K. export market for cycles.
3 Our regressions were based on quarterly data.

TABLE 8.6 *The North-American Cycle Market, 1958-66*

	U.S.A.		*Canada*	
Year	*U.S. cycle imports*	*U.K. share of U.S. imports*	*Canadian cycle imports*	*U.K. share of Canadian imports*
	(U.S. $000)	(%)	(Canadian $000)	(%)
1958	22,577	37·1	3,295	85·7
1959	28,260	28·9	3,329	72·6
1960	32,860	24·7	3,334	82·2
1961	38,877	37·3	3,281	79·3
1962	33,949	41·2	3,996	69·3
1963	34,111	46·6	3,248	65·8
1964	29,669	34·7	3,794	43·3
1965	32,473	26·5	4,599	41·3
1966	27,791	23·3	3,292 *	35·5 *

* Calculated from three quarters only.

overseas and domestic demand as independent variables.[1] Our initial tests showed that for the U.S.A., the coefficient for the overseas demand variable was statistically significant and positive giving a partial elasticity of U.K. exports to the U.S. with respect to overseas demand in the range 0·62 to 1·12. The corresponding elasticity estimates for Canada were also statistically significant and in the region of 0·65. For domestic demand, only for the U.S. market and only when using the unemployment rate for Great Britain was a statistically significant relationship obtained for the pressure variable and the sign of the coefficient was positive: since this result was based on an unemployment measure, it was consistent with the predictions of the pressure hypothesis. However, these initial results, especially for the U.S.A., were not very satisfactory since they gave relatively low Durbin-Watson statistics. In these circumstances, we attempted to eliminate positive serial correlation in our models by fitting a quadratic time-trend.[2] Whilst this modification gave higher Durbin-Watson statistics, the result for cycle exports to the U.S.A.

[1] The basic model was: $X = aM^{\alpha}D^{\beta}e^{kt}$. We used one measure of overseas demand, namely total imports (value) into a market, and two measures of domestic demand, namely the unemployment rate for Great Britain and a measure based on the *volume* of the industry's domestic sales.

[2] Model modified to: $X = aM^{\alpha}D^{\beta}e^{kt+k_1t^2}$.

was that the coefficients for the overseas demand variable ceased to be statistically significant, suggesting multicollinearity with the new time-trend. In comparison, for exports to Canada, the overseas demand variable continued to be highly significant with the partial elasticity estimates rising to the range 0·85 to 0·95. In both markets using our modified model with the additional time-variable, we now obtained a statistically significant relationship between variations in the level of exports and domestic demand, with the signs of the pressure coefficients being consistent with the predictions of the pressure hypothesis. For the U.S. market, both the industry and the economy measures of pressure gave significant results but some of the equations were still bedevilled by relatively low Durbin-Watson statistics. For Canada, only the industry measure performed successfully. Some examples of our results are presented in Table 8.7 below.

For the U.K. cycle industry, the evidence from our level of exports model provides support for the pressure hypothesis. We must now compare these results with those derived from our shares model. Once again, we shall assume that the partial elasticity of U.K. cycle exports with respect to overseas demand is unity. In the case of the U.S. market, some assumption is required in view of the difficulty of obtaining satisfactory elasticity estimates. For the Canadian market, an assumption of unit elasticity is close to the evidence which, if accepted, suggests an elasticity of slightly less than one.

For our shares models two separate series of tests were undertaken. The first series used linear and log-linear regressions of share on domestic demand for the period 1958 I to 1966 III. Our measures of domestic demand were based on the volume of the U.K. industry's domestic sales and the national unemployment rate. Once again, with a time-trend incorporated into the regressions,[1] only for the U.S. market and only when using the unemployment rate for Great Britain, did we obtain statistically significant relationships which were consistent with the predictions of the pressure hypothesis, but our results indicated positive serial correlation. As in our previous model, we attempted to remove the serial correlation by incorporating a quadratic time-trend into the regressions.[2] With such a modification,

[1] The basic models were: (*a*) $S = \alpha_0 + \alpha_1 D + \alpha_2 t$. (*b*) $S = \alpha_0 D^{\alpha_1} e^{kt}$.

[2] The models were: (*a*) $S = \alpha_0 + \alpha_1 D + \alpha_2 t + \alpha_3 t^2$

(*b*) $S = \alpha_0 D^{\alpha_1} e^{kt + k_1 t^2}$.

both measures of domestic demand performed satisfactorily for the U.S. market, each giving the correct sign. For the Canadian market, only the measure based on the volume of the U.K. industry's domestic sales gave a statistically significant relationship and the sign of the pressure coefficient was consistent with the pressure hypothesis. However, for the share of U.S. imports, a substantial amount of positive serial correlation was still present in the equations,

TABLE 8.7 *The Level of U.K. Cycle Exports to the U.S.A. and Canada*

	Coefficients of						
Exports	log *HS*	log *U*	log *M*	*t*	t^2	$\bar{R}^2$	*d*
1. log X_{US}	...	0·89** (0·18)	0·65** (0·21)	0·008 (0·005)	...	0·838	0·71
2. log X_{US}	−0·29** (0·09)	...	0·43 (0·27)	0·07 (0·02)	−0·002 (0·0005)	0·829	0·79
3. log X_{US}	...	0·91** (0·14)	0·02 (0·21)	0·08 (0·02)	−0·002 (0·0003)	0·908	1·50
4. log X_C	−0·11* (0·05)	...	0·95** (0·11)	0·02 (0·008)	−0·001 (0·0002)	0·931	1·65
5. log X_C	...	0·04 (0·11)	0·89** (0·12)	0·02 (0·008)	−0·001 (0·0002)	0·918	1·45

Notes: (1) log X_{US} and log X_C are logs of value of U.K. cycle exports to the U.S. and Canada, expressed in U.S. and Canadian $, respectively.
(2) log *HS* = log of deviations from trend of the *volume* of U.K. cycle industry's domestic sales.
(3) log *U* = log of unemployment rate for Great Britain.
(4) log *M* = log of value of cycle imports. In Equations 1-3, log *M* is concerned with U.S. cycle imports (U.S. $), whilst in the remaining equations it relates to Canadian imports (Canadian $).
(5) *t* = time-trend, 1958 I to 1966 III.
(6) Dummy variables were used for seasonal adjustment.
(7) Standard errors are shown in brackets.

** Significant at the 1 per cent level.
* Significant at the 5 per cent level.

suggesting the influence of some additional variables not incorporated into the model. Examples of our results are presented in Table 8.8. Subject to the qualifications about the results for the U.S.A., it can be seen that in both markets, where the coefficients of the domestic demand variable is statistically significant, it performs in the way predicted by the pressure hypothesis.

TABLE 8.8 *The U.K.'s Share of U.S. and Canadian Cycle Imports 1958-66*

Share of market	*Coefficients of* *HS*	log *HS*	log *U*	*t*	t^2	$\bar{R}^2$	*d*
1. log S_{US}	...	−0·31** (0·09)	...	0·04 (0·02)	−0·001 (0·0004)	0·255	0·84
2. log S_{US}	...	...	0·73** (0·18)	0·02 (0·01)	−0·0006 (0·0003)	0·359	0·76
3. S_C	−0·0004* (0·00014)	...	...	0·52 (0·39)	−0·06 (0·01)	0·907	1·29
4. log S_C	...	−0·12* (0·05)	...	0·02 (0·008)	−0·001 (0·0002)	0·903	1·61

Notes: (1) Share figures are based on percentages.
(2) S_{US} = U.K. share of U.S. cycle imports.
(3) S_C = U.K. share of Canadian cycle imports.
(4) *HS* = volume of U.K. cycle industry's domestic sales.
(5) Remaining details are the same as for Table 8.7.

Owing to the effect on the results of the unusual share figures for the U.S. market during the period 1958-66, we undertook a second set of tests based on a different time-period. For these tests, we used linear regressions of share on domestic demand for a shorter time-period, namely 1961 III to 1966 III.[1] Our measures of domestic demand included both the value[2] and the volume of the U.K. industry's domestic sales, together with the unemployment rates for the industry, the Midlands region and Great Britain. Each

[1] The model was: $S = a_0 + a_1 D + a_2 t$.

[2] Value figures for the domestic sales of U.K. pedal cycles were only available from 1961 III onwards: this was one reason, together with the pattern of the U.S. share figures, which led to our choice of the period 1961-6.

equation contained a linear time-trend together with dummy variables for seasonal adjustment. For the Canadian market, the results for the period 1961-6 can be easily described: none of the measures of domestic demand produced a statistically significant pressure coefficient.[1] In contrast, the equations for the U.S. share were much more satisfactory. For a start, the regressions generally gave much better 'fits' than for the period 1958-66 but, in view of the variations in the U.K.'s share of U.S. imports, such an improvement was not surprising.[2] From our tests, using different measures of internal demand applied to the U.S. share, only the unemployment rates for the Midlands and Great Britain gave statistically significant relationships which supported the pressure hypothesis. The remaining measures, including two and three quarter lags for the volume of the U.K. industry's domestic sales, failed to provide a statistically significant pressure coefficient. A typical equation for the U.K.'s share of U.S. cycle imports, 1961-6 was:

$$S_{US} = \underset{}{32{\cdot}14} + \underset{(2{\cdot}21)}{11{\cdot}29U} - \underset{(0{\cdot}16)}{0{\cdot}59t}$$

$$\bar{R}^2 = 0{\cdot}82.$$

Dummy variables were included for seasonal adjustment.

Standard errors are shown in brackets, with U, the Great Britain unemployment rate, significant at the 1 per cent level.

t = a linear time-trend, 1961 III to 1966 III.

Conclusions

An econometric analysis of the U.K. bicycle industry provides a considerable amount of support for the pressure hypothesis. This support was especially convincing since it was obtained from both the level of exports and the shares models, a point which might reduce some of the doubts associated with a complete reliance on the results of a shares model. Throughout, all the statistically significant coefficients for the pressure variable suggested an inverse relationship between the pressure of domestic demand and variations in either the level of exports to a market or import share. However,

1 Including two and three quarter lags for the volume of the U.K. industry's domestic sales.

2 See Table 8.6.

some of our results, especially for the U.S. market gave relatively low Durbin-Watson statistics and in these cases, doubts arise about some of the pressure coefficients which were accepted as significant. Moreover, the results of the econometric analysis of the industry appear to differ from the relationship at the firm level as indicated by our questionnaire and interviewing results.[1] In these circumstances, owing to the difficulty of holding other things constant in any questionnaire approach, including the influence of any long-run trend factors, together with the absence of supporting data from the firms, we are inclined to regard the econometric results as more satisfactory tests of the pressure hypothesis.

Finally, our econometric analysis of the pedal cycle industry provides two interesting comparisons with the associated motor cycle sector. First, with pedal cycles, the pressure effect tends to operate in the *same* direction in both the U.S. and Canadian markets. Second, by comparing the pedal and motor cycle results for the U.S. market, there is evidence to suggest that a change in the pressure of U.K. domestic demand differs in its effects on short-run changes in the shares of one geographical market obtained by different product groups. As we suggested earlier,[2] such differences might be explained in terms of the objective functions of firms and the degree of capacity-utilization for various product lines.

[1] The conflict might result from the fact that the volume cycle producer was solely concerned with its internal cost position and that its questionnaire reply reflected the effect of movements along a given cost curve whereas the industry results might also reflect the opposite influence of upward shifts in this cost curve due to inflationary conditions external to the firm.

[2] See Chapters 4 and 7 (IV).

Chapter 9

THE U.K. OFFICE MACHINERY INDUSTRY

I. A GENERAL OUTLINE

The U.K. office machinery industry is concerned with the manufacture of typewriters, accounting, adding, calculating and punched-card machines, together with cash registers and duplicators. Given this variety of products, it follows that the market for office machinery consists of a number of sub-markets. For the purposes of the survey we have excluded electronic computers manufactured by office machinery firms. In this section we shall provide some general background information on the industry to be followed by sections presenting the interviewing and questionnaire results and the econometric tests of the pressure hypothesis.

During the period 1958-66 there were major changes in the product composition of the industry's output and exports. Typewriters experienced a substantial decline in their share of both the total industry output and total office machinery exports. In the same period, accounting, adding, calculating and punched-card machines increased their share of both total industry output and exports so that by 1966, this group accounted for some 60 per cent of output and 68 per cent of exports. The industry's output and export record is shown in Table 9.1.

Table 9.1 shows that the value of office machinery exports more than doubled between 1958 and 1966, and this growth was greater than that achieved by either total U.K. exports or the exports of manufactures. It can be seen then, that by using the criteria of national averages, office machinery exports represent a growth sector. Moreover, during the period 1958-66, the industry exported between 38 and 58 per cent of its total output. These percentages do, of course, conceal variations between products. For example, with portable typewriters, duplicators, accounting, adding and calculating

TABLE 9.1 *Office Machinery Industry, 1958-66*

Year	*Total output*	*For export*	*Exports as a percentage of total output*
	(£000s)	(£000s)	
1958	53,405	20,837	39·0
1959	60,019	23,147	38·5
1960	70,755	29,708	41·9
1961	75,973	28,565	37·5
1962	75,236	32,017	42·5
1963	72,726	33,735	46·3
1964	67,685	33,273	49·1
1965	73,889	37,584	50·8
1966	79,356	45,646	57·5

Note: Figures before January 1963 include electronic computers and calculators made by office machinery manufacturers. Value figures are in current prices.

Source: Board of Trade, *Business Monitor*.

machines, the proportion of output exported in each year during the period exceeded the corresponding percentage for the whole industry. By 1966, each of these product groups exported over 60 per cent of its output so that domestic sales were proportionately less significant.

In 1958, the industry's major export market was Australia which accounted for 22 per cent of U.K. exports, followed by North America, South Africa, West Germany and France: these markets accounted for 54 per cent of total office machinery exports and by 1966, this figure had increased to some 57 per cent. United Kingdom imports of office machinery in the mid-1960s were obtained from such countries as West Germany, Netherlands, Italy, Sweden, France and the U.S.A.:[1] these nations were also the U.K.'s major competitors in the world market. Within the world market, the U.K.'s share of the office machinery trade declined by 5·3 per cent between 1953 and 1961, with above-average losses of share in the non-O.E.C.D. Sterling Area, U.S.A., Australia and the Netherlands.[2]

1 In addition, it must be remembered that a number of U.K. office machinery firms are subsidiaries of U.S. companies.

2 N.E.D.C., *Export Trends*, London: H.M.S.O., 1963, pp. 8-9.

Similarly, for the period 1958-66, it has been estimated that Britain's share of world trade in office machinery declined from about 13·5 to 11·5 per cent.[1]

II. INTERVIEW AND QUESTIONNAIRE RESULTS

Introduction

Our field work was based on a sample of six firms, four of which were owned by United States' parent companies and the remaining two were United Kingdom companies. The firms in our sample manufactured business machines, typewriters, postage-meter machines, addressing, duplicating, and mail-room machines. In fact, for three firms, duplicating machines accounted for over 50 per cent of the value of each firm's output.

The sample was selected after consultation with the trade association and, although we were unable to apply a random-sampling technique for the selection of firms, the sample seems to be reasonably typical of the office machinery industry.[2] The results of the questionnaire are given in the Appendix but the most significant findings will be summarized in a number of major sections namely, allocative decisions, the profitability of exports, pricing policies and exports and domestic demand. Statistical data was also obtained from two firms.

Allocative Decisions

Compared with the pottery, motor cycle and cycle industries, the sample contained no small firms. In fact in 1966, the average size of firm in the sample was 3,770 employees, with the smallest firm employing a labour force of over 900 and the largest, which was a U.S.-owned company, employing 10,000 people in the U.K. Some indication of the international nature of the industry can be assessed from the fact that in 1966 the total world-wide employment for two firms was between 15,000 and 20,000 and that one of the U.S.

1 'The Office Machinery Industry in the U.K.', National Institute *Economic Review*, August 1969. This study concluded, 'The picture which has emerged is that of an industry which . . . suffers from considerable competitive weakness' (p. 52).

2 The interviewing of firms was undertaken during August 1966. Five firms were interviewed and a sixth firm replied to a postal questionnaire.

parent companies employed some 75,000 employees in its international organization.

During the period 1961-6, employment in two of the firms had remained constant whilst the remainder had experienced increases: this was consistent with the growth nature of the industry. For the firms in the sample, labour costs as a percentage of total costs varied between 20 and 65 per cent: the 65 per cent figure, and hence the rather large variation, was attributable to one firm which, compared with other units, appeared to be rather exceptional. However, three firms were more specific in their replies and there appeared to be general agreement that labour costs as a percentage of total manufacturing costs for these firms ranged from 20 to 35 per cent.

For our sample, the proportion of output exported varied between 25 and 75 per cent but there was no relationship between firm size and the proportion of output exported.[1] Compared with the motor cycle and cycle industries, the office machinery firms appeared less dependent upon one single export market. Of the firms which gave a more detailed breakdown of their export markets, only one company (the smallest in the sample) sent most of its exports to North America but this was a result of the U.S. parent company's policy of using its U.K. subsidiary as a specialist producer for the international group. For the remainder, three firms sold between 25 and 50 per cent of their exports to Western Europe and one firm sent 25 per cent of its exports to Africa. The largest U.K.-owned company in the sample exported 25 per cent of its overseas sales to North America and a further 25 per cent to Western Europe. Other export markets for the sample firms included Canada, Australia and the Far East. With some of the U.S.-owned companies, the United States' market was supplied by the parent company which explains the absence of this market from the list of major markets for at least two of the U.K. subsidiary companies. None of the firms had experienced a decline in either the total value or volume of their exports during the period 1961-6.

1 For the engineering industry, evidence suggests that the U.K. subsidiaries of foreign companies consistently exported a much higher proportion of output than other companies in the industry, see Mechanical Engineering E.D.C., *Market – The World*, H.M.S.O., 1968, p. 36. For our sample of office machinery firms, the corresponding evidence was inconclusive.

Although firms listed a variety of factors which prevented an increase in exports, four firms agreed that product prices were a short-run constraint. In one case, it was emphasized that prices were affected by rising costs, especially labour costs. Further constraints on exports included the shortage of efficient salesmen, trade barriers and increasing competition, together with promotional effort and the quality and design of products. The long-run constraints on exports were not significantly different from those listed in the short run.

Four firms had no preference for a different proportionate division of output between exports and home sales. In one case, it was explained that the domestic market was required for 'development and innovation purposes', the point being that in the domestic market new products could apparently be tried with less risk of loss of future sales. Only one firm – a U.S.-owned subsidiary, with the lowest proportion of exports to total output in our sample – indicated a preference for a change in its proportion of exports to home sales: in this case, there was a preference for an increased proportion of exports with a 60%/40% ideal division between exports and home sales, respectively. The firm felt that there was a greater potential in the export market: to this firm, the domestic market was more fully exploited than the export sphere and, in terms of the firm's market shares, it was argued that it was easier to increase the market share from, say, a small percentage (the position in many export markets) than from a much larger share which was the case in the domestic market. However, since the company was a U.S.-owned subsidiary any change in its present position was dependent upon the parent company's decision. In other words, it is possible that in an international organization, a subsidiary's informal maximization objectives might differ from those of the parent company. In fact, it is rather intriguing to speculate on the more general effects of foreign-owned subsidiaries on the U.K.'s exports and imports.[1]

[1] See, e.g. J. H. Dunning, *American Investment in British Manufacturing Industry*, London: Allen & Unwin, 1958. Also, the same author's comments on diversification, namely that, '. . . a firm in a particular industry may well choose to grow horizontally through extending its activities overseas than by branching out to new and unfamiliar lines of production or marketing at home'. *Moorgate and Wall Street Review*, Autumn, 1966, pp. 29-30. Also, C. P. Kindleberger, *International Economics*, Illinois: Irwin, 1963 (4th ed.), Chapter 21.

For example, if because of economies of scale and research and development, a foreign subsidiary located in Britain is more efficient than a U.K.-owned company, then it is probable that the subsidiary will be more competitive in both the U.K. and world markets.[1] However, for the purposes of the present study, the critical issue concerns the export reactions of a foreign-owned subsidiary to a domestic deflation. Within an international organization, foreign ownership might impose product and market constraints upon a subsidiary and we obtained evidence showing that some of the subsidiaries in our sample were only concerned with supplying a limited range of office machinery to specific geographical markets. But, given the objective function and the allocative decisions between home and export sales it seems plausible to suggest that a foreign-owned subsidiary located in Britain will be subject to the same set of pressures as a U.K.-owned company and, within its set of constraints, will respond to demand changes in a similar way. It is, of course, possible to visualize circumstances in which the reactions of a foreign-owned subsidiary might differ from those of a U.K. firm. Here, the circumstances might include differences in objective functions or a change in the constraints imposed by the parent company on the subsidiary. For example, with a decline in its U.K. domestic sales a foreign-owned subsidiary's output might be allocated to any world markets in which excess demand for the product might exist but which were previously outside the subsidiary's designated area: such entry into another market in the short run might only be possible for a member of an international group for which there exists an established world-wide sales organization.[2]

1 For the office machinery industry it has been stated that, '. . . foreign-owned firms seem to be in the forefront, notably in technical development, and their productivity is considerably higher on average than that of the British-owned firms'. Also, in relation to the U.K. industry it is maintained that, 'Had the American companies not developed or extended their activities . . . not only would exports of office machinery now be much lower but the imported element in home consumption would be significantly greater'. The Office Machinery Industry in the U.K., National Institute *Economic Review*. August 1969. See also, J. H. Dunning and M. D. Steuer, 'The Effects of United States Direct Investment in Britain on British Technology', *Moorgate and Wall Street Review*, Autumn, 1969.

2 Our sample also included one U.K.-owned firm which was an international company.

These are some of the possibilities which require testing. In one of the sections below, we shall present some limited evidence on the export response of foreign-owned subsidiaries and U.K. companies at various levels of domestic demand.

In reply to the question on export policy four firms stated that they were concerned with growth and growth was defined as the expansion of sales, although some companies explained that they were concerned with growth and earning profits for further growth. The emphasis on growth explained the negative reply by most of the firms to the question on the proportion of exports in total output. For three firms each of which exported 45 per cent or more of output, it was expected that total sales would continue to increase and consequently whilst these firms desired no change in their export proportion, it was anticipated that total exports would also rise. One firm qualified its growth objective by suggesting that in the future, in response to rising trade barriers, growth will probably involve a greater emphasis on the establishment of overseas subsidiary factories. In the company's own words, 'As nations develop, they tend to establish local paper industries and to a certain extent, to foster local manufacture of duplicating supplies. Such industries are usually protected. Thus, to maintain the market, the company has, in certain circumstances, had to establish ancillary factories locally.' The remaining two firms in the sample explained that their export policy was simply to increase exports: such an objective could be perfectly consistent with the growth objective of their rivals.

The firms used a variety of selling methods but exclusive overseas agents and overseas selling subsidiaries were the most common methods: the latter, of course, reflect the international organization of the industry. As might be expected in a sample dominated by large international companies each with overseas selling subsidiaries, only one stated that it used the Board of Trade export services and the E.C.G.D. (another firm mentioned that it used the Board of Trade service 'occasionally').

The Profitability of Exports

In 1966, half of the firms in the sample stated that there was no difference in profitability between home and export sales and the remainder described their exports as less or slightly less profitable than home sales. Where lower profitability of exports was indicated, the firms agreed that a dominant explanation was the greater competition in export markets. For the smallest firm in the sample, an additional but associated explanation for the lower profitability of exports was that since the U.S. parent company had been a relatively late entrant into international markets, its export prices (and associated lower profitability) had been established at a relatively low level in order to expand its export business. In addition, one firm which exported 45 per cent of output claimed that it recovered its overheads on home sales with a consequent effect on relative profitability – such a pricing policy suggests that the conventional arguments about the domestic market providing an essential 'springboard' for exports might be based upon a policy of using the home market to recover a firm's overhead costs so that in the competitive world markets, its export prices can be related to variable costs.[1]

All the firms felt that exports provided them with the possibility of expansion – an answer which was clearly consistent with their general commitment to growth. In addition, four firms, including the largest in our sample, indicated that there were 'prestige' and diversification benefits of exporting and these benefits were given a high ranking. Once again then, as in the other industries, it would seem that diversification is an important consideration in a firm's export policy.

Pricing

From our field work, we obtained the impression that firms changed the prices of established products in response to rising costs and/or if it was found that increased factory and marketing costs could not be absorbed through increased efficiency. Even here, some firms qualified their replies by stating that price changes were subject to '. . . what the market will stand'. It appears that price changes are infrequent, only one firm admitting that price changes were fairly

[1] The argument about the domestic market providing the base for exporting is frequently based on the principle of achieving minimum unit costs at capacity production. Similarly, a large home market demand might enable a firm to move towards its optimum size. See Chapter 4.

frequent and, whilst this firm probably changed prices in periods of two years, it had '. . . no set period for price changes'. The largest firms in the sample stated that price changes were on a 'selective basis' and not by the same percentage. The smallest firm indicated that during the mid-1960s it changed its prices in an attempt to direct orders into standardized items and so secure the economies of volume production. Previously this firm had tended to supply 'one-off' jobs and, in future, in order to discourage custom-built orders, it indicated that it would only provide such items at increased prices (this firm, which had entered the export market at a relatively late stage, was concerned with export promotion).

With one exception, all the firms in the sample determined the price of a new product on the basis of estimated costs and market conditions. The general price-fixing process for new products involved two basic stages: first, market research indicates the market requirements and possible price of the new product and, in estimating market conditions, attention is given to such factors as competition, possible outlets for the product and its relation to existing products; secondly, engineers are asked to build a product within the price range indicated by the market research survey. Thus, the general approach to pricing new products considered both the market and cost conditions. There was apparently one exception to this approach: one firm stated that new product prices are based solely on estimated costs.[1] This same firm was also exceptional in that it was the only one in the sample in which export prices 'ex factory' were not identical to home prices. The reason given for the difference was that 'export prices are lower to allow for competition, shipping, duty, etc.': an explanation which suggests that market conditions were, in fact, included in the pricing process!

In general, firms modified their export prices for large customers through the use of quantity discounts.[2] In addition, the largest firm in the sample stated that since export prices were partly determined on the basis of competitors' prices, export prices were modified

1 This firm replied to a postal questionnaire and it is possible that the question might have been misinterpreted.

2 It must be stressed that since this part of our survey was only concerned with variations in export prices, we did not consider whether domestic prices were subject to similar variations.

for the price changes of foreign competitors. The fact that only one firm mentioned that foreign competition was a factor in export price modifications does not necessarily mean that it was an irrelevant consideration for the remainder: it is possible that most firms consider this factor in their 'estimate of market conditions' part of the price-fixing process and therefore it was neglected in further answers to the questionnaire.

During the period 1961-6, most firms indicated that there had been little variation in their delivery dates. This might be explained by the growth attitude of firms in the sample – an attitude which results in frequent capacity expansion in order to satisfy the expected increases in demand. At the same time it was suggested that since business machines are a capital good, buyers usually require time to re-organize their factory lay-out and, where suppliers are international organizations, delivery can usually be arranged to meet the customers' requirements. In the event of any lengthening in their order books, firms used a number of methods of determining order priorities such as first-in/first-out, a preference to big customers or to contracts which included a time limit. But apparently for the largest company in the sample, the problem did not arise since, being an international organization, it could use its world-wide production capacity to meet local shortages.

Exports and Domestic Demand: The Pressure Hypothesis

For the majority of firms, it was claimed that exports were not significantly affected during a period of peak domestic demand for their products. Here, one British-owned firm maintained that since it was an international organization with export markets in different parts of the world, 'this tends to provide stability of demand and so insulates the company from changes in the domestic market'. It was also relevant that this company, which stated that there was no difference between the profitability of home and export sales, exported 75 per cent of its output, so that the domestic market was in reality the residual. Only two firms felt that exports were affected by a period of peak demand for their products. In one case, exports were helped because unit costs were lower which presumably reflects the benefits of capacity operation with volume-production techniques. But, at the same time, this company also maintained that exports were adversely affected by rising home costs and prices. Although this results in a rather indeterminate answer, it might be a more accurate reflection of the conflicting pressure on exports associated with a period of peak demand for a volume-producer's products;[1] in such cases, there is a need for a more detailed statistical assessment of the firm's performance but unfortunately it was not possible to obtain the relevant data. Finally, the smallest firm in the sample which was a subsidiary of a U.S. company stated that exports are adversely affected in a period of peak demand because home costs and prices are rising.[2] For this firm it was explained that since it had traditionally been concerned with batch production techniques, there was considerable potential for economies of scale through standardization: it was, in fact, using its pricing policy to encourage such standardization. In the absence of such standardization, the firm felt that the opportunities 'for assisting exports through lower unit costs' were unimportant.

In a period of domestic deflation, the majority of firms claimed that exports were not significantly affected and this generalization applied to both foreign- and British-owned companies. At least two firms emphasized that, at the most, domestic deflations have tended to reduce the *rate of growth* of demand for office machinery rather than actually reducing the absolute level of domestic demand. It was also claimed that during a domestic deflation within the economy, home sales might actually benefit from the capital goods nature of the office machinery industry. The reasoning presented was that in a deflation, firms in the economy are especially concerned with minimizing costs, so that there would actually be an incentive to substitute office machines for labour during these periods:[3] such an explanation implies a 'shock effect' in which 'cost-consciousness' at the firm level is some function of the pressure of demand in the economy. Thus, the argument was presented that the office machinery industry had not experienced violent fluctuations in demand and hence in output; at the time of our field work, it was still a growth

1 For this firm, and indeed for others, the problem was one of movements along a cost curve being 'off-set' by upward shifts in the curve.

2 Rather interestingly, this same firm also stated that in a deflation, 'exports are not significantly affected': a reply which suggests that the export-effect of various levels of demand differs between the stages of the cycle.

3 Logically the converse should apply during a 'boom' period.

industry with expanding market opportunities. However, whilst the exports of the majority of firms were not significantly affected during a domestic deflation, there were a number of qualifications which suggested that the answers could only be interpreted with caution. For example, two firms tentatively surmised that 'exports might be helped by a domestic deflation' and a third stated that since the parent company was the decision-making unit for overseas marketing, exports were not significantly affected in the short term. Here, the emphasis on 'the short term' suggests that expectations about the length of the deflation might be a significant factor in stimulating exports.

From the sample, only one company stated that in a deflation exports are adversely affected because unit costs rise. It might perhaps be significant that this firm was a volume-producer which only exported 30 per cent of its output and, although there was a firm with an even lower proportion of output exported (25 per cent), this latter company used batch production techniques. Thus, it is possible that the nature of the production process and the proportion of output exported might be factors explaining the variations in answers. The remaining firms in the sample exported between 45 and 75 per cent of their output so that to some extent the export market insulated such firms from variations in domestic demand.[1]

With a domestic deflation, most firms responded with an increased sales effort in both the home and overseas markets, although for some of the foreign-owned companies, any increased sales effort directed into the latter markets were dependent on the parent company's decision. It was also interesting to observe that in general, firms apparently responded to a deflation by emphasizing sales effort, so attempting to shift their demand curves, rather than by changing prices or output. For the two smallest firms in the sample, it was emphasized that the answers to the question on their response to a domestic deflation were somewhat hypothetical since, up to the time of the interviews, they had never experienced a recession in the demand for their products (i.e. absolute decline in demand)!

[1] See also, Mechanical Engineering E.D.C., *Market – The World*, H.M.S.O., 1968: 'It is only the marginal exporters who seem to show any appreciable sensitivity to changes in the level of home demand.' p. 5.

Half of the companies in the sample maintained that they would *not* be able to sell more if they could produce more. To these firms, sales represented the dominant constraint on expansion. In one case, the sales-constraint resulted from the fact that selling was primarily the responsibility of the U.S. parent company whilst for a U.K.-owned company, the constraint resulted from the shortage of trained and efficient salesmen. The remaining two firms which answered this question, including the largest company in the sample, maintained that production was the constraint on growth. For the largest firm, which was foreign-owned, it became clear that the size of the U.K. production plant was dependent upon the U.S. parent company's decision. Although the second of these firms was the smallest in the sample and the subsidiary of a U.S. company, it exported 60 per cent of its output and, in this case, a shortage of factory space was the dominant production constraint. Unfortunately, although the company was located on a spacious site to the north of London, it had at the time of our field work, experienced difficulties in obtaining an Industrial Development Certificate for expansion at its existing location. Since the firm exported a relatively high proportion of its output, it seems reasonable to assume that it was efficient and, at the same time, 75 per cent of its exports were directed to the U.S. market! Such an example provides an interesting illustration of the possible conflict in policy objectives between the government's desire to encourage exports and its commitment to 'balanced regional development'.

Conclusions

The U.K. office machinery sector being both a capital goods and a growth industry provides a useful contrast with the other industries in our survey. In assessing our interview and questionnaire results, two points seem worthy of emphasis. First, in considering various aspects of a firm's export behaviour, it might be significant to mention some of the factors which firms did *not* seem to regard as important. For example, no firm in our sample regarded government policies as a factor preventing an increase in exports nor did any firm feel that it was the aim of its export policy to maintain a minimum level of exports. During a period of peak demand, no firm stated that exports were lost due to increasing delivery dates nor during a deflation did exports apparently benefit from quicker delivery. Finally, no company stated that labour shortages represented a production constraint.

Second, at the level of the individual firm, we only obtained limited support for the pressure hypothesis and the majority of firms stated that exports were not significantly affected during periods of peak demand or deflation. We must now compare these qualitative results with our econometric analysis of the pressure hypothesis.

III. AN ECONOMETRIC ANALYSIS

For the U.K. office machinery industry, our tests of the pressure hypothesis were undertaken at both the industry and the firm level, although the latter were extremely limited. As previously, use was made of both linear and log-linear regressions in which the dependent variables were variations in the level of U.K. exports to particular markets and import shares. For the industry tests, our measures of domestic demand were based on the value of the industry's domestic sales and the unemployment rate for Great Britain. Each regression incorporated a time-trend and dummy variables for seasonal adjustment. We proceed by first considering the results of the tests at the industry level.

Initially, we attempted to explain variations in the level of the U.K. industry's exports of office machinery to the Australian and U.S. markets[1] during the period 1958-66. The relevant annual data of total imports and shares for both of these markets are shown in Table 9.2.

For variations in the level of U.K. office machinery exports to Australia, it was found that the coefficient of the overseas demand variable, namely the value of Australian imports was statistically significant and positive, with a partial elasticity in the range of 0·3 to 0·4. From the domestic demand variables used for this market, only the one based on variations in the value of the industry's domestic sales gave a statistically significant coefficient and, being

[1] The choice of markets was determined by data availability and the fact that Australia represented a major market for U.K. office machinery exports. The models used were:

(a) $X = aM^{\alpha}D^{\beta}e^{kt}$

(b) $X = aM^{\alpha}D^{\beta}e^{kt+k_1t^2}$

TABLE 9.2 *Australian and U.S. Office Machinery Imports, 1958-66*

	Australia		*U.S.A.*	
Year	*Total imports*	*U.K. share*	*Total imports*	*U.K. share*
	(£A, 000)	(%)	(U.S. $000)	(%)
1958	11,346	47·7	35,769	9·2
1959	10,629	42·1	48,983	6·1
1960	12,670	38·9	69,719	4·1
1961	12,487	32·7	74,804	9·3
1962	13,854	30·5	84,360	10·3
1963	13,727	35·6	94,839	11·4
1964	24,943	26·8	102,587	9·3
1965	58,473	16·4	136,218	10·7
1966	80,473	10·0	190,473	11·2

TABLE 9.3 *The Level of U.K. Office Machinery Exports to Australia and the U.S.A., 1958-66*

	Coefficients of					
Exports	log *HS*	log *M*	*t*	t^2	$\bar{R}^2$	*d*
1. log X_A	−0·68*	0·30**	0·001		0·619	1·30
	(0·27)	(0·09)	(0·006)			
2. log X_A	−1·06*	0·39**	(0·02	−0·0009	0·623	1·53
	(0·42)	(0·12)	(0·02)	(0·0008)		
3. log X_{US}	1·36	−0·49	0·02	0·0016	0·829	1·40
	(0·78)	(0·51)	(0·03)	(0·0009)		

Notes: (1) log X_A and log X_{US} are logs of the value of U.K. office machinery exports to Australia and the U.S., expressed in Australian £ and U.S. $, respectively.
(2) log *HS* = log of deviations from trend of the value of the office machinery industry's domestic sales.
(3) log *M* = log of value of office machinery imports into a country: Equations 1 and 2 relate to Australia and Equation 3 to the U.S.A.
(4) *t* = time-trend, 1958 I to 1966 IV.
(5) Dummy variables were used for seasonal adjustment.
(6) Standard errors are shown in brackets.

** Significant at 1 per cent level.
* Significant at 5 per cent level.

negative, its sign was consistent with the predictions of the pressure hypothesis. In comparison, the equations explaining variations in the level of U.K. exports to the U.S. market were not very satisfactory. None of the coefficients for the overseas demand nor the domestic demand variables were statistically significant, with the former result being somewhat surprising. In the case of exports to this market, it is possible that the result arises because of the presence in the industry of a number of U.K. subsidiaries of U.S. companies: the parent companies might be largely supplying their own home market to the exclusion of their subsidiaries. Examples of the results are shown in Table 9.3.

With the shares model at the industry level, we considered variations in the U.K.'s share of Australian and U.S. office machinery imports during the period 1958-66, using both linear and log-linear regressions.[1] The results can be readily summarized. For both markets, none of the equations gave a coefficient for the pressure variable which was significant at the 5 per cent level. In each case, the unemployment variable gave the most promising results with signs consistent with the hypothesis but the *t*-values for the pressure coefficients were only in the range 1·50 to 1·89. Some examples of the results are shown in Table 9.4.

At the firm level, the tests of the pressure hypothesis were restricted by the fact that we only obtained data from two firms, *A* and *B*, both being subsidiaries of U.S. companies. The two firms provided quarterly data for home and export sales but, unfortunately, we were not able to obtain the country distribution of these exports and consequently, we were obliged to select the overseas markets for each firm on the basis of information received from the interviews and questionnaires. The measures of internal pressure were the same as for the industry with the addition of a measure based on the value

[1] The models used were:

(a) $S = \alpha_0 + \alpha_1 D + \alpha_2 t$

(b) $S = \alpha_0 + \alpha_1 D + \alpha_2 t + \alpha_3 t^2$

(c) $S = \alpha_0 D^{\alpha_1} e^{kt}$

(d) $S = \alpha_0 D^{\alpha_1} e^{kt + k_1 t^2}$.

In each case, our measures of domestic demand are based on the value of the industry's domestic sales and the national unemployment rate. As previously, the shares models are based on the assumption of a partial elasticity of U.K. office machinery exports with respect to overseas demand of unity.

TABLE 9.4 *The U.K.'s Share of Australian and U.S. Office Machinery Imports, 1958-66*

Share of market	Coefficients of *U*	log *U*	*t*	t^2	$\bar{R}^2$	*d*
1. S_A	4·78 (3·09)		—0·89 (0·12)		0·686	1·53
2. log S_A		0·43 (0·25)	0·02 (0·02)	—0·0015 (0·0005)	0·677	1·35
3. S_{US}	1·96 (1·06)		0·08 (0·15)	0·002 (0·004)	0·274	0·99

Notes: (1) S_A = U.K.'s percentage share of Australian office machinery imports.
(2) S_{US} = U.K.'s percentage share of U.S. office machinery imports.
(3) U = Unemployment rate for Great Britain.
(4) Remaining details as for Table 9.3.

of the firm's home sales. The basic form of the equations was also identical with those used for the industry.[1]

For firm *A*, the choice of overseas markets was easily determined since most of its exports went to the U.S.A. In fact, in the absence of more accurate data, we assumed that all the firms' exports went to this market. For variations in the level of firm *A*'s exports to the U.S.A., it was found that as with the industry results for this market the coefficient of the overseas demand variable was not statistically significant. Like the pottery industry, it is possible that the result reflects the influence of factors which are peculiar to an individual firm. In this case, our interviews revealed that the U.S. parent company's policy resulted in its U.K. subsidiary selling the bulk of its exports to the North American market and this might explain the lack of a statistically significant result for the overseas demand variable.[2] As for the pressure variable in the level of exports model,

[1] That is, level of exports and shares models, the former in log-linear form and the latter in both linear and log-linear form.

[2] The overseas demand variable is based on the value of imports: presumably, for this firm a more accurate measure of overseas demand would be domestic demand in the U.S.A.

we obtained some significant coefficients but their signs were not consistent with the predictions of the pressure hypothesis. Examples of the results are shown in Table 9.5. Here, it is interesting to observe that for this firm, our qualitative results based on interviews showed that in a period of peak demand, exports are adversely affected whilst in a deflation, exports are not significantly affected: results which apparently conflict with those from our econometric analysis.

TABLE 9.5 *Firm A and the Level of Exports to the U.S.A., 1958-65*

	Coefficients of						
Equation	log *HS*	log *U*	log *M*	*t*	t^2	$\bar{R}^2$	*d*
1	1·43 *		0·29	−0·11	0·005	0·848	1·14
	(0·66)		(0·48)	(0·04)	(0·001)		
2		−0·59 *	0·31	−0·04	0·002	0·849	1·41
		(0·26)	(0·46)	(0·04)	(0·001)		

Notes: (1) The dependent variable is log of firm *A*'s exports (value).
(2) log *HS* = log of deviations from trend of the value of the industry's domestic sales.
(3) log *M* = log of value of office machinery imports into U.S.A.
(4) Based on quarterly data for the period, 1958 I to 1965 IV.
(5) Remaining details as in previous tables.

When firm *A*'s data were incorporated into linear and log-linear shares models, the results were inconclusive. In general, the pressure variables did not produce any coefficients which were significant at the 5 per cent level. For example, the unemployment variable gave a coefficient which had a negative sign but it was only significant at the 10 per cent level. Thus, the tests based on estimated market share failed to provide any support for the pressure hypothesis but, at the same time, the results were consistent with those derived from the level of exports model for firm *A*.

For firm *B*, the problems of testing the pressure hypothesis were much greater, the major difficulty being the choice of overseas markets. Since a number of European countries formed its leading export markets, we examined the E.E.C. and West European markets, each being considered separately for the period 1959 I to 1963 IV: in each case, it was assumed that the relevant market absorbed the whole of firm *B*'s exports. With the level of exports model, the only significant coefficient for the overseas demand variable had the expected positive sign, with a partial elasticity of firm *B*'s exports with respect to overseas demand of substantially less than one. At the same time, the various measures of internal pressure including measures based on the value of the industry's and the firm's home sales suggested a positive relationship between variations in the firm's exports and domestic demand, and hence a complete lack of support for the pressure hypothesis. This result was also confirmed by the shares model, where it was found that the majority of the coefficients for the pressure variables showed either no significant relationship or a positive relationship between short-run movements in share and domestic demand. Such results are difficult to reconcile with the views expressed in interview, where it was stated that firm *B*'s exports were not significantly affected by domestic demand: there is, in fact, some evidence from the regressions to suggest that domestic demand made some contribution towards explaining variations in the firm's exports to particular markets, even though the contribution was *not* in the direction predicted by the pressure hypothesis. Examples of the results for firm *B* are shown in Table 9.6.

TABLE 9.6 *Firm B and the Level of Exports, 1959-63*

	Coefficients of					
Equation	log *HS*	log *U*	log *M*	*t*	$\bar{R}^2$	*d*
1	1·17 ** (0·36)		−0·46 (0·33)	0·03 (0·02)	0·422	1·65
2		−0·31 (0·18)	0·12 (0·29)	0·005 (0·021)	0·156	1·23
3	0·86 * (0·40)		−0·09 (0·39)	0·01) (0·02)	0·339	1·44

Notes: (1) Dependent variable is log of firm *B*'s exports (value).
(2) In Equations 1 and 2, log *M* is the log of E.E.C. imports (value); in Equation 3, log *M* is the log of office machinery imports into Western Europe.
(3) Based on quarterly data for period 1959 I to 1963 IV.
(4) Remaining details as in Table 9.5 and previous tables.

Conclusions

At the level of the industry, our tests provided some support for the pressure hypothesis. There was also an indication that for the U.S.A. during the period 1958-66, the pressure of domestic demand in the U.K. made no contribution towards explaining variations in the industry's exports to this market. Once again, then, there is evidence of possible differences in the pressure effect between various overseas markets. At the firm level, there was no support for the pressure hypothesis but, in the absence of more accurate data on the country distribution of exports, any refutation of the hypothesis can only be tentative. Moreover, at this level, the econometric results appeared to be in conflict with those derived from the interviews with the two firms. Even if accepted, the regression results only apply to two firms in the office machinery industry: for the industry as a whole, there was some limited support for the pressure hypothesis. The difference in the results for the industry and for the two firms, *A* and *B*, might reflect the heterogeneity of firms and, in particular, the different marginal cost conditions between firms and between various product lines within a firm.

Chapter 10

DOMESTIC ELECTRICAL APPLIANCES

INTRODUCTION

Any study of domestic electrical appliances raises practical problems of definition and coverage. There is a definitional inconsistency between international trade statistics and the United Kingdom Census of Production. Section 725 of the Standard International Trade Classification, 'Domestic Electrical Equipment' includes domestic refrigerators in addition to washing machines, vacuum cleaners and other appliances with motors, cookers and heating appliances. However, the manufacture of domestic refrigerators is not included within the Domestic Electrical Appliances Industry in the Census of Production, so that it is difficult to relate the activities of the industry as described in the Census to the export performance as measured in international trade statistics.

There is a further problem relating to Census of Production data. The Census is based upon establishments and consequently obscured one feature of the industry: that a number of firms are concerned also with the manufacture of wide ranges of products outside the domestic electrical appliances field. In these circumstances, there are considerable difficulties of a practical and conceptual nature in any analysis of the performance and output of domestic electrical appliances in isolation. Productive capacity for appliances might be affected by variations in the position regarding other quite different products and the relation between a firm's export sales and home demand for appliances may be satisfactorily accounted for only in the wider context of an examination of an individual firm's whole production. Moreover, aspects of exporting policy as regards domestic electrical appliances might make sense only against the background of a firm's policy aims for its exports as a whole. Thus, an apparently unsatisfactory export performance in domestic appliances may reflect a deliberate switch of emphasis to other more profitable products.

It was doubtful whether any simple quantitative study such as was within our resources would throw much light on the questions we were interested in, apart from the problem that in an industry dominated by a few large firms, they might be reluctant to disclose sufficient statistical data to make an econometric study viable. In spite of these difficulties, it seemed worth while to try to explore, if only in discussion, how firms themselves saw the relation between export performance and home demand. Home sales of domestic electrical appliances, along with other consumer durables, have been particularly subject to regulatory economic policy measures. Controls on hire purchase deposits and instalments have been used to affect directly the level of home sales of consumer durables. And indirectly, spending on consumer durables is particularly sensitive to variations in consumer incomes.

Because of these difficulties we decided to limit the scope of the enquiry in two ways. First, we made no attempt to cover the industry either completely (which was more than enough for our resources) or on a sampling basis (for which we did not have enough information and would in any case have been vitiated by non-response). Secondly, it was decided to concentrate in discussions with firms on three principal products of the industry: domestic refrigerators, washing machines, and vacuum cleaners. The following section sets out the general background to the industry, particularly as regards its international trade position. Then follows a description of the results of interviews with firms. It has not been possible to carry out a study at industry level of the relation between export performance and the pressure of demand owing to insufficiently long runs in the trade statistics of relevant overseas countries.

I. GENERAL OUTLINE

Over the period under review (1958-66), and particularly during the later years, United Kingdom producers of domestic electrical appliances have faced increasing competition both on the home and export markets.

TABLE 10.1 *U.K. Statistics Relating to Domestic Electrical Appliances*

	Supplies to home market (£m)				*Proportion*
	Deliveries from U.K. production	*Imports †*	*Total*	*U.K. exports **	*of output exported*
				(£m)	(%)
1958	101	...	...	22·0	22·0
1959	138	...	...	21·0	15·0
1960	130	14·0	144	29·0	22·0
1961	138	9·0	147	29·0	21·0
1962	144	8·0	152	31·7	22·0
1963	165	8·4	173	35·6	21·5
1964	166	9·0	175	34·6	20·9
1965	152	8·8	161	32·2	21·1
1966	157	14·9	172	28·6	18·2

* 1958–61 figures estimated from partial data.
† 1960–2 figures estimated from partial data.

The whole period 1958-66 divides naturally into two parts. In the first, up to around 1963, there was a very sizeable increase in supplies to the home market of nearly three-quarters in value terms.[1] During this period, imports were not as a whole important although they were rising at a faster rate than home production. Between 1963 and 1966 the home market has remained roughly static but imports have risen and domestic production fallen. In 1965, imports accounted for nearly 10 per cent of the home market compared to 5 per cent in 1963 and a smaller proportion in 1958 (precise comparable figures are not available for 1958). United Kingdom experience in the export market appears to have reflected the situation on the home market. Between 1958 and 1963, when exports reached a peak, there was an increase in value terms of roughly 60 per cent. But between 1963 and 1966, they fell by one-fifth.

Commodity Composition

Aggregate statistics for 'domestic electrical appliances' (code 725 in the United Kingdom trade statistics and Standard International

[1] Figures in constant price terms are not available and indeed their computation presents considerable technical problems because of changes in kinds and qualities of products. However, price changes over the period under review as a whole have not been substantial and the value figures are probably a fairly accurate reflection of the volume changes.

Trade Classification) comprise domestic refrigerators (725.01), washing machines (725.02), vacuum cleaners, food mixers, fans etc. (725.03), shavers (725.04) and various cooking and heating appliances (725.05). In our discussions with firms, we decided to concentrate particularly on three products: refrigerators, washing machines (which form part of the home laundry category) and vacuum cleaners. These are picked out in the following tables:

TABLE 10.2 *U.K. Imports of Domestic Electrical Appliances, 1960-66*

£ million

	1960	*1961*	*1962*	*1963*	*1964*	*1965*	*1966*
Refrigerators	(5·3)	(1·6)	0·63	0·81	1·47	1·95	2·53
Washing machines	(2·0)	(1·01)	1·02	1·80	1·62	1·37	0·96
Vacuum cleaners, etc.	...	...	1·72	1·07	1·47	1·57	3·14
Shavers, etc.	...	...	0·42	0·71	0·94	0·93	0·94
Heaters, etc.	...	...	...	3·98	3·57	3·03	7·31
Total	(14·0)	(9·0)	(8·0)	8·4	9·0	8·8	14·9

Note: Figures in brackets partially estimated and not strictly comparable with those of subsequent years. Statistics not available for 1958–9.

TABLE 10.3. *U.K. Exports of Domestic Electrical Appliances, 1958-66*

£ million

	1958	*1959*	*1960*	*1961*	*1962*	*1963*	*1964*	*1965*	*1966*
Refrigerators (01)	(9·9)	(7·8)	(9·0)	(7·0)	6·05	5·12	4·55	4·45	3·70
Washing machines (02)	(5·8)	(5·4)	(8·8)	(10·1)	(12·0)	14·07	12·09	9·66	7·03
Vacuum * cleaners, etc. (03)	(5·3)	(6·1)	(8·1)	(9·6)	8·63	8·45	9·90	9·72	8·96
Shavers, etc. (04)	...	...	...	...	2·15	1·97	1·69	1·44	1·97
Heaters, etc. (05)	...	...	...	...	2·90	5·99	6·37	6·93	6·94
Total	(22·0)	(21·0)	(29·0)	(29·0)	31·7	35·6	34·6	32·2	28·6
* Of which:									
Vacuum cleaners	(1·5)	(1·7)	(2·2)	(2·9)	3·20	3·48	3·96	4·22	3·60

Note: Figures in brackets partially estimated.

Over the period 1958-62, imports of most appliances reflected very closely the rise and fall of the business cycle. In the boom year of 1960 refrigerators and washing machines in particular reached a peak of over £5 million and £2 million respectively, which were not attained in any later year. Following the deflationary measures of 1961, imports fell back to a low point, for some in 1962 and for others in 1963. It is interesting that over this period, exports of most kinds of appliances showed a marked and fairly steady rise. Exports of washers and vacuum cleaners around 1962 were running at twice the level of 1958, though exports of refrigerators showed a more variable experience. In short, there is no obvious sign in the figures of export performance being affected at that time by the pull of the home market. Certainly the simplest explanation of the movements in imports and exports at that time is that the surge in imports was a temporary one which filled the supply gap on the home market at the time of high pressure of demand around 1960. The expansion of exports suggests that British manufactures were maintaining their competitive position.

No similar straightforward explanation for the period since 1963 is supported by the data. Apart from washing machines, all imports of all commodity groups have moved fairly steadily upward. Between 1963 and 1966, imports of refrigerators more than trebled, as did commodities in group 725.03 (vacuum cleaners, floor polishers, etc.). And these increases took place at a time when deliveries to the home market were in general either stable or falling. By and large, imports were gaining an increasing share of many parts of the United Kingdom market. At the same time, the growth in exports, so marked before 1963, ended. There were sizeable falls in exports of refrigerators and washing machines while exports of other commodity groups showed a fairly level trend.

To sum up, the picture suggested by the production, import and export figures is that in the later part of the period, there has been some worsening in the competitive position of the United Kingdom industry. In spite of restrictions on consumer demand, the import surcharge and declining or static United Kingdom export sales, foreign suppliers have managed to increase their share of the home market.

The rise in imports between 1963 and 1966 was uneven, not only as regards the individual types of appliances but also the sources of supply. The rise in imports of domestic refrigerators was almost wholly accounted for by increased imports from Italy; in 1966 Italian imports were valued at £1·9 million with a 78 per cent share of U.K. imports market. The Italians also increased their share of the declining level of imports of washing machines with sales of £0·5 million, or 60 per cent of imports from all sources. Imports of vacuum cleaners rose relatively little between 1963 and 1966 but in this case the French achieved a share in the total of 65 per cent with their imports valued at nearly £0·5 million.

II. INTERVIEW AND QUESTIONNAIRE RESULTS

Interviews were granted by four of the firms which we approached; they took place between July and October 1966. The firms were all extremely helpful in frankly discussing the position and policies of their firms. Only two firms, however, felt able to provide statistics about their sales performance on the home and export markets and even here the data, which came readily out of their accounts, was not sufficiently detailed to allow any econometric analysis of the effect on export performance of the demand situation in the home market. As in the case of other industries, the crucial gap in the available data was a breakdown of export sales according to country of destination.

Of the four firms interviewed, only one, referred to as firm *A* below, almost exclusively manufactured and sold home laundry equipment and vacuum cleaners. Firm *B* manufactured a wider range of appliances, although over two-thirds of its output were of home laundry, vacuum cleaners and refrigerators; a short time before the interview took place, this firm had merged to become part of a wider grouping but the interview related to the situation before the merger. The main business of the third firm, *C*, was the manufacture of gas and electrical cookers and fires and only some 6 per cent of output comprised home laundry equipment. The last, firm *D*, was a large firm with wide interests inside and outside of the electrical industry; our interview related only to the division manufacturing domestic electrical appliances, where production was divided roughly equally between home laundry, refrigerators and cookers. The size of the firms was substantial. Their total labour forces were between 2,500 and 12,000 although in each case only part was attributable to the products under study.

Allocative Decisions

Only firm *A* had a substantial stake in exports with 40 per cent of output exported. The other three exported between 5 and 8 per cent of total output; for these firms in no case did the proportion of output exports of any of the three product groups exceed 17 per cent. Three firms, *A*, *C* and *D*, had experienced a falling trend in exports, by volume and value, in the five years previous to the time of the interviews in 1966. Firm *B*'s exports had risen to a peak in 1963, but the value (though not the volume) had since been falling; we were told that this decline was the consequence of their policy of establishing overseas production and distribution.

Each of the four firms said it would prefer, and was aiming at, a larger proportion of production going to exports than the current level. Understandably, they were reluctant to quantify this preference but two of the respondents among the 'small' exporters thought an export proportion in the range 15 to 25 per cent would in some sense be ideal. This response was a little unexpected in view of the lower profitability of exports (see below) and their current exporting experience. We explored first the reasons for this policy aim and second the measures being taken to try to bring it about.

The general desire to increase exports, both in absolute terms and as a proportion of total output, was a consequence of their general policy aim of growth; they all took the view that growth could only come from sales to export markets, with little scope for growth in home sales. This was the main benefit of exporting which they all cited. Another benefit suggested, though not by all, was the security exporting offered through diversification of markets. At the same time, none of the firms envisaged any quick progress towards a greater emphasis on the export market, not surprising in view of the recent falling trend in exports. One firm pointed to the formidable difficulties in moving from the current 5 per cent export share of total production to what it viewed as the ideal level of 25 per cent: an expansion of exports requires first a careful planning exercise and second a substantial investment of real resources including sales promotion, setting up of service facilities and the design of new products or the modification of existing products for the overseas markets. This kind of investment was difficult to justify in a situation where the home market was both highly competitive and non-expansionary. The three 'small' exporters all identified two main factors hindering export expansion: the competitive pressure on prices (see the section on export profitability below) and the problem of producing the right product design for the market. One of the 'small' exporters had carved out a niche for itself in a number of relatively minor sterling area markets. These markets have the advantage that U.K.-type products are acceptable but provide no satisfactory base for export expansion. The firm already exporting 40 per cent of its output was less pessimistic about the prospects for export expansion. One of its main products has a special design feature which gives it a strong competitive edge, but this firm also saw product prices as an important limiting factor over the rest of its product range.

We asked what steps firms were taking to attain a growth in exports. In the light of the above discussion any measures could not be expected to have a quick impact. Indeed, the firm which had said it would prefer an export-home sales division of 25 to 75 per cent took the view that in the current economic situation there were no feasible steps which could be taken. The others spoke of improving overseas selling effort and methods particularly by way of setting up wholly-owned overseas distributors. Apparently only one, firm *B*, was setting out to design products specifically for overseas markets. The other facet of this firm's overseas policy was to increase its stake in local manufacture abroad which would, if anything, work against exports, though of course ultimately show benefits to the balance of payments in other sectors.

Export Profitability and Pricing Policy

Each firm was clear that exports were less profitable than home sales. One respondent estimated that the net profit on turnover was 10 per cent for home sales compared to only 1 per cent on exports. They all agreed that the primary reason was the greater degree of price competition. The firms' pricing policies were flexible in both the home and export market and prices were arrived at after striking what was thought to be an acceptable balance between costs and the market situation. In general, export prices were below home prices, product for product. There was no support for a marginal approach to export pricing, even from the 'small' exporters. The view was expressed that a company would be uncomfortably vulnerable to changes in the market situation if any sizeable part of production were not making its proper contribution to overheads.

For these firms, export profitability was also being squeezed on the cost side. In general, domestic electrical appliances sold on the home market are not suitable for overseas without significant design modifications, particularly in European and American markets. As a consequence, design and production costs are higher. Two of the 'small' exporters also mentioned the small size of export orders and additional selling costs as contributory factors to lower export profitability.

Exports and Home Demand: The Pressure Hypothesis

The central feature of the four firms' experience in recent years was that over no significant time-period had they experienced a situation of unsatisfied demand. In reply to our question about the variation in the length of the order book over the previous five years, two said that there had not been one to vary, and the others that the variation had been very small. It was suggested by one respondent that technical hold-ups on the production line were a more significant cause of temporary unsatisfied demand than fluctuations in demand itself. Firms said that they were in a position to quickly adjust production up or down to meet variations in total demand. One firm pointed out that the level of demand need not be taken as given: to a certain extent they could influence it in the short run by advertising and sales promotion methods generally. It was inevitable therefore that our discussion of the effect upon exports of variations in home demand would be related to factors other than the consequences of capacity limitations.

There was a fair consistency of view about the effect of domestic deflation and the firms' response to it. All four gave as their immediate response to domestic deflation a reduction in total output. Only one firm said that there would be any voluntary production for stocks and that only in the short term. All said there would be increased sales effort in the home market though only one said it responded by way of lowering product prices in the form of discount offers and sales promotions linked with gift offers. (Casual observation, however, suggests that this is a common procedure.) Two of the firms, including firm *A* exporting a large proportion of output, said they would make increased sales effort in overseas markets. But in all the interviews the point was made that it was difficult or impossible to achieve any increase in exports in the short run to take up slack on the home market. Home sales people cannot be switched to export promotion because they do not know the markets. Nor indeed can production lines geared to home market products necessarily easily be changed to turning out export products.

As to the effects on exports related to variations in home demand, three firms, *A*, *C* and *D*, offered the typical response of the volume-producer, suggesting that exports are adversely affected at a time of deflation and conversely that exports are helped at times of peak demand. Firms *A* and *D* attributed this to the movements in unit costs. Firm *C* also thought that exports were not benefited at times of deflation as the generally lower level of profitability meant that more emphasis was put upon home sales at the expense of the less profitable export market. Firm *C* also made a related point: exports often entail non-standard production runs and, as a consequence, these are more acceptable economically at times of peak output though it was acknowledged that exports are easier to fit in physically at other times. Only firm *B* took a different view. Although they thought that exports were not significantly affected at a period of peak demand, they said that in a deflationary phase, exports might benefit since more attention can then be paid to them.

Conclusion

We interviewed only four firms in the domestic electrical appliance industry though there was such a consistency of experience and view between them that one is tempted to think they might fairly reflect the wider population. Taking the results of the interviews as a whole, they suggest that, at the time of the survey, exports were significantly less profitable than home sales and yet, because of better growth prospects, firms would be ready to see a greater commitment to export sales. However, an increase in exports would not be easily come by, particularly in the case of the 'small' exporters, due to the investment which would be required. As for the effects of high pressure of home demand upon exports, capacity limitations have not been important. On the whole, firms took the view that at times of high pressure of demand exports were if anything helped by the reduction in unit costs and the greater profitability of both home and export sales. And at times of relatively low home demand, exports could not benefit, because production and sales of home and export models could not readily be interchanged nor could new markets quickly be developed.

Chapter 11

CONCLUSION

The central aim of this work has been to study the influence on firms' short-run export performance of variations in the pressure of home demand. Given the limited research resources the study has been confined to four industries: pottery, motor cycles and pedal cycles, office machinery and domestic electrical appliances. Our investigations have, if only incidentally, also thrown light upon related matters, such as the allocation of production between exports and home sales in the long run, and the role of pricing policy. We do not, however, claim to have made a comprehensive examination of these wider issues: a study of pricing policy and its relation to export performance in particular would have required a very different methodological approach, much greater research resources and, for that matter, a degree of co-operation and assistance from firms which could not be expected by private investigators.

There have been three strands to the methodology. The main one has been a series of interviews with senior managements of samples of firms in the selected industries. Much of the information gathered in these interviews has been of other than a straightforward factual nature as will be clear from the industry chapters above. There are, of course, serious difficulties in the way of eliciting meaningful responses to questions about attitudes, about hypothetical situations, and about the nature of causal relationships when the respondent has imperfect knowledge and when it is difficult to know how far other things are being held constant. There is, for example, the problem of communication, in that a straightforward question-and-answer procedure may fail to elicit important qualifications or indeed may fail to ask the right questions. So far as possible we guarded against this by conducting the interviews as discussions, the questionnaire providing a framework and to some extent the questions being formulated as the interview proceeded.

One particularly difficult area to explore in discussion, and one directly relevant to the theme of this study, was the relation between a firm's export performance and fluctuations in demand as understood by the businessman. Information of this kind may, of course, tell one little about the real nature of the relation, even if the respondent were perfectly informed about the dependence of his firm's exports upon the various variables specific to the firm, such as level of capacity-utilization and prices and costs. For his judgment might inevitably involve only a partial approach, taking the situation external to the firm as given; he might, for example, be unable or unlikely to assess the effect on the firm's exports of movements in costs arising out of variations in the general level of demand. The interview and questionnaire approach tends to provide information on what businessmen *think* to be the relationship between domestic demand and exports but, for a satisfactory test of the pressure hypothesis, it is necessary to observe the actual relationship between these variables. The point has been made in another context when it was stated that the direct questionnaire approach '. . . can definitely refute an hypothesis about what people *think* they do. *But what it cannot do is to provide a refutation of an hypothesis about what, in fact, people do*.'[1] Nevertheless, in spite of its limitations, useful information can emerge from this kind of enquiry. Businessmen will be aware of many of the relevant short-run factors such as the sensitivity of their exports to price changes and variations in delivery times, the ordering of priorities between home and export sales and generally the role of capacity limitations in their firm's export performance. Furthermore, whatever the basis and validity of businessmen's understanding of the situation, it is important in that it will in itself influence business behaviour. One final point needs to be made. We have referred to 'interviews with firms' but of course one interviews individual members of the firm. In large organizations, the response may depend much upon the person interviewed and his position in the firm; the export manager may have a very different viewpoint from that of the chief accountant. In

[1] R. G. Lipsey, *An Introduction to Positive Economics*, London: Weidenfeld and Nicolson, 1963 (1st ed.), p. 260; also, 2nd ed., London, 1966, p. 393.

general, however, we were fortunate to effect interviews with senior management and often we spoke with representatives of different interests.

Apart from the interview approach, the two other strands of this project have been econometric studies of short-run export performance in relation to the pressure of demand at firm and at industry level. The study at firm level had only limited success owing to deficiencies in data. Only in the case of pottery was it possible to proceed to a detailed study and even here the outcome was not conclusive. In general, the deficiencies in data were not due to lack of co-operation by managements but rather to the fact that firms' accounting procedures did not readily yield all the data we needed. The main gaps were lack of quarterly data and of statistics of exports according to country of destination.

RESULTS

In a pilot study of this nature it has been possible perforce to examine only a negligible part of British industry. The chosen industries – pottery, motor cycles and cycles, office machinery and domestic electrical appliances – account for only about 2¼ per cent of net output of manufacturing industry and some 3 per cent of exports of manufactures. But although the study can give little guide to what is happening aggregatively at a national level, the characteristics of the chosen industries span a sufficiently wide range to give some idea of the range of possibilities, and we have in fact studied firms which are very different to each other as regards type of product, size of firm, importance of exports in total sales, and long-run levels of capacity-utilization. Thus the pottery industry is one where small firms still play an important role; according to the 1963 Census of Production, 28 per cent of net output was accounted for by enterprises with between 25 and 400 employees whereas the corresponding percentage for the domestic electrical appliances industry was 12 per cent. The proportion of output exported in 1963 varied from 15 per cent for domestic electrical appliances to 54 per cent for the motor cycle and cycle industry combined. As regards long-run export performance, the industry characteristics include ones maintaining or increasing export sales as a proportion of output (pottery, motor cycles, cycles and office machinery) and ones experiencing a substantial degree of foreign competition in both home and overseas markets (motor cycles and domestic electrical appliances). Experience of pressure on capacity-utilization in the short and long run also varied much. At one extreme, many pottery firms had experienced full order books and full capacity working over a long period of years and at the other, the domestic electrical appliance firms we interviewed had no delivery waiting times of any significance even at times of generally high pressure of home demand. Some of the characteristics of the industries in our sample are shown in Table 11.1.

TABLE 11.1 *Characteristics of the Sample Industries, 1963*

	Pottery	*Motor cycles and cycles*	*Office machinery*	*Domestic electrical appliances*
Number of enterprises	314	120	49	194
Number of establishments	400	134	72	237
Average size of establishment	151	183	421	280
Employment (000)	60·2	24·5	30·3	66·4
Net output per head (£)	846	1,021	1,164	1,423
Exports (£000's)	14,500	16,914	33,735	35,600
Proportion of Output exported (%)	40	54	46	15

Sources: Report on the Census of Production, 1963.
Board of Trade, *Business Monitors.*
U.K. trade accounts.

The econometric results at both firm and industry level have been variable but certain tentative generalizations may be offered which are supported, though hardly substantiated, by the analyses. First, most of the industry-market analyses suggest a short-run elasticity of United Kingdom exports with respect to overseas demand of less than unity; that is, in the short run, and after allowing for U.K. pressure of demand effects, United Kingdom exports tend to show less response to fluctuations in overseas countries' import demand than do the exports collectively of competing countries. So far as this is so it has implications, as pointed out in Chapters 2 and 5, for econometric tests of the pressure hypothesis based upon the performance of the share of U.K. exports in world trade. An estimated short-run elasticity of less than unity could be attributed at least in part to bias in the estimation procedure (see Chapter 5). But in so far as it is correctly estimated, a number of possible explanations may be offered. In the case of an industry such as pottery with a long-run shortage of capacity, it is to be expected that export deliveries would not respond fully to fluctuation in overseas demand. It is more difficult to offer an explanation for an industry such as motor cycles which has experienced a long-term decline in the total volume of output. Perhaps in the short run, growth products in world trade are the more responsive to fluctuations in the internal demand of a country.

Secondly, there has been little consistency in the estimated pressure of demand effects and the results suggest a variety of experience not only between industries but also between different overseas markets for the same industry. Nevertheless, as a rough generalization, effects running the same way as the pressure hypothesis dominate. This is consistent with results of most econometric tests of the pressure hypothesis at the national level.

When we turn to the information gathered in the firm interviews a different general picture emerges. As is to be expected, again there was a variation in the response between the industries studied and to some extent between firms in the same industry. But on the whole, respondents generally believed that exports were not significantly affected by the level of domestic demand. We have referred above to the problem of evaluating the views of and information from businessmen, but in so far as there is a conflict between their assessment and econometric analysis it requires explanation. There are, it seems, at least three possibilities. First, as we have remarked above, the businessman will tend to ignore the effect on his firm's short-run export performance of changes in factor prices associated with the general level of demand. Secondly, he may have considerable difficulty in distinguishing between short- and long-run influences on exports. Thirdly, factors peculiar to the individual firm may dominate the firm's export performance.

The study has also shown some of the benefits of disaggregation. We found that within the administrative classification of an industry there was a substantial amount of product heterogeneity, a fact which means that for the pressure hypothesis, home and export sales might not be perfect substitutes. In addition, and not surprisingly, we discovered differences in the attitudes and export performances of firms not only between different industries but also within the same industry. Such differences might result from the different objectives of firms and the very disparate market conditions facing products within an industry.

At various points we have commented on the possible significance for the pressure hypothesis of such characteristics as the proportion of a firm's output exported, a firm's attitude towards this proportion, the degree of capacity-utilization and the nature of the production process, namely the distinction between mass production and batch production. In terms of the theory of the firm, these factors would be included in a more detailed analysis of the objective functions of firms, their market and cost conditions. In this respect, the traditional objective function, namely profit-maximization, provided a most satisfactory framework for some of our analysis of the short-run *output* relationship between exports and domestic demand: it was especially useful for specifying the increasing marginal cost conditions for the operation of the pressure hypothesis.[1]

Our survey of the export behaviour of firms gave some interesting results which provide the basis for further research.[2] It appears that more research is required on the determinants of the 'ideal' proportion of output exported, on whether, as claimed, exports actually result in 'security through diversification of markets' and on the determinants of a firm's queuing policy: here, it would be interesting to test the hypothesis that firms with a relatively large proportion of output exported give preference to export customers in their queuing policy. In the field of pricing, it was observed that in response to a domestic deflation, a relatively large number of firms indicated that they would not change home and/or export prices: evidence which is difficult to reconcile with the predictions of the profit-maximizing hypothesis. However, our interviews provided explanations for this apparent price 'rigidity', and some of these accounts, if valid, might

1 See Chapter 4. A detailed analysis of a firm's marginal costs is, in itself, a major project and one which was certainly beyond the resources of our study.

2 See also, P.E.P., *Firms and Their Exports*, London, 1964.

be compatible with the traditional objective function. For example, firms explained price rigidity in terms of doubts about price elasticities, the cost of changing prices and the associated effect on consumer goodwill; other firms were more specific in claiming that they were not attempting to maximize profits.[1] In addition, to explain export performance, it would seem relevant to compare any rigidity of product prices between nations, and, where significant differences are observed, explanations are required: here, differences in the objectives of firms and hence in their pricing provide possible explanations. As for the pressure hypothesis, there is considerable scope for extending our tests to a much wider range of industries.

Finally, we consider briefly the public policy aspects of our study. In Chapter 1, we summarized the arguments which have been advanced for expecting that deflationary policy measures at times of peak demand can be expected to act favourably upon U.K. export performance. The emphasis in the present study upon a disaggregative approach points to the highly variable and complex nature of the impact of the national level of demand upon the short-run export performance of individual industries and firms, particularly on the supply side. Thus, many firms emphasized that even when deflation initially created excess capacity, exports could not be expanded in the short run; not only might there be imperfect substitutability between home and export products, but also overseas marketing may require substantial investment of a long-run nature. Firms exporting a relatively high proportion of output made the point that they were insulated from the effects of deflation, and firms exporting a low proportion of output expressed an unwillingness to venture into untried export markets at a time of unfavourable and uncertain prospects in the home market. In these circumstances, where there is a high degree of variability between firms, general government deflationary measures are not immune from criticism. However, the question of whether a policy of operating generally on domestic demand is the least-cost method of achieving the objectives of public policy is something which our study cannot answer. We

1 For further qualifications, see R. G. Lipsey, *An Introduction to Positive Economics* (1st ed.), London, 1963, Chapter 22; also, 2nd ed., London, 1966, Chapter 29.

have merely identified the short-run export effects of variations in the pressure of internal demand for a limited number of industries. Whether there are any long-run effects on export competitiveness and whether, on the whole, these effects are beneficial, remains an open question.

Appendix A

QUESTIONNAIRE PROFORMA AND INTERVIEW DATA

This part of the appendix includes the questionnaire proforma used in the firm interviews together with tables summarizing the responses to the more important questions by each firm in the industries covered, namely, pottery, motor cycles and cycles, office machinery and domestic electrical appliances. As explained in the text, the questionnaire was used as a basis for discussion and so the tables setting out the firm responses do not give a comprehensive account of the information gathered in the interviews.

Notes to the industry tables

1. The question numbers are those of the questionnaire proforma. A brief indication of the nature of the question is given.
2. The lower-case letters refer back to the multiple choices set out on the questionnaire proforma. Any ordering of multiple responses is not set out. The letters *s* and *l* relate to short- and long-run responses respectively; thus, *as* means factor (*a*) operates in the short run. There are some blank entries either because the question was inapplicable or because the response could not adequately be fitted into the questionnaire scheme.
3. For questions 2 and 11, relating to trends in employment and exports respectively, *U* = up, *D* = down, *C* = constant, and *F* = fluctuating. For question 17, *a* generally means 'to increase exports'.
4. Additional notes follow each industry table.

QUESTIONNAIRE PROFORMA

1. What, in round figures, is your firm's present labour force? ....

2. How has it changed in the last five years:
   Up/down/constant.
   If a fall or rise, by how much? ....%

3. When does your accounting year end? ....

4. What was the valuation of net assets at the end of the last accounting year? ....

5. What are labour costs as a percentage of total costs? ....%

6. How is the value of your total output divided in percentage terms between the following types of commodities?

7. What proportion of total output is exported? ....%

8. With which countries do you do most export business?

9. What are the most important factors preventing an increase in your exports?

   Please mark in order of importance.

	In the short term	*In the long term*
(*a*) Prices of your products.		
(*b*) Quality and design of products.		
(*c*) Delivery dates.		
(*d*) Promotional effort.		
(*e*) Availability of export finance.		
(*f*) Government policies.		
(*g*) Shortage of capacity.		
(*h*) Other: please specify and add any comments.		

10. The answer to question 9 will relate to total exports. How would the answer vary if related to the individual commodity groups in question 6?

11. What has been the trend in total exports in the past five years?

In value terms.	Rising/steady/falling.
In quantity terms.	Rising/steady/falling.

12. Have any of the commodity groups in question 6 shown a trend different to the broad trend described in question 11?

13. If the trends in questions 11 and 12 were all rising or steady, is there any commodity or kind of commodity which has shown a significant export fall over the past five years?

14. Would you prefer a different proportionate division of your sales between exports and home sales? Yes/No

15. If 'Yes' to question 14, what would be an ideal split?

    Exports ....%, home sales ....%

16. If 'Yes' to question 14, what action, if any, can you take or are you taking, to change the present position?

17. Please indicate which of the following statements describe facets of your export policy.

    (*a*) To (i) increase/(ii) decrease exports.
    (*b*) To prevent exports falling below some minimum level.
    (*c*) To encourage exports as a way of diversifying markets.
    (*d*) To build up a market before establishing a foreign subsidiary.
    (*e*) Other: please specify and add any comments.

18. Which of the following selling methods, and aids to selling, do you use for exports?

(*a*) Export sales representatives.
(*b*) Exclusive overseas agents.
(*c*) Other overseas agents.
(*d*) Export department.
(*e*) U.K. export merchants.
(*f*) Overseas selling subsidiaries.
(*g*) Export Credit Guarantees Department.
(*h*) Board of Trade export services.
(*i*) Other: please specify and add comments.

19. How would you describe the profitability of exports as compared with home sales?

(*a*) Less profitable, (*b*) slightly less profitable, (*c*) no difference, (*d*) slightly more profitable, (*e*) more profitable.

20. If exports are generally less profitable than home sales, please mark the following reasons in order of importance:

(*a*) Greater risk of loss in export markets.
(*b*) Additional selling costs and paper work.
(*c*) Small size of export orders.
(*d*) Greater competition in export markets.
(*e*) Longer period of payment for exports.
(*f*) Other: please specify and add any comments.

21. Please mark in order of importance any other benefits of exporting:

(*a*) Prestige.
(*b*) Security through diversification of markets.
(*c*) Possibility of expansion, which is harder (or impossible) to achieve at home.
(*d*) Stimulus to introduce new products and/or new production techniques.
(*e*) Other: please specify and add any comments.

22. Describe how prices of established products are changed. In particular, is it the normal practice to change all prices simultaneously by the same percentage?

23. How are prices of new designs or products determined?
    (*a*) Solely on the basis of estimated cost.
    (*b*) Some other method: please specify.

24. Are export prices 'ex factory' identical to home prices? Yes/No

25. If 'No' to question 24, what determines export prices?

26. Does your firm make any modifications in export prices for?
    (*a*) Large customers.
    (*b*) New customers for existing products.
    (*c*) Old established customers.
    (*d*) Orders placed at convenient times of year.
    (*e*) Price changes of foreign competitors.
    (*f*) Price changes of U.K. competitors.

27. What has the normal lapse of time been in the last five years between?
    (*a*) Receipt of order and despatch and what has the range of variation been.
    (*b*) Despatch and receipt in U.S.A.
    Canada.
    Australia.

28. Which of the following statements is more appropriate for a period of peak demand for your products?
    (*a*) Exports are helped because unit costs are lower.
    (*b*) Some exports are lost because of lengthening delivery dates.
    (*c*) Exports are adversely affected because home costs and prices are rising.
    (*d*) Exports are not significantly affected.

29. Which of the following statements is more appropriate for a period of sharp deflation (the stop part of stop-go)?
    (*a*) Exports are adversely affected because unit costs rise.
    (*b*) Exports benefit because, with lower home sales, more attention can be paid to exports.
    (*c*) Exports will benefit from quicker delivery.
    (*d*) Exports are not significantly affected.

30. What is your firm's response to domestic deflation (rising bank rate, increased taxes, etc., as in 1964-5)?

(*a*) Increased sales effort in home market.
(*b*) Increased sales effort in overseas market.
(*c*) Changed product prices in home market.
(*d*) Changed product prices in overseas market.
(*e*) Reduction in total output.
(*f*) Production for stocks.
(*g*) No change in output, prices, sales effort.
(*h*) Other: please specify and add any comments.

31. When the order book is lengthening, how are order priorities decided?

(*a*) First in, first out.
(*b*) Preference to old customers.
(*c*) Preference to export/home customers.
(*d*) Preference to big customers.
(*e*) Preference to new customers.
(*f*) Other.

32. Could your firm sell more (exports) if it could produce more? Yes/No

33. If the answer to question 32 is 'Yes', what are the factors preventing increased production?

(*a*) Shortage of labour.
(*b*) Shortage of capital finance.
(*c*) Shortage of suitable land.
(*d*) Other: please specify and add any comments.

FIRM RESPONSES

1. *U.K. Pottery Industry, 1966*

(a) *Firms Manufacturing Domestic Pottery*

Number of question	*1*	*2*	*3*	*4*	*5*	*6*	*7*
1. Size of labour force	*L*	*M*	*S*	*M*	*M*	*S*	*L*
2. Employment trends	*U*	*D*	*D*	*D*	*D*	*C*	*D*
5. Labour costs as % of total costs	45	56	55	45	50	45	64
7. % of output exported	50	44	30	10	48	46	66
9. Factors preventing increase in exports	*i, k*	*c, i*	*d*	*a*	*j*	*a, c, g*	*e, g, i*
11. Export trends, value and volume	*U*	*U*	*D*	*U*	*D*	*U*	*U*
14. Preference for a different % exports/home sales	Yes	Yes	Yes	Yes	Yes	Yes	No
15. If 'yes', ideal % of exports	66	80	50	45	60	70	...
17. Aims of export policy	*a, e*	*a, c*	*a, c*	*a, c*	*a, c*	*a, c*	*c, h*
18. Selling methods	*e, f*	*e*	*f*	...	*h*	*f*	*e*
19. Profitability of exports	*b*	*a*	*a*	*b*	*e*	*b*	*d*

20. Reasons for lower profitability	*b, f, g*	*b, d, e, f, g*	*b, e*	*g*	...	*b, e, f*	...
21. Other benefits of exporting	*b, c*	*b, d*	*a, b, d*	*b*	*b*	*a, b*	*b*
23. Price determination	*a, c*	*a*	*a*	*c*	*a, b*	*c*	*a*
24. Export prices identical to home prices	Yes	Yes	Yes	Yes	Yes	No	Yes
26. Modifications in export prices	*a*	*a*	*a*	...	...	*a*	...
28. Exports and peak demand	*a, d*	*b*	*b, al*	*d*	*b*	*a, b*	*d*
29. Exports and deflation	*a, c*	*c*	*b*	*d*	*c*	*a*	*d*
30. Response of firm to deflation	*a, b, e, f*	*b, d, f*	*a, b, f*	*a, b, f*	*f*	*a, b, e, f*	*e, f*
31. Queuing policy	*a, c*	*a, d*	*c, d*	*a, c*	*a, d*	*a, c, f*	*c*
32. Could firm sell more	Yes	Yes	Yes	Yes	Yes	Yes	Yes
33. Production constraints	*a*	*a*	*a*	*a*	*a*	*a*	*a, b*

Notes: Question 1: L = over 1,000: M = 500-1,000: S = less than 500.
Question 9: i = shortage of labour: j = development of tariff-protected overseas industries.
Question 17: h = to maintain present proportion of exports.
Question 18: only e, f, g, h, responses recorded here.
Question 20: g = special production requirements.
Question 23: c = joint costing and market situation.
Question 31: c = preference to exports.

(a) *Firms Manufacturing Domestic Pottery* (continued)

Number of question	*8*	*9*	*10*	*11*	*12*	*13*	*14*
1. Size of labour force	*S*	*S*	*S*	*L*	*S*	*M*	*S*
2. Employment trends	*U*	*C*	*U*	*D*	*C*	*F*	*D*
5. Labour costs as % of total costs	50	50	50	45	56	42	55
7. % of output exported	66	8	33	75	30	63	60
9. Factors preventing increase in exports	*g, h*	*b*	*j*	*i*	*b, g, i*	*g*	*i*
11. Export trends, value and volume	*U*	*U*	*D*	*U*	*U*	*U*	*C*
14. Preference for a different % exports/home sales	No	Yes	Yes	Yes	No	Yes	Yes
15. If 'yes', ideal % of exports	...	40	50	70	...	less	more
17. Aims of export policy	...	*h*	*a, c*	*a, c*	*a, b*	*c*	*e*
18. Selling methods	*g, h*	*g, h*	*e*	*f, i*	*h*	*g*	*f*
19. Profitability of exports	*c*	*c*	*d*	*b*	*a*	*a*	*a*
20. Reasons for lower profitability	...	...	...	*b*	*b, c, d, g*	*b*	*b, d, f*

21. Other benefits of exporting	*a, b, d*	*b, c*	*b, d*	*a, b, d*	*b*	*a, b, d*	*c*
23. Price determination	*c*	*c*	*c*	*b*	*c*	*a*	*a*
24. Export prices identical to home prices	Yes	Yes	No	Yes	Yes	Yes	No
26. Modifications in export prices	*a, b*	*d*	...	...	*a, d*	...	*e, f*
28. Exports and peak demand	*d*	*al, ds*	*a*	*d*	*d*	*d*	*a*
29. Exports and deflation	*d*	*al, ds*	*a*	*d*	*cs, dl*	*d*	*d*
30. Response of firm to deflation	*e*	*a, b, f*	*e, f*	*a*	*c, f*	*g*	*f*
31. Queuing policy	*c, d*	*c, g, d*	*b, c*	*b*	*a, b, c*	*h*	*d, e*
32. Could firm sell more	Yes	Yes	Yes	Yes	Yes	Yes	Yes
33. Production constraints	*a, b*	*b, c*	*a*	*a*	*a, b*	*a*	*a*

Notes: Question 1: L = over 1,000: M = 500-1,000: S = less than 500.
Question 9: i = shortage of labour: j = development of tariff-protected overseas industries.
Question 17: h = to maintain present proportion of exports.
Question 18: only e, f, g, h, responses recorded here.
Question 20: g = special production requirements.
Question 23: c = joint costing and market situation.
Question 31: c = preference to exports.

(a) *Firms Manufacturing Domestic Pottery* (continued)

Number of question	*15*	*16*	*17*	*18*	*19*	*20*	*21*
1. Size of labour force	*S*	*S*	*S*	*S*	*S*	*L*	*L*
2. Employment trends	*D*	*C*	*C*	*C*	*U*	*U*	*D*
5. Labour costs as % of total costs	62	56	60	63	46	50	50
7. % of output exported	5	15	25	11	75	8	60
9. Factors preventing increase in exports	*d*	*a, j*	*a*	*a, j*	*d, j*	*j*	*a, b, c, d, i*
11. Export trends, value and volume	*D*	*D*	*C*	*C*	...	*D*	*U*
14. Preference for a different % exports/home sales	Yes	Yes	Yes	Yes	Yes	Yes	Yes
15. If 'yes', ideal % of exports	60	60	50	50	66	50	50
17. Aims of export policy	*a*	*a, b, c*	*a, c*	*a, c*	*h*	*c*	*a*
18. Selling methods	...	*h*	*f*	*e, h*	*g, h*	*e, h*	*f*
19. Profitability of exports	*e*	*c*	*e*	*c*	*c*	*a*	*e*
20. Reasons for lower profitability	...	*b, g*	...	...	...	*b, c, d, e*	...

21. Other benefits of exporting	*b*	*b, d*	*b, d*	*b*	...	*b*	*b*
23. Price determination	*b*	*c*	*a*	*a*	*c*	*c*	*c*
24. Export prices identical to home prices	Yes	Yes	Yes	Yes	Yes	Yes	Yes
26. Modifications in export prices	...	...	*a*	...	*a, f*	...	*a*
28. Exports and peak demand	*d*	*d*	*d*	*d*	*a*	*d*	*d*
29. Exports and deflation	...	*a*	*d*	*d*	*cs, dl*	*d*	*d*
30. Response of firm to deflation	*a, b, f*	*e, f*	*f*	*f*	*e, f*	*a, c, e, f*	*e*
31. Queuing policy	*c*	*a, c*	*a*	...	*a, c*	...	*b, c, d*
32. Could firm sell more	Yes	Yes	Yes	Yes	Yes	No	Yes
33. Production constraints	*a*	*a*	*c*	*a*	*a*	...	*a*

Notes: Question 1: L = over 1,000: M = 500-1,000: S = less than 500.
Question 9: i = shortage of labour: j = development of tariff-protected overseas industries.
Question 17: h = to maintain present proportion of exports.
Question 18: only e, f, g, h, responses recorded here.
Question 20: g = special production requirements.
Question 23: c = joint costing and market situation.
Question 31: c = preference to exports.

	Firms Manufacturing						
	(b) *Tiles*			(c) *Sanitary Ware*			
Number of question	*1*	*2*	*3*	*1*	*2*	*3*	*4*
2. Employment trends	*U*	*U*	*C*	*U*	*D*	*U*	*C*
5. Labour costs as % of total costs	30	40	38	38	43	33	30
7. % of output exported	36	40	14	34	13	21	11
9. Factors preventing increase in exports	*j*	*e, f, g*	*a, i*	*a, e, j*	*a, j*	*a, b, j*	*a, j*
11. Export trends: value	*a*	*a*	*a*	*a*	*c*	*b*	*c*
14. Preference for a different % exports/home sales	No	No	...	Yes	Yes	No	Yes
15. If 'yes', ideal % of exports	...	...	...	50	25	...	40
17. Aims of export policy	*a, c*	*a, c, d*	*a*	*a, c*	*a, c*	*a, h*	*a, c*

R 18. Selling methods	*e*	...	...	*e, g, h*	*e*	*e, g, h*	...
19. Profitability of exports	*a*	*a*	*a*	*a*	*a*	*b*	*a*
20. Reasons for lower profitability	*b, d*	*d, e*	*b, d*	*a, b, d, g*	*b, d*	*b, d, g*	*f*
21. Other benefits of exporting	*b, c*	*b, d, e*	*b*	*a, b*	*b*	*b, d*	*b*
23. Price determination	*a*	*c*	...	*b*	...	*c*	*c*
24. Export prices identical to home prices	No	No	No	Yes	No	Yes	Yes
26. Modifications in export prices	...	*a*	...	*a, e, f*	*e*	*a, e, f*	...
28. Exports and peak demand	*d*	*b*	*d*	*b, c*	*d*	*bs, al*	*d*
29. Exports and deflation	*d*	*d*	*cs, dl*	*a, c*	*cs, dl*	*cs, al*	*d*
30. Response of firm to deflation	*d, f*	*a, b, f*	*e, f*	*a, b, e, f*	*e, f*	*a, b, e, f*	*f*
31. Queuing policy	*c, d*	*b*	*c*	*b, c*	*b, c*	*b*	*a, b, c*
32. Could firm sell more	No	Yes	No	No	No	No	No
33. Production constraints	...	*a, b*	...	...	...	...	...

2. *U.K. Motor Cycle and Cycle Industry, 1966*

	Firms						
Number of question	*1*	*2*	*3*	*4*	*5*	*6*	*7*
2. Employment trends	*D*	*U*	*F*	*D*	*U*	*C*	*U*
5. Labour costs as % of total costs	30	33	33	...	10	17	12
7. % of output exported	55	70	66–70	50	55	8–10	10
9. Factors preventing increase in exports	*as, al, h*	*h*	*as, al, cs, es, el, g*	*h*	*gs, h*	*h*	*h*
11. Export trends: value	*D*	*U*	*U*	*U*	*U*	*U*	...
volume	*D*	*U*	*U*	*U*	*U*	*C*	...
14. Preference for a different % export/home sales	Yes	Yes	Yes	No	No	Yes	...
15. If 'yes', ideal % of exports	More exports if profitable	50–60	40	...	...	20–30	...
17. Aims of export policy	*a*	*a, c*	*c*	*c*	*a, c*	*a, c*	*e*
18. Selling methods	*a, c, d, f, g, h*	*e, g, h, i*	*a-e, g, h*	*c, i*	*b, g, h*	*c, e, g, i*	*b, g, h*

19. Profitability of exports	*a*	*a, e*	*a*	*a*	*a*	*a*	*a*
20. Reasons for lower profitability	*b, d, e*	*d, f*	*a, d, e*	*b, d*	*d, f*	*b, d*	*b, d*
21. Other benefits of exporting	*b, e*	*b, c*	*c*	*b*	*b, c*	*b, d*	*a*
23. Price determination	*b*	*b*	*b*	*b*	*b*	*b*	*b*
24. Export prices identical to home prices	No	Yes	No	Yes, U.S.A. No, others	No	Yes	No
26. Modifications in export prices	*a, c, d, e*	No	*a, b, e*	*a*	No	*a, b*	*a*
28. Exports and peak demand	*a*	*d*	*d*	*b*	*d*	*d*	*d*
29. Exports and deflation	*a*	*d* for U.S. *b* for others	*d*	*d*	*cs, dl*	*d*	*d*
30. Response of firm to deflation	*a*	*a, b, e*	*b, c, e, f*	*a-e, h*	*a, b*	*b, f*	*a, e, f, h*
31. Queuing policy	...	*c*	*a*	*c, e*	*d*	*a, c*	...
32. Could firm sell more	No	Yes	Yes	Yes	Yes	Yes	No
33. Production constraints	...	*a*	*a, b*	*a, b*	*a, c*	*a, b*	...

Note: Question 23: *b* = estimates of costs and market situation.

3. *The U.K. Office Machinery Industry, 1966*

Number of question	*Firms* 1	2	3	4	5	6
2. Employment trends	*U*	*C*	*C*	*U*	*U*	*U*
5. Labour costs as % of total costs	...	<50	65	20	35	29
7. % of output exported	50	75	30	25	45	60
9. Factors preventing increase in exports	*as, al*	*as, h*	...	*as, al, bs, bl, ds*	*as, al, h*	*h*
11. Export trends: value	*U*	*U*	*U*	*C*	*U*	*U*
volume	*U*	*U*	*C*	*C*	*U*	*U*
14. Preference for a different % export/home sales	No	No	...	Yes	No	No
15. If 'yes', ideal % of exports	...	...	...	60	...	...
17. Aims of export policy	*e*	*e*	*a*	*e*	*a, c*	*d, e*
18. Selling methods	*c, f*	*b, f*	*a-h*	*b, f*	*a, b, d, f, i*	*a, b, f, i*
19. Profitability of exports	*c*	*c*	*a*	*c*	*a*	*b*

20. Reasons for lower profitability	...	...	*a, d, e*	...	*d*	*b, c, d*
21. Other benefits of exporting	*a-d*	*a-d*	*a-d*	*b, c*	*c*	*a, c*
23. Price determination	*b*	*b*	*a*	*b*	*b*	*b*
24. Export prices identical to home prices	Yes	Yes	No	Yes	Yes	Yes
26. Modifications in export prices	*a, e*	*a-f*	*a*	*a*	*a*	none
28. Exports and peak demand	*d*	*d*	*a, c*	*d*	*d*	*c*
29. Exports and deflation	*d*	*d*	*a*	*d*	*d*	*d*
30. Response of firm to deflation	*a, b, g*	*a, b, f, g*	*a, b*	*a, b, h*	*h*	*a, h*
31. Queuing policy	*d*	*f*	various	*a, f*	*f*	none
32. Could firm sell more	Yes	No	...	No	No	Yes
33. Production constraints	*d*	*d*	...	*d*	...	*d*

Notes: (1) For question 17, *e* = growth.
(2) For question 23, *b* = estimates of costs and market conditions.

4. *Firms Manufacturing Domestic Electrical Appliances, 1966*

Number of question	*Firms* 1	2	3	4
2. Employment trends	*D*	*C*	*U*	*C*
5. Labour costs as % of total costs	11	8–10	...	11
7. % of output exported	40	7	5	8
9. Factors preventing increase in exports	*a*	*a, bs*	*a, b*	*a, b*
11. Export trends: value and volume	*D*	*D*	*D*	*D*
14. Preference for a different % exports/ home sales	Yes	Yes	Yes	Yes
15. If 'yes', ideal % of exports	...	...	25	15
17. Aims of export policy	*a, d*	*a, f*	*al, bs*	*a, c, d*
18. Selling methods	*a, b, d, f, g*	*a, b, c, d, f, g, h*	*a, c, d, g*	*e, h, i*
19. Profitability of exports	*a*	*a*	*a*	*a*
20. Reasons for lower profitability	*d, f*	*a, b, c, d, f*	*c, b, d*	*b, c, d, e*

21. Other benefits of exporting	*c*	*a, c, d*	*b, c, d*	*b, d, e*
23. Price determination	*c*	*c*	*d*	*d*
24. Export prices identical to home prices	No	No	No	No
26. Modifications in export prices	*a*	*f*	*a, b, c, e*	*a, b*
27. Order situation	*c*	*c*	*c*	*c*
28. Exports and peak demand	*a*	*d*	*a*	*e*
29. Exports and deflation	*a*	*b, c*	*a*	*e*
30. Response of firm to deflation	*a, b, e*	*a, b, e*	*a, c, e, f*	*a, e, h*
31. Queuing policy	*c* (exp.)	n. app.	n. app.	n. app.
32. Could firm sell more	No	No	No	No

Notes: For question 17: *f* = increase local manufacture abroad.
For question 23: *c* = market situation, *d* = costs if consistent with market.
For question 26: *f* = each price unique.
For question 27: *c* = no or negligible delay.

Appendix B

MOTOR CYCLES: APPENDICES TO CHAPTER 7

1. THE PRODUCT COMPOSITION OF U.K. MOTOR CYCLE IMPORTS AND EXPORTS, 1961-6

The figures below are based on complete motor cycles. They show quite clearly that the imports of conventional motor cycles have been dominated by small machines, whilst export volume has become increasingly dominated by large motor cycles over 250 cc.

(a) *Volume of U.K. Imports*

	Conventional motor cycles		
Year	*Under 250 cc.* (nos.)	*Total: conventional machines* (nos.)	*Conventional motor cycles under 250 cc. as percentage of total motor cycle imports** (%)
1961	4,513	4,789	5·4
1962	6,802	7,453	10·2
1963	58,095	58,108	39·5
1964	101,623	102,340	54·0
1965	37,741	38,041	46·4
1966	29,003	30,141	49·4

Note: * Total motor cycle imports consist of mopeds, scooters and conventional motor cycles. In the text, the 'other motor cycles' class is equivalent to the conventional motor cycles of the above table.

(b) *Volume of U.K. exports*

Year	Conventional motor cycles Under 250 cc. (nos.)	Conventional motor cycles Over 250 cc. (nos.)	Total: all machines* (nos.)	Conventional motor cycles over 250 cc. as percentage of total motor cycle exports (%)
1961	10,789	18,177	32,705	55·5
1962	9,031	16,312	28,972	56·3
1963	10,289	19,776	32,218	61·3
1964	9,037	23,199	34,286	67·6
1965	6,204	33,936	43,687	77·6
1966	6,619	52,241	60,970	85·6

Note: * See part (a) of table.
Sources: British Cycle and Motor Cycle Industries Association Ltd.
U.K. trade statistics.

(c) *Unit Values of U.K. Motor Cycle Exports*
The unit value figures for the large and small conventional motor cycles which entered the export trade are shown below. It must be emphasized that the figures only refer to conventional machines and exclude mopeds and scooters. The unit values are in current prices.

U.K. Export Unit Values

Year	Unit values of conventional U.K. motor cycle exports: Under 250 cc.	Over 250 cc.
	£	£
1961	101·8	167·0
1962	115·2	176·4
1963	114·6	179·6
1964	115·5	203·7
1965	122·4	215·6
1966	123·1	235·8

2. JAPANESE MOTOR CYCLE INDUSTRY

We feel that the rapid development of the Japanese industry merits some documentation: this Appendix provides background information on one of the world's leading motor cycle industries in 1966.

The Development of the Industry

During the period 1945-65, the Japanese motor cycle industry was characterized by the competitive elimination of firms. In the immediate post-war period, there were approximately 100 companies forming an industry of a large number of relatively small firms. In a competitive process which was not unlike that which occurred in the British car industry, the number of firms was reduced to about thirty by the mid-1950s and to six major manufacturers in 1965. Thus, by the mid-1960s, the industry consisted of a small number of relatively large firms and the major companies had a number of similar characteristics:

1. They were new entrants into the industry in the post-war period and, as such, they were not inhibited by the industrial tradition of the established pre-war companies. At the same time, some of the new entrants employed ex-aircraft engineers, so introducing new technical skills and knowledge into the industry[1]: technical skills which were especially suitable for increasing the speed and reducing the weight of machines.
2. The emphasis upon technical developments. In addition to research and development facilities, most of the existing major companies were the ones which entered their machines in international races: the majority of firms which did not enter such races were the ones which left the industry. In other words, entry into international racing might be regarded as a proxy variable for a company's technical progressiveness: an indicator of its technical ability and its attitude towards technology and marketing.
3. The emphasis on the mass production of standardized models with a consequent reduction in unit costs. The economies of scale achieved by the industry can be illustrated by the fact that in the mid-1960s, the industry had one plant which was mass producing 100,000 units *per month* which was almost equal to the total *annual* output of the British motor cycle industry in 1966!

The rapid development of the Japanese motor cycle industry can be most easily shown by the statistics of production and exports (see table on facing page).

The output and exports of the Japanese industry have been dominated by small motor cycles in the under 250 cc. and especially the less than 125 cc. size range. For example, large machines (over 250 cc.) formed between 1 and 5 per cent of the total annual volume of output for 1961-5, whilst the corresponding range for exports was 5 to 10 per cent. It is rather interesting to note that of the limited production of large machines, more than 60 per cent were exported: this is consistent with the Japanese

[1] By comparison the U.K. aircraft industry remained in existence in the post-war period.

The Japanese Motor Cycle Industry, 1946-65

Year	*Total production (units)* *All motor cycles*	*Machines over 250 cc.*	*Exports (units)*	*Exports as a proportion of total production*
				(%)
1946	211	n.a.	n.a.	n.a.
1950	2,633	n.a.	n.a.	n.a.
1955	200,831	n.a.	n.a.	n.a.
1958	503,087	5,059	5,427	1·0
1959	880,659	5,246	19,484	2·2
1960	1,473,084	7,031	56,268	3·8
1961	1,804,371	8,257	78,449	4·3
1962	1,674,925	18,533	202,090	12·0
1963	1,926,970	22,948	400,385	20·7
1964	2,110,335	35,565	592,737	28·0
1965	2,212,784	104,023	868,756	39·2

Source: Midget Motor Manufacturers' Association of Japan, *Facts and Figures*, 1966.

industry's specialization in the production of small motor cycles. A number of factors have contributed to both this specialization and the rapid development of the industry:

(i) The large population of Japan with its relatively low income levels provided a substantial domestic market for motor cycles. As a result, the industry developed a low-priced product to supply this domestic market. The actual size of the market can be indicated by the registration figures for two-wheeler machines. The number of registrations increased annually from nearly 2 million motor cycles in 1958 to about 8¼ million in 1966 – more than five times the corresponding 1966 figure for the U.K. The size of the Japanese domestic market relative to that of the U.K. can be shown even more strikingly by home market deliveries. For the period 1958-65 the Japanese industry's volume of output for its home market was about twelve times greater than the corresponding figure for the U.K. industry.[1] Here, the important point is that since the size of the domestic market provides an opportunity for achieving economies of scale, it seems plausible to suggest that the Japanese industry will have a substantial unit cost and associated price advantage in world markets.

[1] For 1962-5, the Japanese home market was larger by a factor of about 20!

(ii) Given the existence of a substantial domestic market for low-priced machines, it is still necessary to explain the Japanese industry's specialization in small motor cycles. There were a number of relevant factors. First, since unit values and size tend to be positively associated, the need for a low-priced product meant a market for a relatively small machine. Second, industry experts have pointed out that the stature of the Japanese people requires light motor cycles capable of being easily handled. Finally, the need for a light machine stimulated technical developments in engines, which eventually resulted in the successful production of small, but high performance, motor cycle engines.

Exports

The industry has been exporting an increasing proportion of its expanding volume of output. As might be expected with such an export performance, the industry's index of competitiveness[1] for the period 1958-65 was extremely favourable at about 36,530, which greatly exceeded the index for the British industry. Competitiveness in its broadest sense does, of course, provide the most plausible explanation for this export performance – and here competitiveness is almost certainly a multi-variable concept including price, product and marketing variables. Standardization and mass production have resulted in economies of scale and associated reductions in unit costs. For example, in the export sphere there has been a declining trend in the unit values of Japanese motor cycles throughout most of the period. In addition, technical developments and styling have accentuated product differentiation. The industry also benefited from new capital equipment installed after 1945 and from the relatively low Japanese shipping rates. Finally, the more qualitative and intangible aspects of competitiveness were evident, such as market research, marketing and publicity, international racing and after-sales service. We appreciate that the competitiveness explanation of the Japanese industry's export performance is not very satisfactory, since it merely identifies the variables which have contributed to exports without quantifying their relative importance: such a task is outside the scope of this study. For our purposes, it is sufficient to recognize that the nature of competition in the world motor cycle market might explain the long-run export performance of a nation's industry and this possibility has already been discussed. One further aspect of competitiveness requires noting, namely the relationship between total domestic market sales and exports. A comparison of the volume of output for the home market by the Japanese and U.K. industries between 1958 and 1966 shows that the Japanese industry's exports did not exceed those of Britain until its output for the domestic market exceeded 1·4 million

[1] Exports divided by import values, see page 154.

units. Between 1958 and 1966 British home market sales never exceeded 206,000 units so that before it was surpassed by the Japanese, the U.K. industry was exporting the same or a greater volume, on the basis of a much smaller domestic market.

In 1965, North America received 62 per cent of Japan's motor cycle export volume, followed by South-East Asia with 22 per cent, and Europe accounting for 8 per cent. The three major 1965 buyers were the U.S.A. (over 50 per cent), Taiwan and Thailand. The Asian market is not surprising. What is more fascinating is the fact that, in 1965, 70 per cent of Japanese motor cycle exports were to the advanced industrial nations rather than developing countries. In this context, it seems that motor cycles flow from a lower-cost nation, Japan, to the higher-cost producing nations. Moreover, with the technical developments in the Japanese industry, the trade flow in motor cycle products involves the transfer of the results of technical progress from Japan to the advanced industrial nations.

INDEX